THE TRANSFORMATION OF
MEXICAN AGRICULTURE

The Transformation of Mexican Agriculture

*International Structure and
the Politics of Rural Change*

STEVEN E. SANDERSON

Princeton University Press
Princeton, New Jersey

Copyright © 1986 by Princeton University Press
Published by Princeton University Press,
41 William Street, Princeton, New Jersey 08540
In the United Kingdom: Princeton University Press, Guildford, Surrey

All Rights Reserved

Library of Congress Cataloging in Publication Data will be found on
the last printed page of this book

ISBN   0-691-07693-6 (cloth)
       0-691-02239-9 (pbk.)

This book has been composed in Linotron Sabon

Clothbound editions of Princeton University Press books are
printed on acid-free paper, and binding materials are chosen for
strength and durability. Paperbacks, although satisfactory for personal
collections, are not usually suitable for library rebinding

Printed in the United States of America
by Princeton University Press
Princeton, New Jersey

*To my father
Rupert H. Sanderson,
and to the memory
of my mother
Anna K. Sanderson*

Contents

CONTENTS

List of Figures

List of Tables

Acknowledgments

A study this time-consuming and peripatetic would not be possible without the generous support of many institutions and the intellectual patience of many colleagues. The University of Florida sponsored the first phase of primary research in 1980, with a Faculty Research Grant to conduct field work in Mexico and a Seed Grant to draft a proposal for consideration by other funding sources. Subsequently, the Rockefeller Foundation International Relations Division awarded me an International Relations Fellowship (1981-1982) to conduct the bulk of my work in Mexico, Washington, D.C., and the border area. That award was complemented by a 1981 research grant from the Joint Committee on Latin American Studies of the American Council of Learned Societies and the Social Science Research Council. The two awards provided financial and intellectual support from June 1981 to September 1982. Concurrently, I benefited from a consulting contract from the Sistema Nacional de Evaluación–Sistema Alimentario Mexicano (SINE-SAM), through the Inter-American programs Development Directorate of the American University's Center for International Technical Cooperation. The SAM commissioned me to prepare a study of the U.S.-Mexican frontier beef cattle industry. Arthur Domike and Louis W. Goodman not only contributed to the success of that small commission, but they stimulated me through their own work and our collaboration to understand other areas of international agricultural relations.

David Barkin of the Universidad Autónoma Metropolitana-Xochimilco and the Centro de Ecodesarrollo in Mexico City has, over the past two years, not only improved my techniques of field interviewing and research but contributed greatly to my theoretical understanding of the phenomena described in this study. In addition, he has been a model of academic and personal generosity, sharing data and findings, opening his field notes to me, and commenting on my work at various stages, including a critique of the final manuscript. His collaborator Blanca Suárez and the staff of the Centro de Ecodesarrollo also merit thanks for their indulgence during my visiting fellowship there in the summer of 1981.

Additional opportunities to meet formally and casually with the personnel of the SINE-SAM and with other rural development specialists such as Gustavo Esteva, Arturo Warman, and others helped this project. Lic. Esteva, in particular, has helped me over several years in the area of fresh vegetable exports and CONASUPO policies.

Supporting materials and critical inferences in this study are drawn from over fifty field interviews in Mexico and several more in the United States, which, for their political sensitivity, are not identified or used as primary evidence. However, it is important to acknowledge the cooperation of the Secretaría de Agricultura y Recursos Hidráulicos (SARH), the Compañía Nacional de Subsistencias Populares (CONASUPO), the SINE-SAM, the local offices of the federal irrigation system and the Banco Nacional de Crédito Rural (BANRURAL), the U.S. Departments of Agriculture and Commerce, the Texas State Department of Agriculture, and a number of private and *ejidal* producers from Mexico City to the northern border. Outstanding in this group, both for our long friendship and his diligence in the study of rural development, is Lic. Leonel Argüelles Mendes. As a colleague and friend he was invaluable to this study, though totally innocent of its conclusions. Michael F. Marzick not only contributed to the intellectual directions pursued and discarded in the process of writing this study, but he also wrestled with the unending variations and inconsistencies in data that students of rural Mexico must suffer. His commitment to this project was invaluable. For help in reading drafts and lending support to this study, I am also obliged to Margaretta DeMar, Richard Fagen, Terry

McCoy, John Montel, Donna Roberts, Brooke Schwartz, Kenneth Shwedel, Rose Spalding, Paul Trapido, Mary White, and Charles Wood. LaMond Tullis provided the most thorough and demanding critique of an earlier version of this manuscript, and added to it measurably. To those who are still unidentified, my thanks are due for many of the more concrete insights which may appear in the following pages.

As ever, the real battles are fought at the sacrifice of one's personal life. Many leisure hours have been traded away in favor of this book. I particularly feel the irretrievable loss of time with my parents, to whom I have dedicated this work, as some belated acknowledgment of their tremendous and positive influence on me. Rosalie and Robert have borne the burdens well, looking forward to the completion of this study and a long-overdue chance to dine in peace, without having to attend a permanent seminar on the internationalization of their dinners.

S.E.S.
Washington, D.C.
January 1985

List of Abbreviations

ANDSA   Almacenes Nacionales de Depósito, S.A.
BANRURAL   Banco Nacional de Crédito Rural
CAADES   Confederación de Asociaciones de Agricultores del Estado de Sinaloa
CAASS   Confederación de Asociaciones de Agricultores del Sur de Sonora
CBI   Caribbean Basin Initiative
CCC   Commodity Credit Corporation
CEIMSA   Compañía Exportadora e Importadora de México, S.A.
CEPAL   United Nations Economic Commission for Latin America
CONAFRUT   Comisión Nacional de Fruticultura
CONASUPO   Compañía Nacional de Subsistencias Populares
COPLAMAR   Coordinación General del Plan Nacional de Zonas Deprimidas y Grupos Marginados
DAAC   Departamento de Asuntos Agrarios y Colonización
FAO   United Nations Food and Agriculture Organization
FERTIMEX   Fertilizantes y Guanos Mexicanos, S.A.
FINASA   Financiera Azucarera, S.A.
FIRA   Fideicomisos Instituidos en Relación con la Agricultura
FOJC   Frozen orange juice concentrate
GATT   General Agreement on Tariffs and Trade
IDB   Inter-American Development Bank
IMCE   Instituto Mexicano de Comercio Exterior
IMF   International Monetary Fund
INN   Instituto Nacional de Nutrición
MTN   Multilateral Trade Negotiations

NAFINSA   Nacional Financiera, S.A.
OECD   Organization for Economic Cooperation and Development
PEMEX   Petroleos Mexicanos
PRONAL   Programa Nacional de Alimentación
PRONASE   Productora Nacional de Semillas
SAG   Secretaría de Agricultura y Ganadería
SAM   Sistema Alimentario Mexicano
SARH   Secretaría de Agricultura y Recursos Hidráulicos
SPP   Secretaría de Programación y Presupuesto
SRA   Secretaría de Reforma Agraria
TABAMEX   Tabacos Mexicanos, S.A.
UNPH   Unión Nacional de Productores de Hortalizas
USDA   United States Department of Agriculture
WMVDA   West Mexico Vegetable Distributors Association

THE TRANSFORMATION OF
MEXICAN AGRICULTURE

Introduction

In a small *empaque* (packing shed) in the winter vegetable zone of Guasave, Sinaloa, the manager oversees the labor force (all women from local public sector farms called *ejidos*) as they sort and separate export-quality winter vegetables from culls for local processing and sale. In order to find out if the size and ripeness classifications match those of the U.S. marketing order for tomatoes, I ask the manager about the grading scheme. She replies that the sizes are only three: "small, *mediano, y* large." The international flavor of the *empaque* is further reinforced by the appearance of the label Jesús Takeda on each box of produce the *empaque* sells. The images of agricultural internationalization are vivid.

In Uruápan, Michoacán, the international enterprise Flores Mexicanas, whose high-technology greenhouses produced beautiful clones of carnations in climatically controlled conditions with simulated rain, sunshine, and darkness, is dying. The technological marvel hides a mortal flaw: the absurdity of such artificial environments in the single most appropriate area for outdoor flower cultivation in Mexico. In the face of grinding rural poverty in a state already wracked by high unemployment, relying on low-paid migrant labor in sugar cane, and suffering incursions by avocado plantations on prime land previously farmed for foodstuffs, Flores Mexicanas offers no jobs, no sustenance. The enterprise dies, despite a trilateral technical assistance team from Holland, Colombia, and the United States and despite the infusion of foreign and domestic capital from large investment groups. At the time of my visit in December 1981 huge sheds of freshly cut carnations and chrysanthemums sat wilting in the warehouse. The U.S. market—which was suffering low prices—preferred white flowers for the upcoming holiday season. And, indeed, the carnations were white. The Mexican market, where prices were firmer, preferred colors and rejected the flowers on hand.

In another setting, in Puebla, a rural bank official speaks proudly of giving credit to a new dairy *ejido* in order to create an artificial market for the local feed concentrate mill (which is in competition with Ralston Purina). In Los Mochis, Sinaloa, the local ejidal producers' association (Asociación Ejidal de Productores de Hortalizas del Estado de Sinaloa) confides that potatoes brought the best profits in 1981, not because of local consumption, but because of demand from a local potato chip factory. In the Valle de Santiago, Guanajuato, local hog producers complain of the lack of a breeding registry at the national level and the high cost of going to Lubbock, Texas, annually to buy stock and certify their registration. In Los Reyes, Michoacán, the head of the local federal irrigation district, in turn, complains of the entrepreneurial behavior of FINASA (the national sugar-financing enterprise) in refusing to integrate its water resources into the federal district and in behaving as the old refinery had vis-à-vis the cane producers. Many other producers echo that sentiment, seeing state intervention in agriculture as a process of trading one *cacique* (boss) for another.

Perhaps the most vivid metaphor of the interrelation among state, local economy, and international system appears during a visit in late 1981 to the state of Sonora, where I had spent several months conducting field work in 1976-1977. My visit to the fertile Yaqui and Mayo valleys coincides with the preparations in Navojoa, Ciudad Obregón, and Hermosillo for the arrival of the presidential candidate Miguel de la Madrid Hurtado. Festive local preparations in this most productive area of Mexico hide political tensions, land occupations, and a minor expropriation. The arrival of the candidate stops production, clogs hotels, and taxes the resources and patience of the local population. But as the candidate—who in December 1982 was to become the new president of Mexico—deplanes in Hermosillo for his stay in the state capital, the local secondary school band strikes up a brassy arrangement of "Stranger in Paradise," creating a scene too stagy for fiction. In fact, not to stretch the point too far, the candidate *was* a stranger in the agricultural cornucopia of the Mexican republic. In sad disregard of the serious problems to be treated here, many other Mexico City bureaucrats have never ventured forth to understand the international links that separate the northern river valleys from their inhabitants' needs and tie them, instead, to the United States, to other foreign consumers, and to internationalized agroindustries.

These anecdotal observations, of course, have little place in the formal exposition of this study. Nevertheless, the visitor to the Mexican countryside cannot escape the living reality that is the most serious reason for analyzing the transformation of Mexican agriculture and the new international division of labor. The quest in this piece of field research has been, to a great extent, to merge the analytical presentation of the international system with the mechanics of everyday farm life. In attempting such a synthesis, we will not examine every crop that might be considered "internationalized." Among traded goods, we will ignore sugar, cacao, and coffee, and only mention cotton. In nonexportables, we will give short shrift to internationalized poultry and some processed foods. Mostly, such inattention comes from the desire to make the argument in this study survive the massive amount of data and field work required to defend it. In examining winter vegetables, fruits, livestock, and basic grains, we can offer a preliminary sketch that might not be sustained in every instance for every crop but which can improve our understanding of the international influences on rural change in Mexico.

The Mexican agricultural landscape is everywhere blossoming with symbols of internationalization even more important and systemic than those mentioned in the anecdotes above. Mexico has become the third most important trade partner of the United States in agricultural goods, challenging certain sectors of the U.S. economy with import competition and worrying its own leaders with huge, permanent trade deficits.

For the first time, in 1982, Mexico became a credit customer for U.S. agricultural exports, abandoning a long tradition of cash purchases in the face of overwhelming economic crisis at home. In turn, the Mexican economy is one of the most elaborate networks of multinational investment in agriculture, agribusiness, and related activities in Latin America. Producers, the state, and merchants alike vie to increase their international breadth through trade, agribusiness processing, and stock breeding; through the use of pesticides, fertilizer, and seeds; and through ever more elaborate financing. More subtly, Mexican tastes, consumption patterns, and labor processes are affected by the organization of agricultural production at a global level. As the anecdotes above suggest, one need only visit the Mexican countryside to view firsthand the marks of the international economy on rural society.

This book studies the transformation of the Mexican agricultural system. A once relatively self-sufficient producer and net exporter of basic foodstuffs was transformed in the 1970s into a great net importer of those same foodstuffs. Mexican fields once devoted to satisfying domestic needs were sacrificed to the production of commercially attractive products for the U.S. market, such as winter vegetables, citrus fruits, and tobacco. Many commodities formerly consumed in the countryside became inputs in a transnationalized agroindustrial network. And the cattle industry veered to the export market, drawing domestic resources away from basic foods toward the generation of foreign exchange and the satisfaction of upscale consumer needs.

The principal argument of this study is that the transformation of Mexican agriculture is a product of a systemic internationalization of capital in agriculture and the long-term creation of a new global division of labor. Such a process of transformation—which has implications for other agricultural systems in the Caribbean Basin and Central and South America—affects the entire range of production, distribution, exchange, and consumption of agricultural commodities, not only in rural society, but at the international level as well. The

6

nutritional future of the Mexican population is affected by this transformation, as are the competitive position of U.S. producers of winter vegetables, the export market for U.S. grain growers and livestock processors, and the employment prospects for workers in agroindustries.

The process of agricultural transformation is fundamentally a political dynamic. But the transformation of Mexican agriculture and the new internationalization of the *campo* is not only an important subject of political science inquiry; it requires attention to economics, sociology, and agronomy as well. Such a realization provoked the multidisciplinary synthesis this book pursues. Outside the pioneering efforts of Barkin, Suárez, and Rama, there is virtually no literature that attempts to approach the nature of rural change from an international level of analysis, using at the same time concrete empirical materials from the level of the farm itself. Traditional political science literature has ignored production, as agricultural economics has shunned the politics of rural organization. But the agricultural phenomena to be investigated here are, after all, only the economic representations of rural life itself—statistical metaphors for the daily struggle for survival in a poor, Third World countryside.

This study emanates from a need to understand the high politics of agricultural development as a response to the exigencies of the international system and at the same time as a shaping force in rural life; Mexico presents an excellent venue for such a study. Mexico has had the most thorough agrarian reform program in nonsocialist Latin America. Public investment in agriculture, as the text will show, has remained at high levels throughout the post–World War II era, bringing infrastructure, credit, direct inputs, and political organization (of a certain type, to be sure) to the Mexican countryside. The gains from trade that traditional theory argues are possible for countries specializing in their areas of dynamic comparative advantage have, to some extent, been realized in the Mexican *campo*. And agribusiness has had relatively free rein

7

in the Mexican economy—integrating, coordinating, adding value, and disarticulating production from consumption.

Yet, for all the energy—both programmatic and physical—which has been brought to bear on Mexican tiller and soil, the yield in the *campo* has been as much food crisis as food self-sufficiency, as much economic distortion as articulation, and, in an ultimate irony, as much a threat to the *campesino*'s survival as an aid to his renaissance. In a word, the five decades of rural growth in Mexico since the grand agrarian reform of President Lázaro Cárdenas (1934-1940) have created a system not only incapable of reproducing the conditions for the survival of the rural population but one fundamentally threatening to peasant agriculture and nutrition.

Let us consider briefly the nature of the Mexican food crisis—and its political potential—in more concrete terms. Mexico is facing one of the severest tests of its food system since the rural famines of the late dictatorship of Porfirio Díaz, immediately preceding the 1910 revolution. The food crisis in Mexico is not simply a nutritional shortfall, although that aspect is important. It is a portent of a generalized crisis in agricultural employment, income distribution, uncontrolled urbanization, population growth, and emigration. It must also be considered as an early phase of future difficulties in feeding the growing rural population with an agricultural base less attentive to their needs and a trade base more constrained by external imbalances.

First, and most importantly, the Mexican food crisis is a crisis of nutrition. The National Institute of Nutrition (INN) has estimated that the average active Mexican adult needs 2,750 calories and 80 grams of protein daily. Using such standards, the 1974 National Food Survey showed 18.4 million Mexicans to be seriously malnourished, consuming less than 60 grams of protein and 1,500 to 2,100 calories per day.[1]

[1] Adolfo Chávez, "Nutrición: problemas y alternativas," in Pablo González Casanova and Enrique Florescano, eds., *México hoy* (Mexico: Siglo XXI, 1979), 225.

8

The Sistema Alimentario Mexicano (SAM)—the multiagency food self-sufficiency program directorate established in 1980—has asserted that 90 percent of the rural population suffers some degree of caloric and protein deficiency,[2] or a figure close to 21 million people. According to the SAM, 9.5 million people in 1980 suffered "grave caloric deficit," falling short of needed food consumption by as much as 25 to 40 percent. The Mexican government accordingly included in its object population for the SAM 35 million Mexicans in urban and rural locales, roughly one-third of whom are under the age of nine. A study for the Inter-American Development Bank shows protein and caloric levels to be somewhat higher in the rural population than the SAM admits, but allows that pre-schoolers are particularly susceptible to malnutrition through biases in the ways families distribute scarce foods.[3]

The food crisis and its potential are revealed even more starkly by demographic trends. In 1980, Mexico's rural population totaled 24.5 million.[4] Assuming the same proportion of rural-urban population in 1990, that figure could climb to over 32 million. Population projections are, of course, precarious in a time of declining fertility, and rapid urbanization will probably lower that figure. But, even using the low estimate of projected population calculated by the Mexican government itself, over 33 million people will inhabit the Mexican countryside in the year 2000. As the text will show, rural production has not met population growth, nor have rural inhabitants found remunerative employment in an economy that will need 30 million jobs in the next two decades.

[2] Mexico, Oficina de Asesores del C. Presidente, Sistema Nacional de Evaluación, Sistema Alimentario Mexicano (SINE-SAM), *El Sistema Alimentario Mexicano: primer plantamiento, de metas de consumo y estrategia de producción de alimentos básicos para 1980-1982.* (Mexico: SINE-SAM, 1980), 8.

[3] Inter-American Development Bank (IDB), *Nutrition and Economic Development in Latin America* (Washington, D.C.: IDB, 1978), 27ff.

[4] IDB, *Economic and Social Progress in Latin America* (Washington, D.C.: IDB, 1982), 304.

Of those current and future inhabitants of the Mexican *campo*, we can say little in the abstract, except that current economic, social, and demographic trends indicate that they will feel the measure of the Mexican food crisis more than others in the society. In the 1975 household consumption survey conducted by the Mexican government,[5] it was found that 33 percent of the rural population never eat meat; 32 percent never eat eggs; 37 percent never eat wheat bread; and 59 percent never taste milk. One question facing the Mexican food system involves the future of these people, who never benefit from agricultural modernization and agribusiness industrialization.

The Mexican food crisis is also a crisis of control, raising questions about the ability of the Mexican state and society to guide and manage the national food system in an increasingly internationalized environment. Mexico in its food self-sufficiency drive is once again at least nominally reaffirming its intention to reverse its dependency in favor of greater national autonomy. In attempting to do so in an extremely restricted political environment, however, the partisans of the SAM (and of "food sovereignty" under the new Programa Nacional de Alimentación [PRONAL] of President Miguel de la Madrid) have raised fundamental questions about the sources of decision making in agriculture, the relative leverage of direct foreign investment versus national capital in the national food economy, and the role of the peasant in a modern industrial society. From the perspective of the social analyst, the empirical materials to be presented in this study should also raise even more basic questions about the intellectual integrity of the concept of "national system" in an internationalized regime of capitalist expansion and about the prospects for survival of regimes emphasizing the cooptative power of agrarian patronage.

The food crisis has become a crisis of U.S.-Mexican relations

---

[5] Mexico, Secretaría de Programación y Presupuesto (SPP), *La población de México, su ocupación, y sus niveles de bienestar* (Mexico: SPP, 1979).

as well. During 1982-1983, Mexico entered the United States Commodity Credit Corporation's (CCC) Credit Guarantee Program (GSM-102) in order to find secured loans for basic foods to be purchased from the United States. While the Reagan administration responded quickly and positively to Mexico's requests for credit guarantees in order to sustain huge volumes of U.S. exports in a time of low commodity prices, the two countries have few institutional networks for resolving the difficulties of planning future trade finance agreements.[6] In the absence of Mexican participation in GATT[7] and in the climate of anxiety over U.S. "food power" following the Carter administration's Russian grain embargo, Mexico's relentless dependence on food imports from the United States has become a major policy problem. It stands at the end of 1984 as the most telling critique of the food self-sufficiency drive of President López Portillo, which we shall examine in Chapters 4 and 5.

But this study will argue also that the trade dynamic that confounds bilateral politics is not the single most important focus of agricultural internationalization in Mexico. Though trade in basic grains and fresh produce dominates our attention at times, there is a more subtle process of internationalization taking place, in which Mexico is being inserted into a new international division of labor. The characteristics of that new internationalization and its political consequences for Mexico—a weakening of state power, an increased external dependence, the domination of agricultural decision making by agribusiness concerns, and the removal of food policy from the public realm—are core elements in this study. The Mexican food crisis is simultaneously a crisis of domestic provisioning and a crisis of the new international division of

---

[6] Steven E. Sanderson, "The Complex No-Policy Option: U.S. Agricultural Relations with Mexico," Working Papers of the Latin American Program, Woodrow Wilson International Center for Scholars, Washington, D.C., 1983.

[7] Dale Story, "Trade Politics in the Third World: A Case Study of the Mexican GATT Decision," *International Organization* 36:4 (Autumn 1982), 767-794.

labor, which implies that structural adjustments, national food strategies, and state intervention in the agricultural marketplace must be considered as elements of a global system.

The multifaceted character of the Mexican food crisis has formed the core of this book; both its organization and its analytical strategy are shaped by the subject. As will become obvious in succeeding chapters, the case study approach has proved to be inadequate. The analysis must operate instead at several levels simultaneously in order to capture the nuances of a modernizing agricultural system deeply intertwined with the international system. The monographic literature represented best by Lamartine Yates and the Centro de Investigaciones Agrarias studies of Mexico is no longer sufficiently expansive to capture the Mexican *campo* in its global context. At the same time, however, such detailed farm-level analyses must still be undertaken to avoid an international determinism that vitiates structuralist interpretations of Third World economies and shunts the important political mandate of the Mexican state to the back shelf of agricultural development literature or, worse, considers it to be a "market distortion." Thus, the text will pass among several levels of analysis, from on-site observations of Mexican agricultural production to bilateral relations to occasional regional comparisons to analysis of the changing international system at large.

In such broad movements among interactive levels lies a critical methodological danger: the confusion of case study and international regime. To resolve the occasional disjuncture between local case and international system would have required a multivolume work, with foci that are not fully elaborated here. There is little guidance in traditional literature for such analysis, and the various disciplines whose works are cited here have not generally attempted to cross boundaries or levels in resolving such difficulties. In that sense, this study has the general purpose of providing a new prolegomenon to rural development analysis, challenging mainstream analysts to consider a two-track approach to the problems of food production and rural development in the international system,

12

one track beginning at the local level in selected important national systems and the second track beginning at the highest levels of international integration—in trade, agribusiness development, and finance. In a word, this study seeks to merge case-based empirical work and global analysis, a program so ably laid out as a research mandate in a recent essay by Bruce Andrews.[8] Here the important task is to understand the implications of international integration for domestic policy toward underprivileged groups and disadvantaged producers. It is also important to frame domestic policy-making efforts in the broader context of the international system. Both of these tasks have been avoided by most "world systems" analysis and by *dependentistas*, on the one hand; farm-level analysis, on the other hand, no longer tells the story of the increasing internationalization of production in the 1980s.

While the links established here among those various levels may fall somewhat short of resolving all the gaps between case and international system, those two tracks of analysis will not be joined by more monographs on local production without attention to international factors. Nor does the specific complexity of Mexican (or Brazilian or Argentine) agricultural production and social relations permit us to ignore the absolute necessity of presenting new data and field work from case studies. Thus, rather than being *either* a Mexican case study *or* a study of international factors in rural development—a choice that would deny the relevance of the new international division of labor altogether—this is a book about the specific transformation of Mexican agriculture from the standpoint of an increasingly integrated international system.

[8] Bruce Andrews, "The Political Economy of World Capitalism: Theory and Practice," *International Organization* 36:1 (Winter 1982), 135-163.

CHAPTER ONE

The Transformation of Mexican Agriculture and the New International Division of Labor

THE NEW INTERNATIONAL DIVISION OF LABOR

In the mid-1980s, the production, exchange, distribution, and consumption of many commodities are undergoing profound structural change. World markets frame many goods and labor processes. Those markets govern not only world prices but "worldwide sourcing" for manufactures, "global strategies" of integrated international enterprises, and ultimately the "internationalization" of national economies in new ways. As this "new" world economy challenges U.S. hegemony in trade, the "globalization" of production will figure large on the international political agenda. From OECD economic summits to more prosaic bilateral trade negotiations between the United States and Mexico, trade policy makers worry over the international realignment of production that is making its way into the discourse of economic recovery.

The evidence of this changing productive structure appears across a broad range of social science literature. New studies on the "reindustrialization" of the United States implicitly treat these international phenomena through the special lens focusing on employment in the industrial heartland of America, the composition of agricultural trade with other countries, and the comparative advantage traditionally enjoyed by the United States in consumer manufactures, agricultural commodities, and high-technology goods and services.[1]

[1] See particularly Barry Bluestone and Bennet Harrison, *The Deindustrialization of America* (New York: Basic Books, 1982); Robert Reich, *The Next*

In international relations literature, of course, the "interdependence" of the world has long been recognized.[2] Writers taking widely varying political positions have all contributed to the general understanding of regional and global political integration,[3] the quest for international and transnational economic coalitions,[4] and—in perhaps unrecognized ways the midwife to all these literatures—the realist perception of mutual security interests among allies.[5] At the same time, how-

---

American Frontier (New York: New York Times Books, 1982); Paul R. Lawrence and David Dyer, *Renewing American Industry* (New York: Free Press, 1982); and Samuel Bowles, David M. Gordon, and Thomas E. Weiskopf, *Beyond the Wasteland: A Democratic Alternative to Economic Decline* (New York: Doubleday, Anchor, 1983) for examples of some leading industrial policy analysis in the United States.

[2] The literature on interdependence is voluminous and uneven. Some leading examples and bibliographies may be found in Robert Keohane and Joseph Nye, *Power and Interdependence: World Politics in Transition* (Boston: Little, Brown, 1977); Raymond F. Hopkins and Donald J. Puchala, *Global Food Interdependence: Challenge to American Foreign Policy* (New York: Columbia University Press, 1980); Richard N. Cooper, *The Economics of Interdependence* (New York: Columbia University Press, 1980); and James A. Caporaso, ed., "Dependence, Dependency and Power in the Global System: A Structural and Behavioral Analysis," special issue of *International Organization* 32:1 (Winter 1978), 13-44. A later piece, James A. Caporaso, "Industrialization in the Periphery: The Evolving Global Division of Labor," *International Studies Quarterly* 25:3 (September 1981), 347-384, suggests some important links between national economic development and the global division of labor from within this tradition.

[3] Peter J. Katzenstein, "International Interdependence: Some Longterm and Recent Changes," *International Organization* 29:4 (Autumn 1975), 1021-1034, and Richard Rosecrance et al., "Whither Interdependence?" *International Organization* 31:1 (Winter 1977), 83-105.

[4] Some interesting treatments of global economic associations may be found in Norman Girvan, *Corporate Imperialism: Conflict and Expropriation* (White Plains, N.Y.: M. E. Sharpe, 1976); Joan Edelman Spero, *The Politics of International Economic Relations*, 2nd ed. (New York: St. Martin's, 1981); and Robert L. Rothstein, *Global Bargaining: UNCTAD and the Quest for a New International Economic Order* (Princeton, N.J.: Princeton University Press, 1979).

[5] For a convenient review of this literature, see James E. Dougherty and Robert L. Pfaltzgraff, Jr., *Contemporary Theories of International Relations*, 2nd ed. (Philadelphia: Lippincott, 1980); also, John H. Herz, "Political Real-

ever, other intellectuals have focused on the deep-seated inequality of interstate relations, not only in the political realm, but in development and trade as well. Thus, the dependency and "development of underdevelopment" literatures have contributed to understanding the inequality as well as the depth of North-South integration.[6]

Nevertheless, for the most part the mainstream literature of economic development and international relations does not take us beyond the international framework of analysis to permit us to understand interstate relations in a truly global context. Even in the discussions of specific global regimes,[7] the focus is on institutions and functional analysis rather than the overarching dynamics of change at the global level.

Those who have studied global inequality suffer similar problems of scope and level. The nation-centric "inequality of nations" approach[8] fails to account for underlying dynamics of inequality and ends up with little more than a realist acknowledgment of misery in the international system. Sim-

---

ism Revisited," Symposium in Honor of Hans J. Morgenthau, *International Studies Quarterly* 25:2 (June 1981), 182-197. For an excellent example of "neorealism," see Richard Feinberg, *The Intemperate Zone: The Third World Challenge to U.S. Foreign Policy* (New York: Norton, 1983).

[6] Particularly important contributions to the literature on dependency and underdevelopment include Fernando Henrique Cardoso and Enzo Faletto, *Dependency and Development in Latin America* (Berkeley and Los Angeles: University of California Press, 1979), and Osvaldo Sunkel, "Capitalismo transnacional y desintegración nacional en América Latina," *Estudios internacionales* 4:16 (January-March 1971), 3-61; in English, "Transnational Capitalism and National Disintegration in Latin America," *Social and Economic Studies* 22:1 (1973), 132-176. For a convenient synthesis of dependency literature, see Ronald H. Chilcote and Joel C. Edelstein, eds., *Latin America: The Struggle with Dependency and Beyond* (Cambridge, Mass.: Shenkman, 1974), and Heraldo Muñoz, ed., *From Dependency to Development: Strategies to Overcome Underdevelopment and Inequality* (Boulder, Colo.: Westview Press, 1981).

[7] See Keohane and Nye; Stephen D. Krasner, ed., "International Regimes," special issue of *International Organization* 36:2 (Spring 1982).

[8] Robert W. Tucker, *The Inequality of Nations* (New York: Basic Books, 1977); Robert L. Rothstein, *The Weak in the World of the Strong* (New York: Columbia University Press, 1977).

ilarly, *dependentistas* vacillate between global system and imperialist domination in their analysis of the permanent structural inequality pervading North-South relations.[9] World-systems analysts reify the market as a continuous and all-embracing global institution and fail to account for qualitative transformations in the modes and levels of capital accumulation.[10]

What the world is witnessing in the late twentieth century involves a more mobile, flexible capitalist organization of production itself, whereby a different labor force—less organized, more mobile, in many instances cheaper, and certainly not "entitled" to participation in programs under the rubric of social welfare and services—is employed for the sake of industrial and agricultural rationalization at a global level. The U.S. economy engages Jamaican cane cutters and Central American vegetable pickers in Florida. Undocumented agricultural and service sector workers from Mexico appear throughout the United States to "supplement" or replace local labor. Mexican, Caribbean, and Asian garment workers populate the sweatshops of Los Angeles, San Francisco, New York, and Miami. The new international division of labor means the migration of people from their homes to foreign sites of employment.

The internationalization of labor implies far more than the

[9] Such a contrast is evident even in the early writings of Sunkel (see above) and Johan Galtung, "A Structural Theory of Imperialism," *Journal of Peace Research* 2 (1971), 81-118, which has some of the flavor of frontier theory literature.

[10] The most famous world-systems advocate is Immanuel Wallerstein, whose best-known work is *The Modern World-System: Capitalist Agriculture and the Origins of the European World-Economy in the Sixteenth Century* (New York: Academic Press, 1974). Eric Wolf, in his much-acclaimed new book *Europe and the People without History* (Berkeley and Los Angeles: University of California Press), takes Wallerstein to task in this vein, as well as others, and even lumps Wallerstein together with André Gunder Frank, whose early work *The Development of Underdevelopment* (New York: Monthly Review, 1966) is something of a landmark in dependency analysis. For a provocative critique of the world-systems approach, see Andrews.

simple movement of labor forces, however. If the international division of labor is genuinely new, it is partly because of the system's growing ability to reproduce the most advanced labor processes throughout the world, and thereby to integrate not only commodity markets but people themselves. Tastes, work styles, household employment, and status values all respond to the expanded international system, even within very specific national traditions, values, and customs.

These processes of internationalization, whether in the form of direct foreign investment in agribusiness, migrating labor forces, or export processing in manufactures, create systemic pressures on trade policy, investment regulations, immigration policy, and rural development designs. In turn, new forms of protectionism against Third World competitors within the developed capitalist economies change the language of commerce from free trade to domestic job protection. In a word, the mutual integration of the North and the South has also meant a certain homogenization of nationalist trade and investment strategies—even with a generous allowance for specific national experiences.

But, if it is easy to itemize elements of the new international division of labor, it is more difficult to conceptualize it and describe its motor force. Implicit in such a broad conceptual scheme is the "level of analysis" problem, in which the specific dynamics to be described must be linked to broader global processes and institutions. The tradition of comparative politics, immigration studies, international relations, and international economics has emphasized an international or crossnational focus. While such foci have their place, they ignore the critical core of the new international division of labor: the transnational organization of labor processes and commodity production. Many firms known as multinational corporations in the 1970s are transnational corporations in the 1980s, given their organizational transition to global corporations (as opposed to national companies with overseas operations). The terms "transnational associations" and "integrated international enterprises" found in leading journals such as *Business*

Week attest to the difficulty of nation-centric analysis in our era of globalization.

Nevertheless, social science has responded in some ways to the recognition that the international system increasingly mediates national prerogatives of development. Nation-centric models of modernization have given way to international models, emphasizing interdependence, dependence, imperialism, or other theoretical constructs focused more directly on the international system and its impact on national development.

Before examining such phenomena in the Mexican setting, we must establish some of the key elements of the new international division of labor. First, internationalization no longer means foreign domination in the same sense as it applied during the epoch of colonial rule or the heyday of agricultural export enclaves in the late nineteenth century. Internationalization does not observe the canons of the old "international division of labor," in which Great Britain and the United States presided over the bulk of world trade, and the economies of the Third World imported virtually all their manufactured products and much of their capital and technology from center countries.[11] Currently, many Third World countries, especially in Latin America, display high levels of intraregional trade outside the United States, Britain, and other center countries (e.g., Argentina, Brazil, and the Andean countries).[12] The new international division of labor implies a domination by trade relations and by the transnational integration of production itself, not in the context of empire, but through the medium

[11] Celso Furtado, *Economic Development of Latin America*, 2nd ed. (Cambridge: Cambridge University Press, 1976), part 2. An excellent case study can be found in A. G. Ford, "British Investment and Argentine Economic Development, 1880-1914," in David Rock, ed., *Argentina in the Twentieth Century* (Pittsburgh: University of Pittsburgh Press, 1975), 12-40.

[12] For specific evidence, see Inter-American Development Bank (IDB), *Economic and Social Progress in Latin America: The External Sector* (Washington, D.C.: IDB, 1982), and Business International, *Trading in Latin America: The Impact of Changing Policies* (New York: Business International Corporation, 1981).

of the less nation-bound internationalization of productive capital.

Analysts of the internationalization of capital and the new international division of labor agree that these two related concepts both stem from a structural transformation of the world economy, which has been acknowledged and worried over since the beginning of the 1970s. Institutional upheavals such as the death of the Bretton Woods monetary system, the oil shocks of 1973 and 1979, the structural change in the trade bill of the United States, and the competitive successes of Japan and the German Federal Republic have all been thrown together in loose descriptions of the new international division of labor. Even recent discussions of the debt crisis have assumed a language of economic integration: debtor countries are described as being more deeply and more "rationally" drawn into the international economic system, guided by the IMF, OECD trade policies, and national directors of fiscal and monetary austerity.

After that simple agreement, however, analysts soon part company. In an enormously oversimplified way, even leading international banks concede that the international system is increasingly "penetrated" by competitive products from "developing countries."[13] The decline of American competitiveness in the export of manufactured goods and the successes of East Asian and Latin American rivals have become the single common denominator of this literature. And, in the dialogue about the recovery of debtor countries such as Brazil, Chile, Argentina, Peru, and Mexico, the problems of OECD protectionism and the uneven export performance of Latin American manufactures mark the general acceptance in the banking community of the "interpenetrated" trade system.

Other international organizations more concerned with the developing-country analog, of course, focus on the "internationalization of Third World economies," a theme found

[13] Kredietbank, "The New International Division of Labor," Kredietbank *Weekly Bulletin* 33:37 (October 6, 1978).

particularly in literature from the FAO and CEPAL.[14] But most of these interpretations focus on trade, especially export platforms, and imply that the international division of labor is new mainly for the reversal of the old division of labor in the international system. That is, these analysts maintain that the new international division of labor restructures the system so that the previous hewers of wood and drawers of water— the Third World raw materials providers—now export a substantial amount of manufactured and processed goods, and quite often are importers of raw materials from developed countries. The cases of Brazil and Mexico certainly fit this description. Brazil imports a broad array of raw materials inputs for agroindustry and other consumer goods; Mexico imports inputs even to the extent of depending on trade in seeds and seedlings to produce agricultural exports competing with foreign truck farm goods. Now, for the first time, developed capitalist countries are threatened with competition in a number of sectors of industrial and agricultural activity in which they enjoyed advantages for generations. The United States, a traditional exporter of beef, begins to import beef and live cattle. U.S. and continental European citrus are threatened by Brazilian and Mexican competition. Brazilian poultry exports threaten the traditional U.S. and European domination of Middle Eastern markets. And in wearing apparel, textiles, leather goods, and food and beverage processing—all dependent on primary inputs from agriculture—more value is added in Third World countries and less in the developed capitalist world. The developed capitalist countries, it appears, are losing some of their economic preeminence to Third World parvenus.

This study hopes to propose a more sophisticated under-

[14] Gerson Gomes and Antonio Pérez, "The Process of Modernization in Latin American Agriculture, CEPAL *Review* 8 (August 1979), 55-74; Hector Assael, "The Internationalization of the Latin American Economies: Some Reservations," CEPAL *Review* 7 (April 1979), 41-55; Aníbal Pinto, "The Periphery and the Internationalization of the World Economy," CEPAL *Review* 9 (December 1979), 45-67.

standing of the internationalization of the world economy than the above literature permits. These international changes will be described as a function of the expansion of capital, its valorization and reproduction at a global level, cast in the local settings of Mexican agriculture.[15] According to this understanding, the new international division of labor is a product of the global transformation of labor processes, in this case focusing on the Mexican countryside. The scholarship on this question incorporates much of the best of earlier studies of multinational capital based on the gains from and productive implications of international trade,[16] the product life cycle,[17] institutional imperatives for transnational expansion,[18] and similar explanations documenting the expansion of production itself beyond national borders. But the important difference in this approach rests on explaining change less through industrial organization and the locus of equity than through the changes felt at the local level of production. We will never stray entirely from the realities of rural lives.

This is not to ignore nation and national economy as important forces; it does suggest that we should concentrate on

[15] David Barkin and Carlos Rozo, "L'Agriculture et l'internationalization du capital," *Revue tiers-monde* 88 (October-December 1981), 723-745; Barkin and Blanca Suárez, *El fin de autosuficiencia alimentaria* (Mexico: Editorial Nueva Imagen, 1982); Stephen Hymer, "The Internationalization of Capital," *Journal of Economic Issues* 6:1 (March 1972), 91-111; Christian Palloix, *Las firmas multinacionales y el proceso de internacionalización* (Mexico: Siglo XXI, 1977).

[16] G. K. Helleiner, "Transnational Enterprises and the New Political Economy of U.S. Trade Policy," *Oxford Economic Papers* 29:1 (March 1977); H. Myint, "The Gains from International Trade and the Backward Countries," *The Review of Economic Studies* 22:2 (1954).

[17] Stephen P. Magee, "Information and Multinational Corporation: An Appropriability Theory of Direct Foreign Investment," in Jagdish Bhagwati, ed., *The New International Economic Order: The North-South Debate* (Cambridge, Mass.: MIT Press, 1977); Raymond Vernon, "International Investment and International Trade in the Product Cycle," *The Quarterly Journal of Economics* 80:2 (May 1966).

[18] Theodore H. Moran, "Foreign Expansion as an 'Institutional Necessity' for U.S. Corporate Capitalism," *World Politics* 25:3 (April 1973).

a nation's insertion in the global capitalist system. But rather than considering domestic development policy and external payments and trade disequilibria to be phenomena of closed national systems, this approach concentrates on the interaction of national economies in a transnational system. Specifically, the new international division of labor as used here implies the transformation of labor processes at the international level; the standardization of work and the differentiation of work processes in national contexts; the mobility of capital for the sake of worldwide sourcing, regional comparative advantage, local market enhancement, and other well-known institutional imperatives for expansion; cross-sectoral integration and coordination of production, which often replace equity control of transnational production; a "deepening" of international integration beyond simple commodity trade integration; and the mutual structural adjustment of developed and underdeveloped countries in the new international division of labor.[19]

Beyond these initial premises, the analysis will focus on a little-considered aspect of the new international division of labor: the reorientation of state power. Because most of the phenomena listed above are economic in nature, their definition has advanced beyond political analysis focusing on state strategies of development and the complications of international relations emanating from the new international division of labor. Nation-states have, of course, borne a heavy responsibility for exchange rate management, trade promotion, and foreign policy, as well as rural development and industrialization. But such responsibilities have not necessarily enhanced state power, as is often assumed. The state has often been forced to act as the authorized agent of the international system and to adopt a very restrictive menu of political choices at home. As is the case with Mexico, the state experiences an

[19] For a fuller discussion of these themes, see Steven E. Sanderson, ed., *The Americas in the New International Division of Labor* (New York: Holmes and Meier, 1984).

expansion of its apparatus and responsibility toward the international financial community and individual capitalists exposed in portfolio or direct investment, but at the same time finds that its opportunities to exit from economic crisis are shaped more narrowly in the form of a recipe for deeper integration into the international economic system. In this respect, at least, the power of the state can actually decline, when defined as the enacted capacity to enhance national economic decision-making autonomy or to negotiate the terms of national participation in the international division of labor.

Concretely, that means that the nation-state cannot negotiate from strength for commodity trade agreements in a time of low world prices and beggar-thy-neighbor trade and investment policies. "Obeying nurse"[20] by subscribing to IMF stabilization programs precludes traditional economic nationalism, domestic protectionism, or other time-honored remedies for the structural inequality of the international system. Regardless of its successes and failures, economic nationalism has been the single historical response of Third World nations faced with unremitting and unqualified economic integration into the international system. The vulnerability that comes as a result of this political weakness came first to Mexico in the realm of food policy and agricultural internationalization.

The "New" Internationalization of Agriculture in the Americas

In many ways, the agricultural sector is the most advanced representative of these new labor processes, partly for its importance to most nations of the world and partly for its relatively early entry into the international trade system. But if its role in international integration is secure, the nature of internationalization in agriculture is still complex and elusive. In the post–World War II world, the commodity trading ar-

[20] "Hands Off the IMF," *The Economist* 284:7253 (September 4, 1982), 15-16.

rangements of the "old" international division of labor still endure to a great extent. Argentina still exports the staples it developed in the nineteenth century to its old trading partners in Europe, especially to Great Britain. And the Caribbean nations are still tied to traditional exportables such as sugar, cacao, cotton, and rum. Nevertheless, the sector displays important and subtle changes. New commodities have appeared in the international system, changing relations of production in the countryside. Input industries have generated technologies so significant to Third World development that Mexico and Brazil have developed exports in patented processes, high-technology agricultural infrastructure, and other services never known before.

Agriculture has shown a new face in agroindustry, which has internationalized its production in the wake of import substitution industrialization, beginning with commercial contracting in such traditional crops as tobacco. Such integration has spawned a whole new mode of industrial integration through production contracting, technological "packaging" for whole industries, and nonequity forms of international control over agricultural production. It has also meant that the distinction between national and transnational agribusiness processors has begun to give way to the homogenization of production and technology. The tastes and values of "center" country consumers and agribusinesses have been internalized by Third World populations. The relations of production governing rural cropping and manufacture have become standardized in keeping with their international analogs. The shape of agriculture in the Americas is, to varying extents in different countries, dictated as the international level, in sales, procurement, technological inputs, cropping, and processing agricultural raw materials. No longer is the imperialist model of transnational corporate encroachment satisfactory as an explanation of international integration. The international system is moving "on beyond imperialism."

Given the long history of Latin American primary commodity exports, this thesis is hardly surprising. From the first colonial export enclaves in Brazil, New Spain, and the vice-royalty of Peru, agricultural growth in Latin America has been understood to be an export dependent phenomenon in the grand architecture of relationships with the "center" countries of world commerce. To propose that agriculture in Latin America functioned as a growth pole or generated an "engine of growth" for import substitution industrialization or, alternatively, halted or delayed industrialization in smaller economies, is hardly an improvement over the broad literature on plantation economies, agricultural modernization, and staple crops. To assert that the relations of production in export dependent agriculture determine to some extent the generalized benefits of agriculture for the economy at large does not improve significantly on traditional analysis of the region's economic history.

The character of internationalization in the Mexican agricultural sector has changed from that old mode, however, to reflect a *new* mode of regional integration in the world economy since World War II. Mexico—and to a great extent other large agricultural producers in Latin America—experiences today a *new* internationalization of agriculture at the level of production itself. The rural sector is no longer a simple product of commodity circulation through trade but a fully integrated element of internationally dependent economies. The forces of such internationalized productive capital encourage the *mutual* integration of North and South America (specifically, the United States and Mexico) that transcends simpler models of agribusiness imperialism or central-periphery relations.[21]

Likewise, the idea that such corporations and merchants have a "home" country or national allegiance is increasingly

[21] This departs from the mainstream of dependency perspectives by insisting on the transformation of the center as well as the periphery in the process of agricultural internationalization. Likewise, the argument suggests that the forces of internationalization are less national business forces than transnationals, embodying a "new" form of economic expansion without recourse to empire.

difficult to defend, both as a general principle of industrial organization and as a state planning principle for "host" countries. To DeKalb Seed or Massey Ferguson or Ralston Purina, the nationality of tomato production or farm machinery markets or soya and sorghum supplies, respectively, has little relation to corporate philosophy beyond the desire to stimulate new markets and to continue the valorization of capital and the reproduction of labor processes critical to corporate activities. To the Latin American state—nationalist fulminations aside—the international standardization of agribusiness capital is likewise relatively less important than the desperate need for those industrial and farm processes which yield employment, value-added, and foodstuffs for urban consumption or generate foreign exchange. Internationalization does not depend on the transnational or national character of individual firms but on the process of production itself.

Obviously, such internationalization takes place partly through trade in the private sector and partly through export promotion programs of host country governments. However, one important element in the internationalization of agriculture—the internalization of agricultural production processes and foodstuff products—shows that the internationalization of Latin American agriculture does not depend exclusively on the transnational corporation or on trade. Whether the yield of the countryside is processed or purchased by a transnational corporation or a competing domestic firm makes little difference to the rural poor in Latin America or to the successful agricultural producer.

To the poor, the destination of agricultural commodities processed or sold by agribusiness enterprises is irrelevant: whether white asparagus or strawberries or beef make their way to the tables of the urban middle sectors of the same country or to the equally discriminating kitchens of North American and European consumers, the separation of the producer from his crop is equal. Likewise, in North America, the producer's reliance on the leaders and beneficiaries of internationalized agricultural growth does not vary with a company's transnational affiliation or domestic equity content. Rather, the important issue for the farmer and for his relation to the agribusiness and the world market involves the relations of production in the countryside, which to an increasing extent have been standardized across boundaries through transnational direct investment, technology transfers, and vertical integration and coordination.

THE STRUCTURE OF AGRICULTURAL INTERNATIONALIZATION IN THE AMERICAS

When we speak of the agricultural internationalization of the Americas, we must specify that not all countries are equally important, in either a productive or a trade dimension. Seven countries dominate the production and trade profile of Latin America. Brazil, Mexico, Argentina, Venezuela, Colombia, Peru, and Chile account for nearly 90 percent of the region's gross domestic product. Likewise, these same countries account for four-fifths of regional exports and 88 percent of the gross debt.[22] As we would expect from the thesis that the new international division of labor is not simply a function of trade dependence, none of these countries has a particularly high reliance on the external sector of its economy, relative to the rest of the region. Brazil and Mexico, for example, show the lowest level of reliance on their external sectors of any economies in Latin America.[23] Among these countries, only Mexico shows great vulnerability to the United States, due to its extraordinary reliance on bilateral trade as a proportion of its foreign commerce. The other countries have more diversified markets, less trade reliance on the United States, and high levels of intraregional trade.[24] But bilateral reliance is only one indicator of transnational integration into the new international division of labor.

[22] IDB, *The External Sector*, 23.
[23] Ibid., 24.
[24] Ibid., 30-31.

We can center the analysis further if we consider the scale of activities in agricultural exports and agribusiness involvement in the region. Chile has a modest level of agricultural exports and a small domestic market. Its principal claim to prominence among the trading nations of Latin America comes from traditional mineral exports and the import consequences of the "free market" philosophy of the military dictatorship since 1973. Likewise, Venezuela is a modest provider of agricultural commodities to the international system. Its prominence in the external sectors of the region comes principally from its reliance on imports since the oil boom and its growing exports of petroleum and petroleum products. The clear agricultural leaders among the seven largest economies in the region are Brazil and Mexico, followed by Argentina, Colombia, and Peru. Brazil and Mexico are both major producers of coffee, soya, and citrus, as well as hides and leather goods, sugar, and meat. Argentina, of course, is well known as a major world contributor of wheat and beef, and produces coarse grains, maize, sugar, and a growing volume of soybeans for the international market. Colombia is a growing producer of beef, a major exporter of coffee, and has contributed to regional exports of bananas, sugar, cotton, and even improved seeds in recent years. Peru provides a broad range of agricultural crops to the international system as well, though it is not as prominent an exporter of any single crop. Nevertheless, Peru has participated significantly in sugar, cotton, and other primary exports.

Other regions and nations participate in this web as well. The Caribbean islands have become new targets of trade promotion and agroindustrial investment in the 1980s, and the volume of food imports from the United States to the Caribbean alone equaled 1.2 billion dollars in 1981.[25] But, even if we refine our analysis one step further, by concentrating on transnational corporate presence in the leading agricultural

[25] Mary Revelt, "Developing the Caribbean: Its Implications for U.S. Agriculture," *Foreign Agriculture* 20:6 (June 1982), 4-7.

29

export economies of the region, we once again return to Brazil, Mexico, Colombia, and Argentina. Transnationals in the food- and beverage-processing sectors concentrate their efforts, in the above-named countries, in meat-packing, dairy, and animal feed industries. In addition, of course, the major economies of the region also have their own agroindustrial complexes created largely under import substitution industrialization strategies after World War II. In the cases of Colombia, Mexico, and Brazil—and as part of the long tradition of Argentine export growth—agroindustrial exports have become major influences in these national economies. From refined soya oil in Brazil to soluble coffee in Colombia and canned pineapple in Mexico, these countries have integrated the agroindustrial growth model into their external sector as well as into their processing and marketing for domestic consumers.

The importance of agricultural transformation and international integration is especially clear in Mexico. Home of the most thoroughgoing agrarian reform in nonsocialist Latin America, birthplace of the Green Revolution, vanguard of food self-sufficiency campaigns in the region, and largest Third World agricultural trade partner of the United States, Mexico sets itself apart from the rest of Latin America, not by its exceptional abilities to avoid the pitfalls of export dependence and agroindustrial integration, but by its wholesale embrace of the modern technology of agricultural enterprise and trade, in the face of some of the most egregious extremes of rural life. This study is about Mexico, of course; but not about Mexico as a unique example. If the origins of agricultural internationalization lie at the regional and global level, Mexico is not an exception to the experience of the other countries mentioned here. If the final answers to the regional "agrarian question" lie in more serious cross-national case work and country analysis throughout the hemisphere, this study can at least lay out the issues as they pertain to one of the countries most integrated into the new international division of labor.

The Role of Agriculture in the Mexican Economy

Agriculture has been the backbone of economic life in Mexico for much of the last century. From the early days of the Porfiriato (1876-1911) the colonization, survey, and trade projects of the regime established a permanent place for Mexican agriculture in the development of national well-being. Of course, to a certain extent the expansion of agricultural enterprise under the dictatorship of Porfirio Díaz was a ratification of reality, a confirmation of the history of U.S.-Mexican trade that began with Spanish colonization. The economic success of Pacific Mexican ports was linked intimately to the westward expansion of the United States after the Gold Rush, and the great cattle empires of the northern frontier coincided with the U.S. range cattle boom of the post–Civil War period.

During the Porfiriato, agricultural capitalism blossomed in certain export enclaves, and the value of exports boomed, despite the uneven swings of the last quarter of the nineteenth century.[26] These primary goods exports represented almost all consumer goods exports during the Porfiriato as well as the bulk of traded production goods. Together, agricultural exports represented almost half of total export value—a striking proportion, given the contemporaneous resurgence of mining. Mexico, as a growing provider of raw materials to the industrial nations, grew in trade at a much faster rate than other providers.[27] Part of that growth, as would later be true in the trade expansion of the 1980s, came in the form of increasing food imports.

Not surprisingly, the Porfirian boom coincided with the U.S. movement west after the Civil War. To American expansionists, who were transforming their antebellum lust for the "gor-

[26] El Colegio de México, *Estadísticas económicas del porfiriato*, Vol. II, *Fuerza de trabajo y actividad económica por sectores* (Mexico: El Colegio de México, 1963).

[27] Fernando Rosenzweig, "El comercio exterior," in Daniel Cosío Villegas, ed., *Historia moderna de México*, Vol. VII, Tome I, *El porfiriato: la vida económica* (Mexico: Editorial Hermes, 1974).

geous prospect" of the "annexation of all Mexico"[28] into a less territorial form of economic dominion from the 1860s to 1880s,[29] Mexico represented "one magnificent but undeveloped mine ... the bridge of commerce of the world."[30] The adventurous capitalists of western railroad companies—the International Railroad Company, the Mexican Central, the Mexican National, the Crédit Foncier, among others—saw fortune and trade opportunities in Mexican rail lines, beginning in the 1860s.[31] The increased trade of the Porfiriato and the resurgence of mining in the greater Southwest confirmed their expectations.[32] The ensuing rail networks also shaped the commodity markets of Mexico and split the frontier states from the Mesa Central.

The railroad expansion of the Porfiriato, which joined the "last great American frontier and the paradise of Sinaloa,"[33] also guided the first attempts to rationalize land tenure and exploitation in the fertile river valleys of the Pacific Coast and on the broad expanses of cattle land in the states of Sonora, Chihuahua, and Coahuila. With the expansion of exports of henequen, vanilla, coffee, cacao, watermelon, garbanzos, resins, and other important agricultural products from diverse regions came the dispossession of the peasantry in areas central to the boom.[34] This historical conjuncture of frontiers

[28] Quote from the *New York Herald*, October 8, 1847, cited in John D. P. Fuller, *The Movement for the Acquisition of All Mexico, 1846-1848* (Baltimore: The Johns Hopkins University Press, 1936), 82.

[29] See Thomas Schoonover, *Dollars over Dominion: The Triumph of Liberalism in U.S.-Mexican Relations, 1861-1867* (Baton Rouge: Louisiana State University Press, 1978).

[30] Alexander D. Anderson, *Mexico from the Material Standpoint* (n.p., 1884, pamphlet), cited in David M. Pletcher, *Rails, Mines and Progress: Seven American Promoters in Mexico, 1867-1911* (Ithaca, N.Y.: Cornell University Press, 1958).

[31] Fred W. Powell, *The Railroads of Mexico* (Boston: The Stratford Company, 1921).

[32] C. L. Sonnichsen, *Colonel Greene and the Copper Skyrocket* (Tucson: University of Arizona Press, 1974).

[33] Pletcher, 276.

[34] George McCutchen McBride, *The Land Systems of Mexico* (New York:

provided the opportunity for agricultural and mining capital to enter Mexico; the settlement of the U.S. West and the industrialization of its economy broadened trade opportunities for Mexico as well. The new railroad links helped agricultural and mineral exporters forge trade relations northward.[35] By 1878, these links were so substantial as to generate a fear in Mexico that more of the northern frontier would be lost to the Yankees.[36] That fear, of course, was built on the earlier loss of approximately half Mexico's territory, including Texas, California, New Mexico, and part of Arizona.[37]

But, for reasons of national security and territorial protection, as well as to provide an alternative to early colonization failures in the North, Porfirio Díaz welcomed railroad, survey, and land concessionaires from the United States. The new rail links stimulated by the legislation of the 1880s in Mexico now connected the Mexican North with the U.S. Southwest and its expanding trade potential, leaving earlier, fragile market links with the central and southern regions of the country to atrophy.[38] The Mining Act of 1884, the 1883 Colonization

---

Condé Nast Press, 1923); Luis Cossío Silva, "La agricultura," in Cosío Villegas.

[35] J. Fred Rippy, *The United States and Mexico* (New York: Alfred A. Knopf, 1926); John Coatsworth, "Railroads, Landholding, and Agrarian Protest in the Early Porfiriato," *Hispanic-American Historical Review* 54:1 (February 1974), 48-71; Ray A. Billington, *Westward Expansion: A History of the American Frontier*, 4th ed. (New York: MacMillan, 1974).

[36] Rippy, 321.

[37] Seymour V. Connor and Odie Faulk, *North America Divided: The Mexican War, 1846-1848* (New York: Oxford University Press, 1971); Orlando Martinez, *The Great Landgrab: The Mexican-American War, 1846-1848* (London: Quartet Books, 1975); Gene M. Brack, *Mexico Views Manifest Destiny, 1821-1846: An Essay on the Origins of the Mexican War* (Albuquerque: University of New Mexico Press, 1975).

[38] Eric B. Ross, *Beyond the Myths of Culture: Essays in Cultural Materialism* (New York: Academic Press, 1980); Walter Ebeling, *The Fruited Plain: The Story of American Agriculture* (Berkeley and Los Angeles: University of California Press, 1980); I. A. Dyer and C. C. O'Mary, eds., *The Feedlot* (Philadelphia: Lea and Feiberger, 1977); Richard J. Arnould, "Changing Patterns of Concentration in American Meatpacking, 1880-1963," *Business His-*

and Survey Law, and the elimination of the *alcabala* (a local tax on commerce) in 1896 all served to stimulate interstate and international trade.[39]

Equally important in the long term was the completion of the U.S. transcontinental railroad in 1869, which shifted the economic center of the country westward. As more rail links integrated the far western territories into the mainstream of the American economy, important changes occurred. Texas and other western states became large producers of range cattle, as well as producing feeder cattle and stockers for midwestern feedlots and grasslands. Rail transportation opened up the possibility of large regional packing houses and a greater integration of expanded grain production, lot-fed cattle, and the packing industry.[40]

The durable and crucial aspect of nineteenth-century agricultural development in Mexico was the split in the market system created by the modernization and expansion of North-South trade. Through the internationalization of money and commodity capital, the northern tier of states was separated commercially from Mexico and linked to the markets of the United States. Nogales, Tucson, El Paso, Laredo, and Brownsville became the hubs of north Mexican commerce, not Guadalajara and Mexico City. The settlement of the lower Rio Grande area of Texas in the first half of the nineteenth century (coinciding with the first Mexican colonization grants in Texas and building on a century of cattle raising in New Spain) began a modern frontier cattle economy emanating from Mexico, which presaged windmill irrigation, barbed wire fences, sci-

---

tory Review 45 (Spring 1971), 18-34; Mary Yeager Kujovich, "The Refrigerator Car and the Growth of the American Dressed Beef Industry," *Business History Review* 44 (Winter 1970).

[39] Donald D. Brand, "The Early History of the Range Cattle Industry in Northern Mexico," *Agricultural History* 35:3 (July 1961); U.S. Department of Agriculture (USDA), "The Mexican Beef Cattle Industry," *Foreign Agriculture* 8:11 (November 1944).

[40] Sergio de la Peña, *La formación del capitalismo en México*, 2nd ed. (Mexico: Siglo XXI, 1976); Cossío Silva.

entific stock improvement, the introduction of shorthorn and Hereford cattle, and forage cropping on both sides of the Rio Bravo.[41] As a by-product of the great range cattle boom of the early 1880s and its demise in the blizzard of 1886-1887, land speculators and foreign *latifundistas* such as Senator George Hearst and Lord Beresford, *hacendados* such as Luis Terrazas and the Sánchez Navarros, land companies such as the Palomas Land and Cattle Company, and grand robber barons in the persons of Collis P. Huntington and Nelson Aldrich poured their dollars and pesos into modern cattle and mining enterprises rivaling the largest in the world at the time.[42]

In local agriculture, the Porfirian laws of the 1880s, along with the U.S. push to the Pacific, made the Sonora and Sinaloa river valleys lush gardens for vegetable and fruit exports. Guaymas boomed by the 1890s, stunted in its commercial growth only by repeated Indian wars and the militarization of the Sonoran agricultural heartland.[43] The importance of the isthmian canal and the consolidation of the western frontier under the "open door" of the last decade of the nineteenth century again coincided with a commodity price stability in the 1890s that further stimulated agricultural exports from Mexico. But, after two decades of that export experience, the advent of the Mexican revolution and later the Great Depression crushed economic growth in Mexico and ensured that export agriculture in the North would know its true potential only in the expansion of trade with the United States after World War II. In the course of the great revolutionary disjuncture, agricultural production fell precipitously in 1911

[41] Walter Prescott Webb, *The Great Plains* (Boston: Ginn and Co., 1931).

[42] Edward Everett Dale, *The Range Cattle Industry* (Norman: University of Oklahoma Press, 1930), 127ff.; Brand, 135.

[43] Héctor Aguilar Camín, *La frontera nómada: Sonora y la Revolución mexicana* (Mexico: Siglo XXI, 1977); Claudio Dabdoub, *Historia del valle del Yaqui* (Mexico: Editorial Porrúa, 1964); Steven E. Sanderson, *Agrarian Populism and the Mexican State: The Struggle for Land in Sonora* (Berkeley and Los Angeles: University of California Press, 1981).

and 1912, regained three-quarters of its value in the period 1914-1919, and then fell again during the 1920s (see Table 1.1). Only in 1937, after the *cardenista* land reform began, did agricultural production surpass levels of value achieved in 1910. In volume of output, the agricultural economy did not surpass Porfirian levels after the revolution until the 1940s.

In the 1940s, agriculture began to reclaim its place as "engine of growth" of the Mexican economy, but this time as a financial promoter of the new wave of import substitution industrialization which accompanied World War II and the rapid recovery from the Great Depression. That role for agriculture, as engine or handmaiden of growth, has been de-

TABLE 1.1
Indices of Mexican Agricultural Production, 1900-1944
(1929 = 100)

	Volume	Value	Prices
1900	87.9	51.3	58.3
1905	106.8	63.3	59.2
1910	143.4	124.2	86.6
1915	109.3	91.9	84.1
1920	87.6	69.4	79.2
1925	109.4	114.8	105.0
1930	90.3	83.2	92.1
1935	106.3	92.4	87.0
1936	117.8	120.1	102.0
1937	109.9	136.2	123.9
1938	110.6	138.6	125.4
1939	125.0	157.1	125.7
1940	115.1	139.4	121.2
1941	150.9	175.1	116.1
1942	154.7	227.2	145.6
1943	142.0	261.2	190.2
1944	175.5	353.9	224.6

SOURCE: Mexico, NAFINSA, *La economía mexicana en cifras*, 1981, 105.

scribed in great detail elsewhere.[44] For now, suffice it to say that agricultural growth provided a large proportion of the foreign exchange necessary for import substitution in the post–World War II period. In 1950, the nonmineral primary sector (agriculture, cattle raising, forestry, and fishing) contributed 19 percent of the gross domestic product (GDP, Table 1.2) and 47.5 percent of the total value of merchandise exports. Agriculture alone contributed 34.5 percent of the value of merchandise exports in that year (Table 1.3). By 1982, agricultural activities had fallen to a contribution of 7.3 percent of the GDP and 2.7 percent of the total merchandise export value.[45] Even without petroleum exports, agriculture contributed merely one-sixth the total value of merchandise exports in 1982.

Despite the reduced role of agriculture in the economy in general, food production, agricultural inputs to industry, and agricultural export production remained important to the na-

TABLE 1.2

Contribution of Agriculture to Mexican GDP, 1950-1982

	GDP (millions of 1970 pesos)	Primary Sector (%)	Agriculture (%)	Cattle (%)	Food (%)
1950	124,779	19.1	11.6	6.2	6.2
1960	225,447	15.9	9.8	5.2	7.0
1970	444,271	12.2	7.1	4.4	6.6
1980	841,854	9.0	5.2	3.2	5.9
1982	903,839	8.8	5.1	3.2	n.a.

SOURCE: Mexico, NAFINSA, *La economía mexicana en cifras*, 1970, 1984.

[44] See especially Clark W. Reynolds, *The Mexican Economy: Twentieth Century Structure and Growth* (New Haven: Yale University Press, 1970); Richard W. Parks, "The Role of Agriculture in Mexican Economic Development," *Inter-American Economic Affairs* 18:1 (Summer 1964), 3-27; and Ricardo Torres Gaytán, "Sector agropecuario y desarrollo económico y social de México," *Comercio exterior* 31:6 (June 1981), 619-626.

[45] Unpublished data from Banco Nacional de México and the USDA.

TABLE 1.3

Value of Mexican Agricultural and Merchandise Exports, 1950-1980
(millions of pesos)

	Agricultural Exports (1)	Merchandise Exports (2)*	(1)/(2) (%)
1950	1,498	4,339	34.5
1960	3,690	9,247.3	39.9
1970	9,306.7	17,457.3	53.3
1975	14,270.6	37,526.2	38.0
1980	42,327.4	351,306.7	12.0

SOURCES: 1950-1960, Centro de Investigaciones Agrarias (CDIA), *Estructura agraria y desarrollo agrícola en México*, 1974; 1970-1980, Mexico, NAFINSA, *La economía mexicana en cifras*, 1981.

* Excluding petroleum.

tional growth plans of all governments following World War II. Public investment in agriculture (Table 1.4) remained relatively high throughout the years of the "economic miracle" (1940-1970) and increased markedly during the oil boom of 1977-1981. Private sector investment, in particular, modernized agricultural support industries such as fertilizer, farm machinery, seeds, and pesticides. Public infrastructure investment created huge dams, irrigation canals, and federal districts for water control. But the role of agriculture changed over the period 1940-1980, not only in the products the system yielded and the land tenure and social relations it sustained, but also in its importance to national growth. No longer was the agricultural sector primarily designed to produce fresh foodstuffs for the domestic population; it functioned now more as an "input" sector for agribusiness and trade. Likewise, the main function of agriculture shifted from feeding the rural population in widely varying market and nonmarket relations to feeding the enormous urban populations, who were without access to the means of food production themselves. As the economy shifted from a rural to an urban setting and from agriculture to industry after World War II, the shape

TABLE 1.4
Public Investment in Mexican Agriculture, 1940-1980

	Average Annual Total (millions of pesos)	Percent of Total Public Investment (5 yr. average)
1940-44	75.93	16.4
1945-49	1,376.96	20.7
1950-54	571.20	17.8
1955-59	705.77	13.0
1960-64	1,228.76	10.1
1965-69	2,103.78	10.6
1970-74	6,106.38	15.3
1975-79	30,002.99	17.4
1980	70,401.92	16.6

SOURCES: Barkin and Suárez, *El fin de autosuficiencia alimentaria*, elaborated from data from Mexico, NAFINSA, *La economía mexicana en cifras*, 1978; José López Portillo, *Cuarto informe de gobierno* (Mexico: Secretaría de la Presidencia, 1980).

and meaning of crop and cattle production also shifted. Agriculture was no longer the engine of growth for the Mexican economy; it was instead the adjunct of industrialization. Basic food production was no longer the principal goal of the agricultural system; it was geared increasingly to support agribusiness processors, retailers, and intermediaries, whether at the international or the national level. And, significantly, the agricultural sector was no longer the locus of reform sentiment and redistributive policy under the revolution; it was, in the end, a holding tank for the marginally employed, a buffer for an economy whose structure encouraged the elimination of the peasantry but whose absorptive capacity in wage labor did not permit the transition from peasant to proletarian.

By 1980, agriculture's role—however described—was in grave crisis. Agricultural exports could not keep up with increasing imports of other agricultural commodities which had been marginalized by that very same trade model of agricultural development. Agribusiness not only failed to absorb rural labor displaced by agricultural modernization and industrialization, but it also failed to improve the nutritional profile of the Mexican population. Basic grain production failed to keep up with per capita needs and effective demand, and grain relinquished much of its social role as nonwage economic provider to the deprived peasantry. State policy toward agriculture—whether in its technical and commercial mandate as promotor of agricultural capitalism or in its reform mandate as guarantor of the struggling *agrarista* tradition—was obviously seeking alternatives to the vicissitudes of the trade-agribusiness development model, which reinforced dependent relations with the United States and encouraged the concentration of capital in agriculture domestically. The state was seeking to avoid, as well, the limited land reform strategies of the Echeverría government, which had precipitated one of the deepest political crises in modern Mexican history. Before mapping that state-led quest for a coherent agricultural development policy, however, let us concentrate first on the specific nature of the transformation of Mexican agriculture.

The Transformation of Mexican Agriculture

In addition to the important changes in the role of agriculture in the national economy—from export enclave to industrializing force, then to adjunct of that industrialization—the internal character of agriculture itself underwent profound transformation. In several dimensions—in crop mix, cattle raising, trade content, and agribusiness value-added—the Mexican agricultural system changed internally over the period 1940-1980. The lines of change are relatively easier to sketch than to explain. First, trade in agricultural commodities became more important as the sector assumed its role as engine of growth for import substitution in the 1940s. That trade—principally with the United States—continued to expand over the four decades since 1940, even after the importance of agriculture as the fountainhead of financing for industrialization had waned. Second, trade generated a more complex set of agribusiness relationships—contract farming, vertical integration and coordination in certain crops and in cattle, and technological packages disseminated from processors, retailers, and marketing intermediaries—which permanently affected the rural relations of production in traded agricultural goods. Basic grain production during the period tended to give way to forage and fodder crops as well as to certain export plantation crops and perennials, such as grapes. The livestock-feedgrain "complex" grew to great importance, challenging basic foodstuffs and the land system which sustained their growth. Finally, the state, through public investment, export promotion, and water and land use policy, stimulated the internationalization of the agricultural economy, the internationalization of that model of growth and its products, and the separation of control over agricultural production from the agricultural producer.

While simply described in the abstract, the nuances of these transformations are subtle, and therefore deserve individual attention. The following discussion will analyze the general lines of each of the above propositions, and following chapters will specify the development of these transformations in the fruit and vegetable, livestock-feedgrain, and basic grain complexes.

Trade and the Internationalization of Mexican Agriculture

Latin American agriculture has always operated under a clear trade imperative. From the agricultural export enclaves of the independence period, of course, come the notions of "classical dependency," based on the old international division of labor.[46] But, even with the rise of import substitution industrialization, agricultural exports maintained their importance

---

[46] For a good description of "classic dependency," see Peter Evans, *Dependent Development: The Alliance of Multinational, State, and Local Capital in Brazil* (Princeton, N.J.: Princeton University Press, 1979).

41

in national economic growth plans throughout Latin America, even as they were being decapitalized and shifted away from domestic foodstuff production. During the "easy phase" of import substitution, agriculture provided the key foreign exchange for importing industrial inputs for transforming the economies of Brazil, Argentina, Colombia, and Mexico. Agricultural modernization became a prime value of the leaders of the rural sector, both for its domestic potential in feeding the burgeoning urban industrial working class and for its capacity to stimulate the external sector's role in import substitution.

During this period, however, the internal terms of trade operated to the disadvantage of agriculture, as did the priorities of the banking system and the strategies of national entrepreneurs. Capital fled agriculture for industry. State finance also favored industry. And individuals sought higher and safer returns outside the primary sector. As industrialization proceeded, agriculture declined in importance as a generator of foreign exchange, although in 1981 the Latin American region still counted on foodstuffs for 45.8 percent of export activity.[47] Likewise, the rural sector employed fewer people, as nonfarm employment skyrocketed.[48] But rural life remained important as an adjunct to industrialization.

The trade imperative in Mexican agriculture, above all, implied the diversion of agricultural resources from basic foodstuffs to the production, exchange, and distribution of traded agricultural goods and processed commodities. In the period since 1940, it has been increasingly evident that the bulk of Mexican agricultural resources has gone to the sectors and regions devoted to trade and agroindustrial manufactures, along with certain luxury produce items. That dynamic is the product of a number of mechanisms, the first and perhaps most important of which involved the creation of the federal irrigation districts and their management for export. Begin-

[47] IDB, *The External Sector*, Table 10.
[48] Gomes and Pérez.

ning with the creation of the Comisión Nacional de Irrigación under President Calles in 1926, the state involved itself directly in the management and development of federal irrigation districts and "units of irrigation" (*unidades de riego*). Detailed analysis of the evolution of that particular mode of state intervention will come in Chapter 2. Here it is important to note that the international market, perforce of its traditional allure in northern Mexico (where the bulk of federal irrigation projects are still concentrated) and through the intervention of the state itself in export promotion, created the irrigation districts as providers of traded agricultural commodities, to the detriment of basic foodstuffs for internal consumption. Second, the state devoted the bulk of all agricultural investment to the enrichment and expansion of the federal irrigation districts, at least until 1980. Finally, the character of general state policy toward trade in agriculture stimulated the irrigation districts to specialize more and more in producing for the exterior, particularly for U.S. markets.

Regarding the creation of the federal irrigation system as an "export platform," it is not necessary to assume that the motivation of state managers in Mexico was to rationalize water use specifically for export. Rather, it is necessary to recognize only that the areas in which the *grandes obras de irrigación* were created traditionally enjoyed a positive trade relationship with the United States. In 1978, seven of the eight federal irrigation districts harvesting over 100,000 hectares were in the northern border states plus Sinaloa. The eighth was in Guanajuato, in the heart of the vegetable-processing and strawberry export complex. Total production in the eight "superdistricts" equaled nearly half the total agricultural value produced in irrigated districts in Mexico, and roughly one-sixth of total agricultural value nationwide.[49] In these irrigation districts, farmers traditionally had exported gar-

[49] Mexico, Secretaría de Agricultura y Recursos Hidráulicos (SARH), *Anuario estadístico: año agrícola 1977-1978* (Mexico: SARH, 1979); SARH, *Econotecnia agrícola: consumos aparentes de productos agrícolas para los años de 1925-1978* (Mexico: SARH, 1980).

43

banzo, vegetables, cotton, cattle, and melons northward to the United States from the time of the Porfiriato. After the great expansion of irrigation works during the Alemán presidency (1946-1952), certain export crops skyrocketed in volume and value. Those crops were, not surprisingly, cultivated in the new irrigation districts, which finally confirmed the Porfirian split in the agricultural system between the north and the center of the country.

The volume of cotton exports at the outset of the Alemán government totaled a mere 47.6 thousand tons; a decade later Mexico exported 421.8 thousand tons, near the peak levels achieved in 1966.[50] Another export commodity springing from irrigation districts in Sinaloa—tomatoes—yielded only 88.2 tons in 1946, and 50.3 in 1956. But by 1966, Sinaloa had blossomed as a fresh vegetable exporter, and tomatoes led the way with exports of over 231 tons. In the aftermath of the "Florida tomato war," the Mexican government has, for various reasons, tried to limit tomato production for export, which by 1978 had grown to nearly 500 tons.[51] Grapes and strawberries appeared as new irrigated crops for export in the postwar period, as garbanzos maintained their century-old position in the trade bill.

The point, whether illustrated by winter vegetables, cotton, or citrus crops (which also showed remarkable increases in the 1950s and 1960s) is that the federal irrigation system grew mainly to serve U.S. markets for fresh produce, rather than internal markets for similar primary commodities. Its role as

[50] Data for 1946-1966 are from Mexico, SARH, *Econotecnia agrícola: consumos aparentes de productos agrícolas para los años de 1925-1978.* Table 1.5 shows the subsequent deterioration of cotton as an export. For more on tomato exports, see Chapter 2.

[51] For details and analysis of the Florida tomato war, see Andrew Schmitz, Robert S. Firch, and Jimmye S. Hillman, "Agricultural Export Dumping: The Case of Mexican Winter Vegetables in the U.S. Market," *American Journal of Agricultural Economics* 63:4 (November 1981), 645-654, and Steven E. Sanderson, "Florida Tomatoes, U.S.-Mexican Relations and the International Division of Labor," *Inter-American Economic Affairs* 35:3 (Winter 1981), 23-52.

TABLE 1.5
Mexican Exports of Selected Irrigated Crops, 1950-1977 (tons)

	Cotton	Grapes	Garbanzos*	Strawberries
1950	162,637	75	11,639	1,632
1960	324,302	26	4,730	13,261
1970	222,681	4,965	8,492	81,990
1975	37,936	4,757	32,006	64,545
1976	179,099	7,625	28,450	38,100
1977	152,809	15,328	46,522	80,429

NOTE: The viability of these data, along with other SARH figures, is thrown into question by the inconsistency of USDA, World Bank, SARH, and Bank of Mexico figures. All the sources do show similar trends, however.
SOURCE: Mexico, SARH, *Econotecnia agrícola*, 1980.
* Includes forage also.

input producer for agribusiness is somewhat more complicated, but that analysis remains for Chapters 2-4. In general, production in irrigation districts after World War II moved away from basic foodstuffs—although wheat is still irrigation-dependent in Mexico—toward oleaginous crops (soya, safflower, and linseed, mainly), export vegetables and fruits, and forage crops (see Table 1.6). This movement was reinforced not only by the heavy investment of the state in those irrigation districts particularly successful in export-oriented agriculture (see Table 1.7) but also by the influences of the growing U.S. market in certain commodities and the relative price structure of Mexican agriculture.

In the 1950s, the Mexican government supported the prices of key foodstuffs in irrigation districts—particularly wheat—through direct price supports and the purchasing policies of CEIMSA and CONASUPO.[52] Likewise, in the healthy economic environment of the 1950s, the Mexican miracle main-

[52] CONASUPO, to be described more fully later, is the National Company for Popular Subsistence; CEIMSA, the Mexican Exporting and Importing Company, was its predecessor.

TABLE 1.6
Area Devoted to Various Crops in Mexico's Federal Irrigation Districts,
1970-1978

Crop Type	1969-70 (%)	1974-75 (%)	1977-78 (%)	Change in Area (ha), 1970-78
Grains	59.50	57.79	53.73	−205,416
Other Foods	3.25	3.23	3.77	+36,375
Forage	4.63	6.72	7.78	+127,084
Oleaginous	12.96	18.67	16.50	+190,898
Textiles	13.39	6.01	9.09	−50,126
Industrial	3.50	4.20	4.61	+56,542
Fruits	1.99	2.36	3.80	+68,916
Flowers	0.08	0.02	0.02	−1,329
Seeds	0.02	0.02	0.04	+677
Other	0.68	0.98	0.66	+3,531

SOURCE: SARH, *Anuario estadístico*, 1979.

tained relatively positive internal terms of trade for certain
key agricultural commodities, due to a stable exchange rate,
low inflation, and the progressive pricing policy of the government. During that period of initial growth in irrigation and
agricultural modernization, key export crops that eventually
were to challenge domestic food production either were not
being produced or were only beginning to find their way into
the irrigation districts for the first time. Soya production was
at low levels, not only because of its lack of tradition as a
crop in Mexico, but because of the lack of water for two-
season cultivation prior to the growth of the great irrigation
districts and their storage dams. Other oleaginous crops were
also relatively minor in the crop makeup of the 1950s in
Mexico. The principal areas of citrus and grape cultivation—
the pump irrigation districts—were generally not capitalized
until the mid-1950s and, as we shall see, did not shift to export
production until later, Most remarkably, sorghum, which
would shortly challenge maize production in every corner of

TABLE 1.7

Participation of Key Sectors and Regions in Mexican Public Investment, 1940-1980

	Total Public Investment (millions of pesos)	% of Total Allocated to Agriculture and Cattle = B	% of B Allocated to Irrigation	% of B Allocated to Son., Sin., & Tamps.
1940	290	15.5	80.0	—
1945	848	17.2	95.8	—
1950	2,672	19.3	72.1	36.2
1955	4,408	13.7	99.2	11.8
1960	8,376	8.0	85.5	33.2
1965	13,049	8.6	98.4	62.9
1970	30,250	13.4	92.5	66.3
1975	95,767	18.1	76.0	77.1
1980	424,108	16.6	59.2	24.7

SOURCES: Elaborated by Centro de Ecodesarrollo with data from annual presidential reports (*Informes de gobierno*), various years 1974-1980; and NAFINSA, *La economía mexicana en cifras*, 1978.

Mexico, did not even appear in the Mexican crop profile of the 1950s.

As an example of the effect of pricing policies, throughout the 1950s and 1960s the government's concentration on wheat expansion tended to challenge maize production nationwide. In the irrigation districts, wheat displaced maize through credit supports, technical assistance programs, and price subsidies. In general, despite the importance of maize to CONASUPO and to the peasant economy, crops benefiting from progressive price support programs and other "modernizing" incentives to agriculture tended to challenge basic food cultivation in peasant areas.[53] Price guarantees in the 1960s, however, became extremely costly to the Mexican government

[53] David Barkin and Gustavo Esteva, "El papel del sector público en la comercialización y la fijación de precios de los productos agrícolas básicos en México" (Mexico, U.N. CEPAL, June 1981, mimeo.).

because of high internal prices, low international prices, and the cost of maintaining large internal reserves of grain produced under the price subsidy program. The price support system then shifted away from its prior mission as a producer incentive to concentrate instead on the more restricted intention to control the price of agricultural commodities to the urban consumer, especially the industrial working class. Thus, the transformation of cropping through the price system—as we shall see in more detail in Chapter 5—had the effect of transforming the state's role in agricultural growth from price maker in basic commodities to agent of international trade and internal oligopolist in basic grains. By the mid-1970s, CONASUPO had entered the international market to import rice, barley, sesame, soya, safflower, and sunflower as well as maize, sorghum, and wheat. Thus, in both pricing policy and official purchases, the international trade regime affected the capacity of the Mexican system to continue a policy of promoting basic foodstuffs, an argument which will be pursued in more detail later.

In addition to pricing policies which—at least in the 1950s—favored wheat production at the expense of maize in the irrigation districts and which also provided more direct incentives to new cultivation of soya, safflower, sesame, linseed, and other oil-bearing seeds, the government concentrated its credit to agriculture in favor of the great irrigation districts. In 1977, for example, agricultural credit for safflower extended to 60 percent of all irrigated land devoted to that crop, but only 25 percent of the rain-fed land for the same commodity. In soya, over 50 percent of the irrigated land devoted to the crop received credit, but only 0.3 percent of the rain-fed area benefited similarly. Even in sorghum, which is primarily known for its drought resistance and adaptability to rain-fed cultivation in Mexico, nearly half of the irrigated area devoted to grain sorghum received credit for the crop, whereas little more than one-third of the rain-fed area found credit for its cultivation.[54] Similarly, for the entire period 1940-1980, public investment in agriculture went in overwhelming proportion to irrigation (see Table 1.7). The balance of public investment in agriculture and cattle raising favored the richest farmers producing the most marketable crops and left over half the rural proprietors without access to credit.[55] The results of this policy and the development of the great irrigation districts over the period 1946-1980 have been stunning. In the crop year 1976-1977, for example, the federal irrigation districts of the North Pacific region alone contributed over 54 percent of the total value from all federal irrigation districts. The index of agricultural production in the irrigation districts (1960 = 100) in 1977 was double that of the base year. Annual rates of growth in those districts exceeded 7 percent at the national level; at the same time agricultural growth in rain-fed districts stagnated (1960-1977).[56]

Agricultural trade from the irrigated districts responded also to some fundamental changes in the character of the U.S. agricultural system. As the largest market for Mexican exports in general (and the indispensable market for agricultural produce), the United States to a certain extent dictated the conditions of trade in certain crops, through a trade-generated expansion of agribusiness relationships. As we shall see throughout the text, important changes in the geography of U.S. agricultural production, especially in cattle raising, affected the role of the frontier beef cattle industry in Mexico. Likewise, the growth of the U.S. market for fresh winter vegetables generated an expansion of production in Sinaloa, me-

[54] Steven E. Sanderson, *Trade Aspects of the Internationalization of Mexican Agriculture: Consequences for Mexico's Food Crisis*, Center for U.S.-Mexican Studies, Monograph #10 (La Jolla: University of California, San Diego, 1983), Table VIII.

[55] Centro de Investigaciones Agrarias (CDIA), *Estructura agraria y desarrollo agrícola en México* (Mexico: Fondo de Cultura Económica, 1974), 776.

[56] Mexico, SARH, Dirección General de Distritos de Riego, *Estadística agrícola en los distritos y unidades de riego, 1977-1978*, Table XIX.

diated by brokers and distributors in Arizona and opposed by competing producers in Florida. Partly because of the comparative advantage enjoyed by the United States in basic grain production and its importance in world export markets in such grains, Mexico found itself drawn to a trade model which, ultimately, increased its dependence on foreign providers of basic foodstuffs and diverted the rural food system away from domestic, and especially rural, consumers. The gradual change in roles assigned to the U.S. and Mexican agricultural systems and their increasing integration through trade, agribusiness expansion, and state policy played a large part in the emergence of a "new international division of labor in agriculture," which was a partial expression of historical interaction and a recognition of some fundamental changes in the accumulation of capital in the countryside.

Because of the necessity of assuring markets for traded produce and the complementary desire in the United States to secure regular and reliable high-quality imports from Mexico, a new wave of trade-impelled agribusiness grew up in the frontier area during the three decades since the development of the great irrigation districts. A number of those agribusiness ties will be developed in later chapters; they include purchasing contracts for produce, especially in winter vegetables, future production contracts in cattle, and "packages" of seeds, technical assistance, and credit in a wide range of crops, from maize to tomatoes. Such agribusiness relationships are not restricted to the frontier, however; nor are they necessarily impelled by trade alone. In the case of tobacco, for instance, agricultural producers enter into production contracts with both domestic and international corporations, mediated by TABAMEX, the state tobacco enterprise. As we shall see later, such relationships are not necessarily restricted to multinationals or to the trade sector. In fact, they argue strongly for a broader understanding of the internationalization of Mexican agriculture, based on production itself, as well as trade and state mediation. If trade sometimes stimulates agricultural internationalization, it does not explain it fully.

In short, as the following discussion will show, the dynamics of trade in agriculture, combined with state policy and agribusiness encouragement, have had the effect of transforming the Mexican agricultural sector by turning it away from the production of basic foodstuffs and concentrating efforts instead toward the production of urban goods and commodities for the international market. That production system has also generated a support structure which further disarticulates domestic production from consumption. In the case of cattle, for example, northern agricultural lands—including the irrigation districts—have increased production of cattle feed, in the form of sorghum and soya, as well as fodder grasses. In the case of poultry, which is exclusively for domestic consumption in Mexico, international technology requires a massive diversion of crop land to the production of sorghum for confinement feeding. Even egg yolks are colored by carotene in marigolds (*zempoaxochitl*), traditionally cultivated on rainfed land for ceremonial use on the Day of the Dead.

The New Agricultural Export Enclave

The traditional notion of Latin American agricultural growth has emphasized one of two trends: the export pole led by a staple crop (Argentine wheat, Guatemalan bananas, Brazilian sugar, then coffee, etc.)[57] or the relatively isolated hacienda, only marginally linked to commerce and little affected by international forces (e.g., Mexican cattle before 1850, Cuban sugar before the 1830s).[58] Naturally, for our purposes here,

[57] Two interesting statements of staple theory are Melville H. Watkins, "A Staple Theory of Economic Growth," *The Canadian Journal of Economics and Political Science* 29:2 (May 1963), 150-158, and John Fogarty, "Staple Theory and the Development Experiences of Argentina, Australia and Canada," paper delivered at the International Congress of Americanists, Manchester, England, September 1982.

[58] See for example, François Chevalier, *Land and Society in Colonial Mexico: The Great Hacienda*, trans. Alvin Eustis, ed. Lesley B. Simpson (Berkeley and Los Angeles: University of California Press, 1963), and Furtado, Chapter 7.

the former is more interesting to compare with current agricultural export enclaves. The new export enclaves differ from traditional circumstance in several respects. First, the new agricultural exports are to a much greater extent governed by internationally standardized technological requirements. All citrus exported fresh from Mexico to the United States passes through U.S. Department of Agriculture certified inspection and packing stations.[59] All beef packed in Latin America for shipment to the United States must meet USDA standards for hygiene and slaughter.[60] And, for reasons of market appearance and appeal, products emanating from the Americas in general must mimic the fastidious requirements of consumer markets abroad. To a great extent, such demands are possible only in the current epoch of revolutionary transformation in shipping, disease control, and communication.

Second, the new agricultural export enclaves are much more likely to be productively integrated via contracts and long-term productive relationships than were most auction markets or primary commodity arrangements of the old order (Spanish mercantilist restrictions and later British domination notwithstanding). In the case of Mexican winter vegetables—one of the most famous cases of export enclave integration in recent years—producer technology, financing, and sales all transcend mere episodic market interaction and involve contract relationships, transnational brokerage, and consignment sales to prearranged markets. The same is true of strawberries. The fluctuations of commodity markets dictate with great sensitivity the annual planting priorities of Mexican producers and the marketing prerogatives of their U.S. distributors.[61] The same is true of live cattle exports from the Mexican north, which respond to the brokers' and feedlots' expectations of market performance but revolve around production contracts

[59] USDA, *Citrus in Mexico*, Foreign Agricultural Service Report, May 1981.

[60] I refer to P.L. 90-201 (81 Stat. 584) "The Wholesome Meat Act," Section 10, which amends provisions of the Federal Meat Inspection Act of 1964 (52 Stat. 1235).

[61] The evidence for this will be presented in Chapter 2.

and forward contracts for custom feeding across borders.[62] Likewise, in Brazilian and Colombian coffee production, state trading arrangements and an international convention dictate the international marketing strategies of producer countries in accordance with a relatively refined understanding of the market and other variables of production. This articulation of agricultural exports with the international market stands in stark contrast to the weak interventions of the Brazilian valorization schemes of the first half of the twentieth century, which served principally to manage the marketing of existing stocks rather than to attune production to market conditions per se.

Third, the new agricultural export enclaves have more direct impact on domestic markets than in classic cases, with, perhaps, Argentine beef as the outstanding nineteenth-century exception. While most agricultural export enclaves of the old regime seemed to operate relatively apart from domestic market considerations, the current incarnation of the export enterprise directly relates to provisioning requirements for populations increasingly "sophisticated" (at least in a value-added sense) in their food demands. Exports of Mexican cattle bring about shortfalls in domestic supplies. Winter vegetables threaten basic foodstuff production in irrigation districts. Pineapple exports undermine the popular consumption of fresh fruit at a low price. And sugar exports (in Brazil, at least) must be attentive to increasing domestic demands. To the extent that the export enclave is more sensitive to domestic political and consumer considerations than previously, the growth prospects and nature of state intervention in agroexport activities become more problematic, as we shall see.

Finally, the new agricultural export enclave must survive in a much more politically sophisticated atmosphere. The old model of agroexport activities came from a historical circum-

[62] Steven E. Sanderson, "The Emergence of the 'World Steer': Internationalization and Foreign Domination in the Latin American Cattle Industry," paper presented at the 44th International Congress of Americanists, University of Manchester, England, September 1982.

stance in which the Latin American state had little bureaucratic weight and less power. The current state has, since then, weathered the rise of import substitution, presided over the creation of massive social service and social capital investment structures, and acted as midwife to agricultural capital formation in post-Depression Latin America. No longer does the export entrepreneur encounter the client state perhaps more fondly remembered by United Fruit or Standard Brands. Now, if one can concede that the virtue of many Latin American states is too easily breached, the politics of state management from the exporters' perspective have become much more complicated and interactive with domestic considerations.

Agribusiness Development and the Internationalization of Mexican Agriculture

Agribusiness, defined as a vertically organized food chain made up of producers, intermediaries, and processors,[63] includes not only relationships driven by shared trade interests, of course, but also integrative mechanisms that operate on behalf of more general institutional interests of the agribusiness enterprise. In fresh produce, the form of agribusiness tends to be rather straightforward commercial mediation between farmer and consumer, whether at the local, national, or international level. In winter vegetables and some fruits for export, the mediation takes place across national boundaries through "complexes" of production, exchange, distribution, and consumption.[64] Food and beverage processors tend to govern the market through forward contracts to producers; grains are also subject to such contracts, but less frequently

[63] The term agribusiness was elaborated by Ray Goldberg in *Agribusiness Management for Developing Countries—Latin America* (Cambridge, Mass.: Ballinger, 1974). See also James E. Austin, *Agribusiness in Latin America* (New York: Praeger, 1974). Roger Burbach and Patricia Flynn, *Agribusiness in the Americas* (New York: Monthly Review Press, 1980), offer a contrasting evaluation of agribusiness activities in Latin America.

[64] See Chapter 2.

by U.S.-based brokers and multinational corporations. Seed production is perhaps the clearest case of multinational corporate influence over a commodity which is basically for domestic consumption but produced according to global strategies with international technologies, capital, and management.[65]

The state is also involved in agribusiness, as we have already mentioned in connection with CONASUPO. In fact, distinguishing agribusiness in the private sector from peasant agriculture in nonmarket economies and state supported activities in a mixed economy is as difficult as finding the nationality of transnational corporations. Mexico presents some special problems in this regard, as we shall see in the areas of feedgrains and foodgrains, fresh produce, and cattle.

Agribusiness, especially agroindustry, serves as one of the most significant elements of the dynamic of internationalization. Agroindustries, of course, are hardly new to Latin America. From the *aurora yucateca*[66] of the nineteenth century, or the rise of bottling, beer, and soft drink industries at the turn of the twentieth century, or even the redoubtable sugar refinery of emerging agricultural capitalism in the Caribbean, Brazil, and Mexico, agroindustries have played an important role. They have focused the generation of value-added in the countryside, the articulation of production with the market, and the rise of state intervention and foreign direct investment in the primary sector. The progressive integration of such industries at the international level, however, has led to a qualitative change in their composition since World War II. First, as in the case of the new agricultural export enclave, agroindustries are more likely to be integrated into an inter-

[65] Louis W. Goodman and Arthur Domike, *The Improved Seed Industry: Issues and Options for Mexico,* A Document of the Joint Program of the SINE-American University, Center for International Technical Cooperation (Washington, D.C.: The American University, 1982).

[66] Howard Cline, "The 'Aurora Yucateca' and the Spirit of Enterprise in Yucatan, 1821-1847," *Hispanic American Historical Review* 27:1 (February 1947), 30-60.

national standard of technology, labor process creation, and valorization than before. Concretely, that integration has had a twofold effect at the level of production: first, the agroindustrial goods are implicitly more acceptable to international markets; and second, the technology of production, determined to a great extent outside the national boundaries of the Latin American "host" nation, are not necessarily the most appropriate for national agricultural production.[67]

The more painful corollaries to these statements involve the generation of agricultural product lines and goods inappropriate for domestic consumption, or unnecessarily expensive from the viewpoint of domestic requirements. Likewise, another corollary involves the strain on productive resources imposed by internationalized technologies. In the first case, as may be seen in the export promotion of frozen orange juice concentrate or confinement-fed purebred beef cut to international standards (although, with slight variations, we could include frozen strawberries from the Mexican Bajío, cut flowers from Colombia, canned pineapple from Veracruz, granulated sugar from Brazil, or refined safflower oil in Sinaloa), the productive apparatus of Latin American agroindustries tends to be geared to global markets and technologies, at the expense of low-income domestic consumers. Although Latin America has been cited as a locus of increasing domestic animal protein consumption,[68] data from leading countries in the region show that per capita consumption of beef has not consistently increased with herd growth (a relationship which, itself, even understates the separation between the "modern" beef industry and the average consumer). In the case of the poultry industry, the leading hosts for the chicken boom, Mexico and Brazil, both validate our observations. In Mexico, virtually no one in the lowest income strata eats poultry, eggs,

[67] Barkin and Rozo, "L'agriculture et l'internationalization du capital" and Sartaj Aziz, ed., *Hunger, Politics and Markets: The Real Issues in the Food Crisis* (New York: New York University Press, 1975), Section V.

[68] Winrock International, *Technical Report: The World Livestock Product, Feedstuff, and Food Grain System* (Morrilton, Ark.: Winrock International, 1981).

or any other animal protein on a regular basis.[69] In Brazil, rapid growth in modern poultry production has also been accompanied by a declining proportion of production domestically consumed.[70] In the first case, Mexican poultry has failed to address the food needs of the nutritionally deprived, all the while being touted as a cheap source of popular protein. In Brazil, poultry production has joined the legions of export platform industries, provisioning European markets while denying the domestic consumer improvements in diet. In both cases, of course, the demands for sorghum, soya meal, and other balanced feedstuffs essential to the confinement feeding of poultry strain agricultural resources further.

In the case of orange juice concentrate, Brazil has a relatively privileged position in the international market as the world's second-largest producer of citrus and frozen orange juice concentrate (FOJC).[71] While the foreign exchange consequences (U.S. $609 million in 1981) of such activities are clearly important to a country such as Brazil, once again we find a Latin American agroindustrial experience being dedicated to foreign exchange generation, quite removed from the needs of much of the domestic population and dependent on futures markets dictated by the caprices of weather, the value of land in Florida, the appearance of citrus canker in Mexican (then Florida) groves, and similar uncertainties. In the case of Mexico, a recent entrant in the FOJC sweepstakes, the costs of production are even clearer. Mexico is still much more dependent on imported technologies for processing citrus, still straining to produce all the varieties necessary for a palatable "international grade" FOJC, and still without leverage as a producer of concentrate, compared with the United States and Brazil.

[69] Mexico, SPP, *La población de México*.

[70] U.S. estimates state that domestic consumption of Brazilian poultry declined from about 90 percent of production in 1979 to about 75 percent in 1981. Exports at the same time increased as a percentage of production from 8 percent to 20 percent. USDA, "Brazil: Agricultural Situation, 1981," Foreign Agricultural Service Report (American Embassy, Brasilia, March 5, 1982, mimeo.), 11.

[71] Ibid., p. 23. Brazilian production of FOJC totaled 533,000 tons in 1981.

At the same time, Mexico shows little domestic demand among consumers below the middle strata, for reasons of both income and prices, as well as lack of refrigeration.

In all these cases, the agroindustrial growth of the economy, impelled by agribusiness relationships in general, has also meant the diversion of scarce public resources to externally oriented enterprises or to enterprises targeted toward a small upper stratum of domestic consumers. We will treat this by-product of agroindustrial growth more carefully in future chapters; suffice it to say here that there is a gradual drift of public credit and incentives away from domestic food needs, as a "natural" concomitant of comparative advantage and agroindustrial growth. Only in halting fashion did Mexico attempt to counter that diversion through the now-defunct Sistema Alimentario Mexicano.

In Mexico, Brazil, Argentina, and Colombia, one of the primary functions of the state is to arbitrate the successful capitalization of agribusiness, in the form of both primary goods marketing and agroindustrial processing. Central to the "new wave" of *export* substitution engaging many Latin American economies—by which they attempt to integrate their manufactures into the international system through trade liberalization and production incentives programs—is the idea of adding value to agroindustrial exports. Those strategies span the full range of national economic alternatives, from economic stabilization, with its great emphasis on exchange rate and credit incentives for export, to the industrialization drive of Mexico in the late 1970s, which sought to expand agroindustrial exports to stave off the petrolization of the external sector of the economy. We shall introduce the political consequences of such agroindustrial incentives shortly, and explore them more fully in Chapter 5.

The Agroindustrial Satellite

As suggested in the brief description of the poultry industry, the rise of agroindustry and export enclaves involves the "satellization" of the agricultural economy in general. Such vertical and horizontal linkages into input and support activities distinguish the modern internationalization of agriculture from the classic case. The most illustrative examples of the agroindustrial satellite may be found in the balanced feed and sugar industries, though similar cases in barley, maize, manioc, and other crops could be cited. In the case of modern sugar production, the mode of producer dependence differs little at the local level from that of the old refinery of the Caribbean or Mexico or Brazil. The cane producer is typically a client of a refinery to which he is beholden not only for the critical processing of his cane but for production financing, water rights, transport, and the like. However, we could hypothesize here that the greater the industrial growth of the national economy of sugar-producing nations in the region, the greater the change in the commercial relations of sugar production. That is, in Brazil, Colombia, and Mexico, as well as Argentina, sugar production is less important as an export crop (as compared with nontraditional exports) than as an agroindustrial input and a domestic commodity in refined form. While the satellite producers have stayed the same, their integration into the international economy has changed.

In the case of the livestock feed industry, the dynamic is different, fundamentally for the lack of a transnationalized balanced feedstuff industry in the classic mode of export enclaves. The rise of feedmills and their producers has come with the rise of modern beef, poultry, and pork industries, emphasizing confinement feeding over range and *traspatio* modes and demanding improved protein content in the feedstuffs for the sake of faster growth rates, better marbling characteristics, lower death rates of livestock, and the like. Immanent in such a rise of sorghum, soya meal, and maize production is the satellization of traditional peasant producers and some small farmers into the livestock-feedgrain complex, especially in the form of contract production for feedmills and oilseed processors. They become satellites to a highly mechanized and integrated poultry industry, as well as to the feed mills dedicated to other livestock feeding. Of course, the consumer market for animal protein—overwhelmingly income-determined—returns us to the question of who is raising what for whom. In this regard, the essence of satellite production for integrated agroindustries is the deepening disarticulation of the producer from national and local needs, the upward income bias of the agroindustry-led food system, and the diminution of local control over production decisions in the countryside.

POLITICAL CONSEQUENCES

Clearly, the processes and modes of international integration described above are not politically neutral, particularly in view of the Latin American state's longstanding involvement in agriculture, the importance of the rural sector to the national economies of the region, and the external trade and payments crises currently endemic throughout the Americas. Unfortunately for attempts to generalize about the political attitudes or policy frameworks guiding Latin American agricultural development strategies, the analyst is undone at first look by the great diversity of state apparatuses in Latin America and their widely varying perspectives on the role of state intervention, the significance of the rural sector for national development, and state capacity to attend to rural imbalances and growth prospects.

In the case of Mexico, we find a state apparatus singularly well equipped to deal with agricultural modernization and its attendant social questions, at least from the common standpoints of historical experience in agrarian matters and installed bureaucratic capacity. As we shall see in Chapter 5, the Mexican state has not been deficient in its presence in the agricultural sector. To the contrary, its presence has been clear and felt by producers and agribusiness interests as well as peasants. Rather, the inability of the state to "manage" the rural crisis that has been building since the 1970s comes from the insertion of the sector into the international division of labor, along lines designed by the Mexican state itself in the import-substitution experience. The agricultural system has been transformed from the "independent variable" of growth to the "dependent variable" of industrialization. Agriculture has deepened its relation with and dependence on agroindustrial development. And the food system has become more vulnerable to changes in demand from the urban consumer and the transnational corporation, irrespective of the objective needs of the countryside itself.

The political consequences of the industrialization of agriculture and its relegation to a subsidiary position in the economy have included a deepening relationship with the forces militating toward a greater internationalization of agriculture. In the first place, the Mexican economy in the 1970s—in keeping with Brazil, Colombia, and especially Venezuela—has fallen into an import dependence in basic foods, at least partly due to the industrial shift in agricultural growth and the inattention of state policy supports to basic foodstuffs producers. Such import dependence in basic foods and agroindustrial raw materials puts great strain on economies suffering trade and payments imbalances. Such is the case with Mexico at this writing (1984).

Also, agroindustries have become increasingly important to the growth and trade plans of the region's economies. Since the beginning of import substitution, one of the goals of Latin American economic growth plans has been to reshape exports in favor of manufactures, once domestic demand has been satisfied and infant industries have matured. "Export substitution" became even more important in the 1970s in Mexico, not because of the oil shock but because of Mexico's own effort to diversify its exports as a buffer against the petrolization of the economy and the fluctuations of commodity prices. While Mexico suffered somewhat from an overvalued exchange rate, it managed to increase its exports of foodstuff manufactures—albeit with substantial petrosubsidies.

In such developments lies the specter of increased state intervention. Whether we consider the "shared development"

61

of President Echeverría's integrated rural industries (1970-1976) or the famous "industrial corridors" of the López Portillo administration or the nascent national development plans of the de la Madrid administration, the Mexican national economy has for decades dedicated itself to greater participation in an international system already weighted against Third World competitiveness and committed to eradicating specifically those kinds of subventions the Latin American state finds itself able to offer the rural sector. This tension-building political drive to involve the state more in the affairs of the agricultural sector has met a contradictory political agenda. With heavy state involvement in agricultural growth and agroindustrial development has also come external reliance on developed-world producers of grains for imports of basic foods. The diversion of scarce resources away from basic foods in favor of the industrialization and export orientation of agriculture has given new ammunition to "food power" advocates in developed countries. And the import content of basic foods supplies has become more directly dependent on the expansion of state spending (exacerbated by demographic characteristics in rural Mexico) and the vicissitudes of international commodity prices and international lending policies. In Mexico's current case, agricultural development policy—dependent as it is on the federal budget—has fallen under the purview of the international banking community's negotiations with the Mexican government over a fiscal austerity package for the de la Madrid administration. And from that vulnerability to U.S. grain supplies and external sector collapse has come a new discourse of dependency versus autonomy, denominated partly by the language of "food power" and "food sovereignty" in strategic foods.

At the heart of these external relationships, however, are more important domestic development problems for Mexico and other Latin American states. The growth of the agroindustrial complex has threatened peasant survival and undercut the production of basic foodstuffs in a self-sustaining rural social environment. Embedded in that growth dynamic is the evaporation of remunerative rural employment, the mass migration of the peasantry to the cities or to the border, the decline in peasant nutrition (especially among the elderly and preschool children), and regional shortages in the labor force stimulating migration from Oaxaca to Michoacán or from Nayarit to Sinaloa and Sonora. The state that faces such current integration into the new international division of labor is a particularly weak—if elaborate—one. It is a state ravaged by fiscal crisis, externally dependent, and late in its attempts to "steer" the nature of agricultural development at a national level.

CHAPTER TWO

The Politics of Produce: Mexico, the United States and the Internationalization of Fresh Fruit and Vegetables

> Florida farmers will not allow themselves to be the sacrificial lambs for a U.S. policy of accommodation with Mexico.
> —Johnnie Goodnight, Florida farmer

> There's no free lunch.
> —Former U.S. Assistant Secretary of Commerce Abraham Katz, in Mexico

> Certainly, we want to be friendly with our neighbors across the Rio Grande River. . . . But they have no right to come in with their cheap labor and dump on our markets—kill our markets—and then become a Tomato OPEC.
> —Doyle Conner, Florida Commissioner of Agriculture and Consumer Services

BILATERAL CONFLICT IN THE FRESH PRODUCE TRADE

The most obvious and painful agricultural trade relationship between the United States and Mexico has focused for some years on the increasing fresh produce trade between the two countries. In the past two decades Mexico has built on its longstanding tradition of fresh fruit and vegetable production for export and challenged U.S. producers in their home market. While that challenge has been concentrated principally in the winter vegetable trade, there are increasing signs of a tense symbiosis across a variety of crops in which Mexico plays the part of a spillover producer for the U.S. market and whipping boy for low commodity prices and oversupply in northern U.S. markets. For a number of reasons to be analyzed here, the two countries have considered this symbiosis to be a product of a straightforward bilateral trade relationship, amenable—to the extent that any agricultural trade is—to remedies designed to protect the principles of free trade and simultaneously to assert the first rights of national producers over foreign interlopers. The reality of the situation, however, differs substantially from the official politics of, say, the bilaterial winter vegetable trade.

The focus of this chapter is on bilateral trade conflict. But bilateral trade in this setting is guided by transnational integration and coordination, which impose multilateral trade and productive agendas on Mexico. To think of the produce trade in traditional terms is unequal to the task of analyzing an increasingly integrated binational agricultural complex. The produce trade is, in fact, an elegant case of the new internationalization of agriculture in the United States and Mexico. Producers react to external stimuli. Transnationals invest in all phases from farm to market. The locus of control is through contracts, technological "packages," and financial aid, not through equity ownership of the land. And the produce trade demands that both the United States and Mexico undergo mutual structural adjustment in a transnational environment beyond the control of a single country's policies. But the most important point is that the politics of produce are not governed by trade alone.

In the first place, it is unclear that trade is actually the prime mover behind the exchange of fresh produce between Mexico and the United States. As we shall see, the impulse for such trade comes from a highly internationalized agricultural sector with partisans and patrons on both sides of the border. Their production priorities are not simply set by market conditions on an auction basis but respond as well to contract relationships, government policies in both countries, and a binational network for production planning. Second, the current political remedies available to the United States and Mexico for disputes in the fresh produce trade are almost strictly unilateral measures, inadequate to the binational—indeed, even global—nature of the commerce in perishables and only marginally linked to the greater political and economic realities of general transborder agricultural integration at the level of production itself.

As I have argued elsewhere,[1] such incongruity between political exigency and productive reality yields a particularly bitter fruit. In the United States, for example, domestic producers have lobbied for more than a decade for more restrictive policies against the free entry of produce from foreign countries. Much of that vituperative battle against alleged foreign threats to U.S. producers has fixed on Mexico's fruit and winter vegetable trade, though the Reagan administration's Caribbean Basin Initiative quickly evoked a similar response toward even small Caribbean economies that might export horticultural products, textiles, or sugar in competition with favored U.S. interests. This angry climate of neoprotectionism tempts economies in trade deficit and recession to "solve" their employment and trade problems by engaging in commercial hostilities with major trading partners, forgetting momentarily the dependence of the entire U.S. agricultural system on unrestrained trade in grains. In the Mexican case, that hostility has mixed with North American nativism to rekindle old U.S.-Mexican antipathies extending far beyond trade issues alone. Thus, in the guise of a commodity trade conflict, U.S. interests portray Mexican produce as unsafe to eat or hostile to the American free enterprise system.

In addition to sectoral concern for the protection of local producers, the U.S. government has added to the political agenda in recent years a revival of the language of "food power," a provocative threat against Third World countries who produce crucial commodities or who are found to be politically reluctant to join the United States on certain political issues dear to its perceived national interest. Due partly

[1] Sanderson, "Florida Tomatoes."

to the character of the transborder agricultural trade, Mexico finds itself particularly vulnerable to U.S. threats to close or restrict trade for political reasons. Interestingly, U.S. producers share the Mexican fear of "being held hostage" by foreign food producers,[2] though such worries are interesting mainly for their demagogic appeal in the struggle for protectionist legislation in the United States.

Food power is a blunt instrument, neither finely controlled nor predictable in its effects. In its more explicit forms, it has not been a particularly successful way of attracting friends or punishing enemies.[3] Nevertheless, food power has taken many forms in U.S. foreign relations. The most recent and recognizable form has involved tying importers of U.S. agricultural commodities to U.S. policies through the manipulation of food supplies. Woodrow Wilson used the promise of food aid as a lever against the westward spread of the Bolshevik revolution in Europe.[4] More recently, Hubert Humphrey recognized the power of food to "get people to lean on you."[5] And, in more imperious fashion, Henry Kissinger and Richard Nixon brought the concept into the realpolitik of the 1970s by using food to broaden ties with the Soviet Union and other socialist countries, while denying food aid to Cuba. Parallel policies included the "Vietnamization" of the Food for Peace program

[2] Wayne Hawkins, "Statement on the Views of the Florida Tomato Industry to the Subcommittee on Trade of the House Committee on Ways and Means concerning Relief from Unfair Trade Practices," April 12, 1978, 2. In this document, Mr. Hawkins echoes Mexican worries that the American/Mexican "people's dependence on many important food items would be at the mercy of the frivolities or caprice of foreign government," unless protection in local markets were to be secured.

[3] See Robert L. Paarlberg, "Food, Oil, and Coercive Resource Power," *International Security* 3:2 (Fall 1978), 3-19, and William T. Weber, "The Complexities of Agripower: A Review Essay," *Agricultural History* 52:4 (October 1978), 526-537.

[4] Dan Morgan, *Merchants of Grain* (New York: Viking, 1979), Chapter 11, passim.

[5] U.S. Congress, Senate Committee on Agriculture and Forestry, Hearings, *Policies and Operations of PL 480*, 84th Cong., 1st Sess. (1957), 129, cited in Burbach and Flynn.

and the interruption of food aid to Chile during the embattled years of the Allende government.[6] Obviously, the most current incarnation of "agripower" American style has come in the form of the Soviet grain embargo begun under the Carter administration.

In Mexico, analysts have realized for some time that their country is a prime candidate for the food-as-weapon tactics of the American government, though the more blatant forms have yet to show themselves. In Mexico, the origins of the Sistema Alimentario Mexicano were marked by an official recognition that the huge bilateral trade in basic grains, cattle, fruit, and vegetables left Mexico vulnerable to the vicissitudes of the international market and to the caprice of U.S. agricultural export policy. It remains to be seen, in an era of vertiginous drops in commodity prices and enormous grain surpluses, whether any U.S. administration could stand the political and economic distress of undercutting Mexico's status as its third-largest agricultural trade partner. In fact, the provisions of the Farm Bill of 1981 make the exercise of food power even more difficult and costly to the United States. In reaction to the Russian grain embargo of President Carter, the Congress stipulated in the new legislation that embargoes not be in agricultural trade alone but across the board, and that U.S. producers must be compensated for resulting losses.[7] Nevertheless, for the Mexican side, the very possibility of being vulnerable to U.S. food power has had a formative influence on agricultural development and trade policy in the late 1970s and early 1980s. The continuing absence of a re-

[6] I. M. Destler, "United States Food Policy, 1972-1976: Reconciling Domestic and International Objectives," in Raymond F. Hopkins and Donald J. Puchala, eds., *The Global Political Economy of Food* (Madison: University of Wisconsin Press, 1978), pp. 57-59; Frances Moore Lappé and Joseph Collins, *Food First: Beyond the Myth of Scarcity* (Boston: Houghton Mifflin, 1977), 358.

[7] United States Agriculture and Food Act of 1981, P.L. 97-98, Sec. 1204-5.

newed Export Administration Act adds to the uncertainty in U.S. policy.

Food power has another, more vivid dimension in Mexico. Agricultural exports have traditionally played an important role in Mexico in generating foreign exchange for industrialization, as we saw in Chapter 1. In the aftermath of the famous "tomato war" with Florida producers, however, Mexican state policy has, in effect, responded to a form of food power, if we define it as the capacity of the United States to coerce or persuade Mexican producers to cut back production of winter vegetables for fear of evoking protectionist laws or the imposition of dumping duties.

A collateral aspect of the U.S. desire to use its coercive power to limit Mexican agricultural exports emanates from U.S. concerns in the Multilateral Trade Negotiations (MTN) and dissatisfaction with Mexico's refusal to join the GATT conventions in which it participated during the Tokyo Round. The resolution of the winter vegetable dispute in favor of Mexican producers and U.S. importers occurred during the Tokyo Round of Multilateral Trade Negotiations, and the GATT negotiations were clearly on the mind of U.S. decision makers, who feared that a favorable resolution to Mexico ". . . may also foster the belief that the U.S. is willing to bend over backwards to avoid straining relations with Mexico. If the *public were led to believe that we could trade tomatoes (or agriculture) for oil, our position in the MTN and future negotiation with Mexico would be severely weakened.* The resolution of the antidumping investigation is closely related to the Mexican decision on GATT accession."[8]

The USDA also worried at the time that a popular proposal to exclude perishables from antidumping statutes might rep-

---

[8] USDA, untitled memorandum, July 17, 1979. For more general comments, see the statement of Alonzo L. McDonald, Deputy Special Representative for Trade Negotiations in the Carter administration, in "U.S. Agriculture's Stake in the MTN," *U.S. Department of State Bulletin* 79 (August 1979), 41-43.

resent an outright concession to Mexico and cause the U.S. to "lose negotiating leverage in the MTN."[9] Mexico's decision in March 1980 not to join the GATT left U.S. officials shocked and angry in light of their view of the winter vegetable dispute's resolution.

Later, through the trade and aid elements of the Caribbean Basin Initiative (CBI) proposed by the Reagan Administration in 1982, the United States encouraged other countries to compete with Mexican exports of horticultural products and, perhaps, even live cattle eventually.[10] An implicit motivation in the CBI was to encourage alternative producers to challenge Mexico's position as exporter of certain commodities to the United States, until such time as Mexico might reconsider its "graduated status" as a newly industrialized country and recant its own protectionist heresies.[11] Perhaps inattentive to the irony, U.S. protectionist agricultural interests, to the extent they are able to weaken the CBI trade initiative, might protect the same producer interests in Mexico which they have so recently fought in other forums.

A final form of food power involves the theory of comparative advantage, which, as U.S. policy has become doctrine. Comparative advantage in the U.S. policy establishment suggests, as we shall see in this chapter, that Mexico "has no business" emphasizing basic grain self-sufficiency over agricultural exports in fruits and vegetables or over the production of other crops in which relative factor endowments favor Mex-

[9] USDA, untitled memorandum from Under Secretary for International Affairs and Commodity Programs to Deputy Secretary of Agriculture, May 30, 1979.

[10] For background on such potential, see Gustavo Uceda, "Prospects for Expanding Beef Production in the Basin," Federal Reserve Bank of Atlanta *Caribbean Basin Economic Survey* 5:4 (September-October 1979), 10-16, and Edward Bee, "Prospects for Basin Fresh Vegetable Exports," Federal Reserve Bank of Atlanta, *Caribbean Basin Economic Survey* 4:4 (July-August 1978), 12-15.

[11] Field interview with Donald Nelson, Office of the Special Trade Representative, Washington, D.C., May 19, 1982.

ico. This logic, which is a reductive position taken from neoclassical trade theory, naturally favors the largest world trader
in basic grains, the United States. Likewise, it favors a "cheap
food policy" in both the United States and Mexico, which
cannot be ignored in the bilateral trade agenda by either country. Advocates on both sides of the border have recognized
that providing cheap food to the urban populace represents
a hedge against inflation and a primary goal in public policy
toward agriculture and trade.[12] To the extent this logic prevents the Mexican state or producer from incurring certain
costs in order to produce basic grains instead of export commodities, Mexico will likely experience tighter integration into
the U.S. grain export circuit and continue depending on the
U.S. grain belt for the sustenance of its people. The potential
hazards in such an integration are many, as we shall see.

From a pure trade perspective, however, the disadvantage
is difficult to see, for the stakes and potential rewards in fresh
produce are great. While, on first glance, an intense focus of
government policy on exotic fruits and winter vegetables may
seem eccentric, Mexico and the United States have tremendous
financial, productive, and social interests engaged in the area.
On the Mexican side, principal crop exports generated U.S.
$917.2 million of a total U.S. $1.5 billion in agricultural trade
value in 1981.[13] In recent years, Mexico has planted in excess
of 60,000 hectares of tomatoes, of which three-fifths are in
irrigation districts.[14] Other winter vegetables double the area
planted in tomatoes, and oranges, limes, and grapefruit alone

[12] In fact, this cheap food mandate was a consideration in the Florida
tomato war, as Alfred Kahn, the President's inflation adviser, personally
concerned himself with the inflationary impact of a finding against the Mexicans. USDA memorandum, May 30, 1979.

[13] USDA, unpublished estimates.

[14] L. P. Bill Emerson, Jr., "Preview of Mexico's Vegetable Production for
Export," USDA, Foreign Agricultural Service Report, 1980; Mexico, SPP,
México: estadística económica y social por entidad federativa (Mexico: SPP,
1981).

contribute another 200,000 hectares.[15] Though tomato production for export has decreased steadily since 1978, receipts
still exceed U.S. $130 million annually, second only to receipts
for coffee.[16] Along with frozen strawberries, tomatoes lead
cash crops in value per hectare farmed.[17] Clearly, the winter
vegetable and fruit trade is lucrative and important to Mexican
agriculture.

Yet, Mexico is now a food deficit nation: its agricultural
trade balance has slipped into deficit every year since 1979,
due at least partly to the relationship between exports of fresh
produce and imports of basic grains. As will be shown in more
detail in Chapter 4, basic grain imports are related to fresh
vegetable and fruit cultivation, in complex ways. Here, it is
important to note that the export value of Mexican agriculture
has been buoyed throughout the 1970s by those sectors least
able to expand—coffee and winter vegetables. Mexican coffee
exports, which lead all agricultural exports, are limited under
the International Coffee Agreement. Those export limitations
have resulted in an uneven performance in coffee revenues
since the mid-1970s.[18] The burden of increasing agricultural
export value in order to keep pace with expected increases in
agricultural imports in the 1980s thus falls squarely on live
cattle, fresh vegetables and fruit, and frozen and processed
fruits such as strawberries and pineapple. As we shall see, the
relationship between basic foodstuff production and agricultural exports is a problematic one, destructive of peasant farming, vulnerable to U.S. trade sanctions, and—to paraphrase
de Janvry—disarticulated from the domestic market.[19]

[15] Mexico, SARH, "Valorización de la producción agrícola, año agrícola
1980" (Mexico, 1981, mimeo).

[16] Gretchen Heimpel, "Mexico: Agricultural and Trade Policies," USDA
Foreign Agricultural Service Report, 1981, Table I.

[17] Mexico, SPP, *El sector alimentario en México* (Mexico: SPP, 1981), Table
I.1.35.

[18] Joel R. Parker, "Basin Exporters Move to Stabilize Coffee Prices," *Caribbean Basin Economic Survey* 6:2 (May-June 1980), 7-10.

[19] Alain de Janvry, *The Agrarian Question and Reformism in Latin America*
(Baltimore: The Johns Hopkins University Press, 1981).

ORIGINS AND STRUCTURE OF THE FRUIT AND
WINTER VEGETABLE TRADE IN MEXICO

Fruits and vegetables have figured in the Mexican export bill for more than a century, finding their origins alongside the cattle industry as the rootstock of frontier development. Melons, garbanzos, oranges, and other products of contemporary northwestern Mexico also flourished in the river valleys of Sonora and Sinaloa on a modest scale before the great irrigation works of the post–World War II period. In fact, Sonora benefited from one of the first irrigation plans in modern Mexico, as a result of a Porfirian speculator and land developer, Carlos Conant Maldonado, who began to create canals and irrigation works in the Yaqui Valley.[20] By 1910 Mexico already had over 1 million hectares under irrigation, although only about 70 percent of this land was being cultivated.[21] After the nationalization of water resources in the revolution, the census of 1930 reported 1.67 million hectares irrigated, the vast majority of which were in private hands.[22] Under the old system, the northwest trade in garbanzos flourished on a world scale with diversified markets beginning in the late nineteenth century, and the petty commodity production of melons and "truck farm" goods became the endeavor of local peasants. That trade benefited from the flow of three of the most important rivers in water-short Mexico: the Yaqui, the Mayo, and the Fuerte. With the advent of pump irrigation and the canalization of the great rivers, the traditional trenches and *norias* (draw wells) that brought water to the crops became anthropological artifacts in one of the most modern agricultural export systems in the Third World.

The modern fresh fruit and winter vegetable trade with the United States has a more recent origin, of great interest to rural development designers and proponents of agricultural

[20] Sanderson, *Agrarian Populism and the Mexican State*; Dabdoub.
[21] CDIA, 864.
[22] Paul Lamartine Yates, *El campo mexicano* (Mexico: Ediciones El Caballito, 1978), I, 160.

modernization. The first stroke foreshadowing the real agricultural export possibilities of the Pacific Northwest came in the form of the first great irrigation districts storing and regulating the flow of the Fuerte, Mayo, and Yaqui rivers. Beginning with the grand projects of the Alemán presidency[23] and continuing throughout the 1950s and 1960s, the Mexican government added more than 3 million hectares of land area improved by federal irrigation works.[24] Of the 2.7 million hectares currently enfranchised as federal irrigation districts, the major districts of Sinaloa and Sonora regularly account for more than a million hectares.[25] The value of irrigated agriculture in those two states represents nearly 40 percent of total irrigated agriculture in Mexico.[26] Sinaloa and Sonora are the leading agricultural states of the Mexican republic, thanks in large part to the productivity of Mexican agricultural labor and farmers but also to the recent availability of water, technical assistance, Green Revolution technology, and United States markets. Likewise, in the hinterland of Michoacán, Guanajuato, and Querétaro, fresh fruits and vegetables and those for processing have reshaped the colonial breadbasket of Mexico as a new agricultural enclave for export produce since the advent of modern irrigation and infrastructure expenditures undertaken by the state.

The Green Revolution also had a formative effect on Mexican agriculture, especially in the Pacific Northwest. The gen-

[23] Oscar Benassini, "Estudio general de gran visión del aprovechamiento de los recursos hidráulicos del Noroeste," *Ingeniería hidráulica en México* 8:4 (1954), 18-31; Adolfo Orive Alba, "Programa de Irrigación del C. Presidente Miguel Alemán: posibilidades de un financiamiento parcial," *Ingeniería hidráulica en México* 1:1 (January-March 1947), 17-32.

[24] Mexico, Nacional Financiera, S.A. (NAFINSA), *La economía mexicana en cifras* (Mexico: NAFINSA, 1981), Table 3.2.

[25] Mexico, SARH, Dirección General de Distritos de Riego, *Estadística agrícola en los distritos y unidades de riego* (Mexico: SARH, various years). Figures vary from year to year, according to available water resources and cropping patterns. This estimate was calculated using the most recent published data, for the crop year 1977-1978.

[26] Ibid.

eral lines of that formation are well known and treated at length in other literature.[27] Here suffice it to say for the moment that the most significant crops of the Mexican Pacific Northwest employ improved seeds and plant varieties, great amounts of fertilizer and pesticides, farm machinery, and irrigation, as well as improved cultivation practices. The Pacific Northwest is the most mechanized agricultural zone in the country, with over 98 percent of farms reporting use of farm machinery as early as 1964.[28] In the Northwest Pacific zone, some 56 percent of all energy in agriculture was employed in machine form, compared with 18 percent nationally, according to the most recent available census.[29] The use of hybrid seeds in wheat, improved stock in tubers, and imported winter vegetable seeds and plants is virtually universal in the federal irrigation districts there. Likewise, the Secretariat of Agriculture and Water Resources (SARH) has created training and extension centers for technical personnel of the ministry as well as individual farmers and merchants. The rural school system in the region is probably as healthy as anywhere in Mexico; many *ejidos* and farm proprietors enjoy agricultural secondary schools either on their own property or nearby, and extension programs from the rural preparatory system are impressive, compared with those in other regions of the country.

[27] Kenneth Dahlberg, *Beyond the Green Revolution: The Ecology and Politics of Global Agricultural Development* (New York and London: Plenum Press, 1979); Cynthia Hewitt de Alcántara, *Modernizing Mexican Agriculture: Socioeconomic Implications of Technological Change, 1940-1970* (Geneva: U.N. Research Institute for Social Development 1976); Keith Griffin, *The Political Economy of Agrarian Change: An Essay on the Green Revolution* (Cambridge, Mass.: Harvard University Press, 1974); Sterling Wortman and Ralph W. Cummings, Jr., *To Feed This World: The Challenge and the Strategy* (Baltimore: The Johns Hopkins University Press, 1978).

[28] José María Dorronsoro, "La mecanización de la agricultura en los distritos de riego en México," *Ingeniería hidráulica en México* 18:1-2 (January-June 1964), 109.

[29] Mexico, Secretaría de Industria y Comercio (SIC), *V censo agrícola, ganadero, y ejidal, 1970* (Mexico: SIC, 1972), cited in Yates, Table 9.13.

For the past two decades, Mexican producers of winter vegetables and other important horticultural products have formed powerful organizations, which, in turn, have collaborated with the Mexican government in, for example, an annual tomato production plan (*programa siembra-exportación de tomate*). Through the key producer association CAADES (Confederación de Asociaciones de Agricultores del Estado de Sinaloa), the largest *tomateros* in Sinaloa plan the production and acreage allocation for tomatoes in a given crop year. They are also the critical agents advising the local water resource allocation board regarding its priorities for water use in the federal irrigation districts.[30] These same producers control the *unidades de riego* (irrigation units) not under federal mandate but merely administrative advisement.[31] The most important winter vegetable producers in Sinaloa also form the heart of the UNPH (Unión Nacional de Productores de Hortalizas), which acts as a political lobby and coequal member with government in the creation of a national tomato production and export plan.

While organizations of such great power do not exist in fruits and other fresh produce cultivation, the government and private sector cooperate in those areas as well, through the CONAFRUT (Comisión Nacional de Fruticultura), parastate agencies for the industrialization of fruits at the state level, and trust funds for technical assistance, merchandising, and industrialization of citrus and other crops. Product-specific producers' associations abound in both the ejidal and private sectors of the federal irrigation districts as well. According to their own estimation, they contribute to the CAADES in Si-

[30] The Comité de Usuarios meets with officials of the irrigation district to determine water use in the area. It is well known that powerful organizations such as CAADES and the UNPH are well represented in such councils.

[31] The *unidades de riego* are those irrigated areas not enfranchised as an official federal district. The SARH has limited authority over such areas, which are increasingly important in Mexico. Their duties extend only to maintenance and conservation of existing works in the *unidades*.

naloa and its analog in southern Sonora (CAASS).[32] At more modest political levels, they also govern avocado production in Michoacán, grapes from Aguascalientes to Sonora, apples in Chihuahua and Durango, and mangoes in Veracruz. One of the most interesting points shared by all these crops and organizations has been the inability of local prices to match international market opportunities, and thus to lure production away from the path of export or agribusiness processing.

THE DAILY POLITICS OF PRODUCE

As is the case with beef cattle and basic grain production (to be treated in succeeding chapters), the mode of cultivating winter vegetables and fruit is an intensely political matter. At the most general level, there is a certain irrationality in an agricultural system that produces luxury comestibles in such abundance for the export market and is unable to feed its own population. Consequently, the determination of the role of comparative advantage and its relation to the politics of rural development forms one central area of political concern for the Mexican state and rural society. On a second and intimately related plane, the realities of production in the Pacific Northwest constantly challenge Mexico's "fit" for the international fruit and vegetable trade. That challenge comes in two basic forms: an external harassment of the winter vegetable and fruit trade by threatened domestic producers in the United States, where 99 percent of Mexican vegetable exports find their destination,[33] and a structural economic crisis within Mexico raising questions about the competitiveness of fresh fruit and vegetable exports under current circumstances of high inflation, exchange rate instability, uncertain economic growth, and fiscal austerity, all of which have impact on the agricultural sector.

[32] This impression is based on numerous field interviews with private farmers and *ejidatario* members of various producers' associations in Sinaloa and Sonora during 1981.

[33] Mexico, SPP, *El sector alimentario en México*, Table III.140.

The ecology of the industry also comes into play as a political factor, in land and water distribution and use, the origins of agricultural day labor, and the prospects for employment in agriculture or the absorption of *jornaleros* in industry. Each of these general areas—the rationality of winter vegetable and fruit cultivation itself, the concrete trade and production issues surrounding the fresh produce complex, and the ecology of production—deserve attention as part of the U.S.-Mexican produce complex

The Nature of Comparative Advantage in the U.S.-Mexican Fresh Produce Complex

Conventional trade theory argues that the "factor intensity" of winter vegetable and fruit production favors Mexico, principally due to the widespread use of internal migrant and resident farm labor at low wages. The availability of such a labor force has been enhanced by the Mexican rural population boom, the decline of agrarian reform grants that in other times occupied rural dwellers outside the wage labor force, the concentration of capital in agriculture generating a broader wage labor market for the marginal rural producer, the abandonment of the *bracero* program, under which many such workers crossed into the United States as international migrants, and many more general forces of the changing international division of labor in agriculture. Complementing such changes in Mexican agriculture was the disappearance of Cuba as a vegetable supplier to the United States after the 1959 revolution. On the U.S. side, increasingly expensive energy for a highly mechanized agricultural system, a durable land boom forcing changes in agricultural land use, and low commodity prices have tended to "wash out" the small fresh produce farmer who might compete in a relatively free trade environment with Mexican exports.

The argument that Mexico should employ principles of comparative advantage in agricultural trade to enhance the export capacity of the sector and to employ scarce resources

78

more efficiently according to relative factor endowments generally focuses on the abundance of cheap labor in the Mexican countryside, the propitious climate for fresh fruit and vegetable production in the Northwest and other semitropical zones of the country, and the lower costs of land, credit, and water for use in such endeavors. Interestingly, as we shall see shortly, the counterarguments from the United States also focus on such elements of comparative advantage, but with a different purpose—to establish that relative price advantages in labor and energy are artificially maintained, as are export prices.

The abundance and low wages of Mexican labor are well known. Many studies of the winter vegetable industry have shown that cost advantages in Mexican agriculture are tremendous, with individual wages as low as U.S. $5.00 per day. Indeed, this figure is grossly inflated, as rural labor rarely manages to earn the official minimum wage on which these calculations are based. Even when paid, the official rural wage rate in the 1978-1979 season was one-fifth the rate in Florida,[34] and the *hourly* agricultural labor cost in the California tomato fields was greater than the *daily* wage in the Baja California tomato fields with which the Californians competed.[35] Yet, these great differentials in labor costs do not yield a cheaper tomato from Mexico than from California, when tariffs and transportation are taken into account. While there are some specific cost advantages in Mexican tomatoes at the level of production (e.g., in labor, land, and water), Mexican production varies in its cost competitiveness with its U.S. counterpart. In essence, the Sinaloa tomato's total preharvest cost of production compares favorably with the Flor-

[34] G. A. Zepp and R. L. Simmons, *Producing Fresh Winter Vegetables in Florida and Mexico: Costs and Competition*, USDA Economics, Statistics, and Cooperatives Service (ESCS) Report, November 1979, 9.

[35] G. A. Zepp and R. L. Simmons, *Producing Fresh Tomatoes in California and Baja California: Costs and Competition*, USDA, ESCS Report, February 1980, 32, 37.

ida product, but Baja California does not compete well with California in tomatoes (see Table 2.1, total preharvest cost).

While some analysts have argued that Mexico's substantial wage advantage over U.S. production is on the wane due to rapid increases in the rural daily wage,[36] that trend is misleading. Despite the nominal increase in wages experienced during the oil boom years (1977-1981), workers' real wages declined every year of the López Portillo sexennium. That weakening of the average minimum wage in Mexico was felt even more strongly by the rural worker, because of the lax supervision of minimum wage payments in the countryside, the transient nature of field labor in export agriculture, and the burgeoning and desperate labor force unable to fight the exploitive power of the employer in the migratory labor circuit.

As of this writing, there are no authoritative accounts of the migratory rural circuit in Mexico. Such accounts as exist[37] combined with this author's experience traveling the migratory route of rural workers along the Pacific Coast of Mexico paint an incomplete but nonetheless dismal picture of the plight of the rural proletarian who constitutes an important advantage in the relative price structure of fresh produce exports to the United States. In interviews from Michoacán to Sonora, on routes crossing crops from sugar to avocados to flowers to tomatoes, a beginning picture of the migrant laborer emerges. The constitutive elements in his or her position in the wage force include, first, a lack of adequate representation by organized labor in official syndicates from Oaxaca to Sonora. Second, the employee is seasonally forced to migrate from one state to another, according to crop cycles. The migrant worker is placed in direct competition with household labor from local *minifundios* and *ejidos*, whose women and children staff the onion fields and packing sheds in response

[36] See, for example, Zepp and Simmons, 1979 report, 50.

[37] Luisa Paré, *El proletariado agrícola en México: ¿campesinos sin tierra o proletarios agrícolas?* (Mexico: Siglo XXI, 1977); Salomón Eckstein, *El ejido colectivo en México* (Mexico: Fondo de Cultura Económica, 1966).

TABLE 2.1

Costs of Producing and Marketing Tomatoes from Four Growing Regions of the United States and Mexico, 1978-1979 Season

Cost Item	California Cost	Baja California Export Cost	Southwest Florida Cost	Sinaloa Export Cost
PREHARVEST	--------------(Dollars/Acre)		--	
Land rent	184.56	150.67	42.50	75.33
Machine Services	59.37	223.72	361.08	170.55
Labor	947.27	312.89	725.61	242.84
Purchased Inputs	1306.00	577.32	1375.10	525.77
Admin. costs	149.83	56.90	112.70	45.64
Interest on operating capital	98.30	66.07	93.21	53.00
TOTAL PREHARVEST	2745.33	1387.57	2710.20	1113.13
HARVEST	--------------(Dollars/100lbs.)		--	
Picking	3.86	—	2.60	2.77
Hauling	0.45	—	0.37	0.20
TOTAL HARVEST	4.31	1.80	2.97	2.97
PACKING & MARKETING	9.77	13.50	6.17	12.03
TOTAL COSTS	19.18	21.40	18.63	19.17

NOTE: The tomatoes are not identical in each region, but are comparable for our purposes.

SOURCE: Zepp and Simmons, 1980, 13 and 18; and Zepp and Simmons, 1979, 18 and 25.

to the variable labor demands of small-scale agriculture in Mexico. Third, the rural worker does not enhance the farm's productivity, compared with the international competition in Florida, Texas, or California, where labor-saving machinery has also been capital-saving through increases in productivity per unit of labor cost. In such lower productivity resides an implicit restraint on the rural wage, governed partly by the Mexican state's management of the minimum wage, which both guarantees an income floor undoubtedly higher than the labor market would bear and at the same time encourages the reproduction of a labor relationship with export agriculture that cannot generate an adequate wage. I will return to this point later.

In addition to differential wages, Mexico subsidizes the production of winter vegetables and fruit through federal programs involving water resources management and price controls on agricultural inputs. Since the creation of the national water system in 1926,[38] the federal government has refused to impose cost effectiveness on the federal irrigation districts. That is, under the federal water law, irrigation district officials are permitted to collect only nominal user fees, not to exceed the basic cost of preserving and maintaining the irrigation infrastructure itself.[39] Not only has the low cost of irrigation water encouraged the abuse of scarce national water reserves, but it has also acted as a subsidy for crops produced in federal irrigation districts, including winter vegetables and fruits for export.

Similar subsidies exist in the form of energy, fertilizer, and credit, and in the wage rate itself. The Mexican government controls the price of fertilizer through a number of policy instruments, including a national fertilizer production company, FERTIMEX (Fertilizantes y Guanos Mexicanos, S.A.); a national plan for fertilizer self-sufficiency; direct producer

[38] The *Comisión Nacional de Irrigación* was formed in that year.
[39] Mexico, SARH, *Ley federal de aguas*, publicación legal #13 (Mexico, SARH, 1972), Chapter Four.

subsidies in fertilizer purchases through the Sistema Alimentario Mexicano; and, indirectly, through the management of the domestic price of energy inputs into fertilizer. Thus, Mexico has not experienced the tremendous price increases in fertilizer suffered by the rest of the Third World since the "oil shock" of 1974; its fertilizer prices are well under world prices, and supplies to producers are secure enough that Mexico has become a net exporter in fertilizers since the oil boom.

In agricultural credit, direct subsidies come in the form of federally controlled credit programs for agricultural producers. Those programs include graduated interest rates for short- and medium-term loans through the FIRA (Fideicomisos Instituidos en Relación con la Agricultura) and more general credit programs executed through the rural credit bank (BANRURAL). Through the years, agricultural credit has favored producers in irrigation districts and been a major force in the structure of cropping and livestock raising in Mexico. Yet, for all its ability to stimulate the federal irrigation districts in general and to guide subsidy payments to key producers, the credit incentive has proved inadequate as a refined political instrument that the state might employ to produce basic commodities.

Finally, an unheralded addition to wage and input subsidies comes in the form of an implicit energy transfer to agriculture. Through the national petroleum-pricing system governed by PEMEX (Petróleos Mexicanos), the competitive position of agricultural goods produced in irrigation districts has been buoyed. The relatively low price of fuels and fertilizer feedstocks derived from natural gas benefits principally the large producers of agricultural commodities for export or for agribusiness processing in the irrigation districts, because of the concentrated national consumption of energy in agriculture, already mentioned. If we isolate the effects of those energy subsidies (in the form of domestic fuel prices lower than international market prices for the same inputs) on the produce complex, we find that, in effect, Mexico is directly subsidizing U.S. consumption of certain agricultural imports through the transfer of national energy reserves embodied in fresh fruits and vegetables. While such a policy appears to be diminishing under the new presidential administration of Miguel de la Madrid, the battle to establish market prices for energy will be hard fought and complex in its effects. The benefits of such subsidies are felt less directly by the Mexican consumer, but they are still an important part of the cheap food policy embraced by every administration for the past two decades.

Yet, with all these subsidies to the production of Mexican export fruits and vegetables, the dynamic of the market in the United States is unclear. The principals in the Florida tomato war, as well as grape, raisin, and citrus producers, argue that Mexican exporters have not been able to compete effectively with U.S. producers. Even with the structure of production heavily infused with government subventions, say the U.S. competitors, the Mexican producers have had to engage in predatory pricing for the sake of undoing their U.S. counterparts. Even if such a presentation is overdrawn, Mexican producers in the two years following the tomato war recognized their increasing input costs and shifted in some great degree away from tomatoes and fruits to basic grains and crops for domestic processing (such as potatoes). Their resurgence after the 1982-1983 devaluations has already provoked a worried response from U.S. competitors, and the tomato war has found new life.

Given that variable experience in U.S. markets, how do Mexican fruits and vegetables manage to intrude into the North American market, and to what extent do they reflect the nature of the fresh fruit and winter vegetable market as opposed to the machinations of the tomato cartel indicted by Florida interests? The first step in answering such questions must take us back to the nature of the export fruit and vegetable industry itself.

The idea of a purely Mexican fruit or vegetable producer for export is, in fact, a misnomer. In the first place, Mexican production is truly internationalized, depending on international corporate inputs, technical assistance, seeds and plants, and markets. Typically, international seed manufacturers produce winter vegetable seeds for Mexican production, from which seedlings are sometimes cultivated. Other times, Mexican producers purchase seedlings directly from distributors.[40] On occasion, direct financial assistance from U.S. distributors is available for growers of winter vegetables as well.

Another main ingredient undercutting the idea of a "national" winter vegetable producer is the U.S. distributor. In the case of winter vegetables, he is found almost exclusively in Nogales, Arizona. In that frontier town, which is the entrepôt for some 85-90 percent of winter vegetable exports from Mexico,[41] the West Mexico Vegetable Distributors Association (WMVDA) acts as the premier importing agent. Recent studies have shown, interestingly, that some of the members of the Nogales importing community are, in fact, companies owned by Mexican growers.[42] In any event, the U.S. distributors, irrespective of their nationality, act as the consignment brokers or contract purchasers of Mexican winter vegetables. Either they develop longstanding relationships with the premier growers of Sinaloa—which is the normal case—or they purchase Mexican exports on a simple commercial contract or on consignment. Each of these transactions creates problems for the presentation of antidumping suits, as we shall see shortly.

In the 1960s and 1970s the expanding market for winter vegetables exported from Mexico to the United States seemed to have no ceiling. Each year Mexican production could ex-

[40] Zepp and Simmons, 1980 report; Goodman and Domike, Appendix E.

[41] Mexico, SARH, *Programa siembra-exportación de tomate, temporada 1978-1979* (Mexico: SARH, 1979), 8; "Affidavit of the West Mexico Vegetable Distributors Association to the U.S. Department of Commerce," May 29, 1979; Humberto Rubio Valdez, "Perspectivas de producción y exportación de tomate a los Estados Unidos y Canadá para la temporada 1978-1979," *Comercio y desarrollo* 8 (November-December 1978), 45.

[42] David Mares, "The Evolution of U.S.-Mexican Agricultural Relations: The Changing Roles of the Mexican State and Mexican Agricultural Producers," Working Papers in U.S.-Mexican Studies, 16 (La Jolla: University of California, San Diego, 1981).

pand to its limit and encounter only episodic resistance in U.S. production circles, thanks to the generosity of a growing market. In fact, it appears that throughout the 1960s and 1970s Mexico represented less a challenge to U.S. producers' prerogatives in their traditional markets than a spillover producer for a blossoming three-country winter vegetable complex that came to include Canada. As Figures 2.1 and 2.2 show for tomatoes, Mexican production never threatened Florida producers except in the years of freeze (most notably the 1976/77 season), and modestly even then. Likewise, it is clear that Mexico's share in the U.S. market traditionally has come at a time during the season when U.S. producers are "on stream" with the bulk of their production, not really challenging the high-priced beginning and end of the season. Regionally, studies have also shown that the bulk of Mexican winter vegetables go to western markets and to Canada, not challenging the territorial domain of U.S. producers in the East.[43] Although

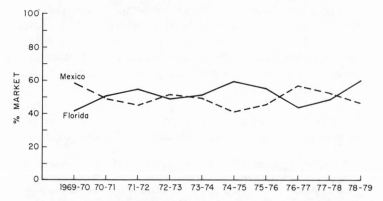

FIG. 2.1   Florida's and Mexico's Shares in the U.S. Tomato Market, by Year, 1969-1970 to 1978-1979

SOURCE: G. A. Zepp and R. L. Simmons, *Producing Fresh Winter Vegetables in Florida and Mexico: Costs and Competition*, USDA ESCS Report, November 1979.

[43] See especially "Brief of Respondents Union Nacional de Productores de

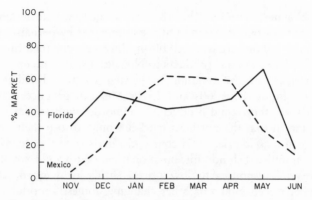

FIG. 2.2   Florida's and Mexico's Shares of the U.S. Tomato
Market, by Month, 1975-1976
SOURCE: Zepp and Simmons, *Producing Fresh Winter Vegetables*, Table 3.

occasional freezes have brought Mexican tomatoes to those
eastern markets in modest amounts, recent fluctuations in
Mexican production seem to threaten even that trend.

Mexican growers show through their market initiatives that
their products are contributors to and not determinants of the
U.S. demand for winter vegetables. Their participation in the
U.S. market is governed by that consideration. CAADES monitors prices in Nogales on an hourly basis to ensure that local
growers receive current market value for their product and to
assess the general cost-effectiveness of exporting winter vegetables. Growers respond, as do other agricultural capitalists,
to past trends and future expectations of the market, based
on price, supply, Florida trends, and their own input expenses.
Interestingly, their main source of information for such decisions is the WMVDA, the U.S. distributor of their produce

Hortalizas and West Mexico Vegetable Distributors Association," submitted
to the U.S. Department of Commerce, 1979, and Richard L. Simmons, "An
Updated Comparison of U.S. and Canadian Prices of Mexican Winter Vegetables," U.S. Department of Commerce, February 1980, mimeo.

in Nogales, Arizona. The Mexican producers, who number more than two thousand but are dominated by perhaps one hundred of the largest vegetable producers among their ranks, generally send their products to Nogales distributors *on consignment*, in the amounts requested by the distributor. Throughout the 1960s and 1970s Mexican producers sent whatever they could produce to the border with the fair expectation that the northern market would absorb their produce at a good price.[44] Of course, the decisive test to uncover the impulse behind this binational market would involve growers' responses to low prices, shrinking demand, and higher-priced inputs or other changing domestic production circumstances. In fact, in 1981 and 1982 we have seen just such changes, which give us new insight into the role of Mexican winter vegetables in the U.S. market and, by extension, their likely future in the Mexican agricultural export bill.

Mexican winter vegetable producers in Sinaloa cut back acreage after 1978, particularly in tomatoes (see Table 2.2) partly in response to U.S. threats to Mexican tomato exports, but also due to much higher guaranteed prices for other crops—principally rice—and low commodity prices for winter vegetables in the United States. Only during the freeze of 1981-1982 were prices strong in winter vegetables, at which time the Mexican producers not only were benefiting from high prices for rice, potatoes, wheat, and other nonexport items under the Sistema Alimentario Mexicano, but also were eligible for federal crop insurance and risk sharing, neither of which was available in winter vegetables. Perhaps the Mexican producers' requests for planting increases in Sinaloan tomatoes for 1983 (estimated at 30 percent) show the most immediate reminder that the industry is truly beyond a single nation's purview.

Such responses confirm the annual flexibility of Mexican produce in general and challenge the idea of a permanent nationalist intrusion of Mexican produce in U.S. markets.

[44] Sanderson, "Florida Tomatoes."

TABLE 2.2
Mexican Exports of Selected Vegetables to the United States, 1971-1980 (metric tons)

	Asparagus	Cucumbers	Eggplant	Onions	Peppers	Tomatoes
1971	0	64,841	10,502	18,648	33,711	258,682
1972	0	69,884	13,066	25,993	27,646	264,124
1973	3,304	75,517	17,761	56,332	40,081	339,801
1974	4,132	76,143	11,885	40,982	39,274	267,897
1975	3,849	55,482	11,706	34,037	28,303	253,605
1976	3,739	89,004	13,480	33,754	40,106	294,198
1977	1,978	107,119	14,457	44,203	51,199	356,251
1978	2,271	129,223	18,942	53,857	65,598	369,283
1979	3,036	134,692	18,009	64,902	61,381	322,170
1980	3,267	135,785	16,443	57,108	75,610	294,601

NOTE: Includes fresh, chilled, and frozen vegetables.
SOURCE: USDA, *Foreign Agriculture Circular: Fresh and Processed Vegetables*, "Vegetables: Trade Statistics in Selected Countries," FVEG1-82, Foreign Agricultural Service, January 1982.

That flexibility also relates to levels of state intervention and the structural limits of Mexican producers' power in the fresh fruit and vegetable export complex, where perishability and external dependence vitiate any potential for market control from the producer side.

First, we can see that the Mexican producers have little pricing power of their own, for several reasons. Even in winter vegetables—the largest crop group exported to the United States—Mexican producers control less than half the winter market in the United States and cannot expect to control prices merely with their produce. Given that the vast bulk of Mexican export produce funnels through the fifty distributors of the WMVDA in Arizona, it would seem impossible for the Mexican growers to control the price of sale on a day-to-day basis by means of controlling supply. Planting decisions are made months ahead, based on earlier market trends; the crop production lag simply does not permit day-to-day manipulation of the market, as it might in nonperishable commodities. Only when prices are extremely low do the Mexican producers divert their smaller tomatoes to the domestic market to buoy prices in the United States. Even in such situations, however, a more likely response for the flexible and well-informed Mexican producer is to change crops and abandon the export market until high prices lure him back.

The winter vegetable market in Mexico, though potentially great, is troubled by ineffective transportation links from producing areas to the central markets of the country, *caciquismo* (bossism) in produce wholesaling reminiscent of turn of the century produce markets in the United States, and low prices reflecting the reduced capacity of the Mexican consumer to purchase export-quality goods. In the Northwest, producers often dump their vegetables on the ground for lack of domestic markets in times of contraction in the United States. Given the lack of public crop insurance for winter vegetables, such actions hardly seem typical of oligopoly price makers, as competitors in the United States would suggest dominate the trade.[45]

Of course, the brokers and retailers in the United States have different interests than the Mexican producers, further limiting the prospect of direct Mexican control of the U.S. market. Once again returning to the winter vegetable trade, we can see that, producer participation in Nogales notwithstanding, the WMVDA is comprised of a U.S. group promoting the distribution and sale of fresh produce in the United States and Canada. The organization was created in 1946 as an American trade association and functions alongside the Food Marketing Institute and other retail associations to market commodities on a national basis.[46] From the brokers' and retailers' perspective, the market for perishables is made difficult by seasonal changes in supply, needs for speedy transportation from field to market, and hourly changes in price at the retail outlet.

In each of these areas, Mexican producers are captive sellers guided by extranational forces. They must sell their produce through agents outside their national territory on the basis of rapidly fluctuating prices, with the expectation of serious spoilage and loss if sales agreements are not rapidly executed. The consignment sale is most convenient for the U.S. brokers, as their obligations to Mexican growers are determined by sale value of the produce; the consignees never actually take possession of the goods but are merely transfer agents between producer and retailer. Such practices have been widely criti-

[45] For these claims, see the statement by Doyle Conner at the opening of this chapter. Equally interesting are the statements by Wayne Hawkins, Executive Vice-President of the Florida Tomato Exchange, especially: "A Statement on the Views of the Florida Tomato Industry to the House Agricultural Committee Concerning the General Agricultural Situation in the United States as it Applies to Florida Tomatoes," February 9, 1978; and "A Statement . . . Concerning Imports of Tomatoes," March 22, 1978. See also Robert Johnson, "The Florida Tomato War," *Florida Trend* (June 1979), 45.

[46] See Affidavit of the WMVDA; Food Marketing Institute Brief to the U.S. Department of Commerce, February 29, 1980.

91

cized by U.S. competitors because they encourage high-volume, quick sales irrespective of price. Thus, the consignment sale becomes the focus of the "dumping" complaints we will treat shortly.[47] Former Secretary of Agriculture Robert Bergland, smoothing the ruffled feathers of Florida growers after their defeat in the Florida tomato war, called consignment sales "an abomination,"[48] equivalent to predatory pricing by Mexican producers.

Interestingly, it is not the Mexican producer who favors consignment sales but the Arizona broker and U.S. retailer, typically large supermarkets and brokers. Obviously, Mexican producers would rather seek a contract price in such a price-sensitive market, instead of the auction price they currently receive. Also, it seems inconceivable that winter vegetable growers in Mexico would not prefer to transfer the ownership of their product at the border, at its peak quality, rather than to wait until retailers bid on the produce. In fact, growers have cited such consignment dependence as one of the weaknesses of the U.S-Mexican winter vegetable trade.[49] The consignment sale, as well as the commercial contract, is principally an instrument of vertical coordination[50] exercised by U.S. interests in order to secure steadier, higher-quality supplies, with less risk to the brokerage houses. If pricing power exists within a single group in this relationship, it rests with the retailer, who acts as an oligopsony buyer of a perishable good. Such pricing power rests not only with buyers but with commercial agents and transnational intermediaries as well.

Each of the members of the WMVDA, by its own testimony, has a contract with a producer group in Mexico to assure

[47] "Strano Farms," a case study prepared for the Harvard Business School (July 1980, mimeo.), 10.

[48] "Consignment Sales Irk Bergland," *The Packer* 87:17 (April 26, 1980), 1.

[49] Interviews with CAADES producers in Mexico City and Culiacán, Sinaloa, November 1981.

[50] Ronald Mighell and Lawrence Jones, "Vertical Coordination in Agriculture," USDA report, 1963.

steady supplies of high-quality winter vegetables. The contracts are not production contracts, however, in the same sense as we see in tobacco and vegetables for processing. Rather, they are simple agreements to purchase, based on quality, delivery dates, size, and other criteria. In this sense as well, the Mexican producers who contract with the WMVDA are not price makers, nor do they control the size or destination of their produce beyond the terms of the contract with U.S. distributors.[51]

Even if we concede, however, that consignment sales from Mexico damage the interests of U.S. competitors, evidence of oligopoly pricing behavior by the Mexicans simply does not exist. The most important shortcoming of this argument involves the nature of the winter vegetable industry itself. Truck farm goods—characterized by many modest-sized producers and no real domination of supplies to the market—are price sensitive in production as well. That is, as prices for such commodities increase, cropping decisions change favorably, increasing supplies and driving down prices. Conversely, when prices fall, small producers wash out of the market, and even some large producers turn to more remunerative crops. If Mexican producers were to engage in oligopoly pricing after driving all competitors out of the market—the presumed motive of the "Tomato OPEC" alleged by Florida competitors—higher prices for winter vegetables would, over the relatively short term, cause competitors to re-enter the market and begin to produce winter vegetables again. What is apparent from the U.S. side is the mutual structural adjustment implied by the bilateral winter vegetable market. Such adjustment—which would undoubtedly come in the form of reduced prices for U.S. produce, or a changing structure of production, or the disappearance of noncompetitive farmers—is consistent with the mutuality of the new international division of labor but inconsistent with the U.S. national goal of protecting domestic production.

[51] Affidavit of the WMVDA, 1.

Although conditions for entry and exit vary in perennial crops such as citrus and grapes, Mexican produce plays similar roles across the board in the U.S. market—as a marginal provider of commodities to the north, an occasional competitor with U.S. producers, and a growing pressure point for mutual economic adjustment driven by trade and transnational integration.

PROSPECTS FOR THE U.S.-MEXICAN FRUIT AND VEGETABLE TRADE

Quite aside from the explicit political factors that might guide or restrict the transborder winter vegetable trade, serious questions have arisen about the viability of the Mexican export produce complex. Those questions relate directly to the influences shaping Mexican cropping decisions and to the role of the export fruit and vegetable sector in the U.S. market.

Clearly the most vulnerable aspect of the industry from the Mexican standpoint involves the structure of input prices. As mentioned earlier, the Mexican state heavily subsidizes many Mexican crops by offering credit, fertilizer, energy, and water resources at lower prices than the market might bear. Although the future of such subventions is problematic in light of the current fiscal and exchange crisis of the Mexican economy, some trends seem to have emerged over the past five years. Importantly, the rate of inflation in the Mexican economy is much higher than that of the United States. It rose to 98 percent in 1983 and was projected to continue at 60 percent for 1984.[52] In the past, domestic inflation in Mexico has required a state response to demands from wage labor for increases in the official minimum wage. Through the entire López Portillo period, wage increases did not match the rate of inflation, and there is little reason to expect the austerity cam-

[52] Mexican inflation rate data are from Banco Nacional de México (BANAMEX), *Examen de la situación económica de México*, various issues, January 1983–January 1984.

paign of the new government to change that trend. But the nominal cost of labor will undoubtedly go up faster than labor costs in the United States, without the improvements in productivity associated with higher-cost labor in the United States.[53]

As the government withdraws from the wholesale support of input prices in agriculture, the cost effects on fruits and vegetables are likely to become more severe. In 1981, the federal government attempted to increase users' fees for water in order to recoup the costs of operation in the irrigation districts; that attempt was unsuccessful, due to the power of the users and the lack of a constituency for such a change.[54] The new government, with its mandate for fiscal austerity, is likely to have a greater capacity to increase users' fees, along with the already-announced increases in energy prices and the proposed elimination of gross subsidies to state enterprises. Such a contraction in public support would undoubtedly affect the prospects of Mexican export produce, especially in winter vegetables, where farmers had already shied from the market after the heyday of 1977-1978. It is ironic that such an austerity-induced mandate has international origins.

Other characteristics of Mexican export produce also project a loss of competitiveness in U.S. markets. For example, Mexican vegetable growers have complained of the lack of new technological innovations to improve productivity. They have not undertaken the practice of using plastic mulch, which has been such a boon to Florida productivity. Nor have they been able to conquer local viruses and fungi attacking their harvests, which they attribute to a combination of high pes-

[53] Those increases in productivity relate mainly to fewer picking days, lowering the quality of the crop, perhaps, but increasing output and lowering the total wage bill.

[54] Interview with SARH officials in the Division of Legal Affairs, Department of Districts and Units of Irrigation, Mexico City, August 19-20, 1980, and August 5, 1981. This impression was confirmed in numerous interviews on-scene and in irrigation district offices in Querétaro, Guanajuato, Michoacán, Sinaloa, and Sonora during November and December 1981.

ticide prices and the lack of new varieties of winter vegetable plants.[55] In the atmosphere of uncertainty currently clouding the future of winter vegetable cultivation in the Northwest, it is doubtful that long-range technical and cultural innovations might be undertaken, rather than a less-risky decision to turn to other crops. Those cropping decisions will reappear in future chapters.

In any event, the prospects for fruit and vegetable exports to the United States are ambiguous. Mexican exports to the United States play a significant role as a complement to U.S. production, especially in the western states and Canada. Insofar as that role continues unrestricted, Mexican production at current levels may be expected to continue as well. But the prospect that Mexican producers might make further incursions on the U.S. market at the expense of the Florida or California producer is far-fetched. It presupposes the continuation of low producer prices, a security in market prices that simply has not characterized the industry in the past few years, and the cessation of trade hostilities. On none of these counts is the future clear, and, as a consequence, neither is the future of the Mexican export produce sector.

THE COMPLICATIONS OF PERENNIAL CROPS AND AGRIBUSINESS PROCESSING

The northwestern winter vegetable industry is clearly the most problematic and noticeable export crop complex in Mexico. But other fruits and vegetables play an important part in the internationalization of Mexican agriculture as well. Their story differs somewhat from that described so far, in region of origin, destination, and social relations of production in the countryside. Because of the diversity of these crops, they are difficult to characterize as a group. Nevertheless, for the

[55] Interviews with CAADES members, Culiacán, Sinaloa, and Mexico City, November 1981 and August 1981, respectively.

sake of analytical organization, let us divide our consideration of these fruits and vegetables into two elements. For now, we will continue with fresh fruits and vegetables; momentarily, we will turn to fruits and vegetables for processing.

Citrus crops are clearly in the forefront of perennials that are used both as fresh produce and as inputs for agribusiness processing. Mexico is the sixth-largest producer of citrus in the world, and the only significant exporter of fresh citrus to the United States, accounting for about 70 percent of total U.S. imports.[56] In contrast to winter vegetables, however, citrus enjoys a large and growing Mexican domestic market, challenging exports, and is often processed for consumption as juice, fruit sections, and oil (e.g., persian lime oil). Citrus production allows us to view an agricultural complex not limited to the northern frontier of Mexico. It represents a case of the international integration of agriculture beyond the geographic limits of the border and, as such, permits a qualification of the argument that Mexican comparative advantage in certain agricultural commodities is mainly the result of a regional or transport advantage vis-à-vis U.S. or other world producers. Mexican citrus production extends from Tamaulipas and Nuevo León in the northern Gulf region to Michoacán and Colima in the central and southern Pacific; it bands the nothern and southern borders of Oaxaca, from the Pacific Coast to the hinterland of Loma Bonita, on the border of Veracruz.

Citrus production for fresh export to the United States—which accounts for about 90 percent of Mexican exports of oranges alone[57]—must pass through packing houses approved by the USDA, where fruits are fumigated and boxed. The Mexican Association of Citrus Packers, who control most of these packing houses, contract for delivery with local pro-

[56] USDA, *Citrus in Mexico*, 1.

[57] Ibid., 21; Mexico, Instituto Mexicano de Comercio Exterior (IMCE), *El comercio exterior y los comités para la promoción de las exportaciones* (Mexico: IMCE, September 1980).

ducers by financing some of their crops, which is also the case in winter vegetable packing.[58]

Until recently, no government incentives existed to stimulate fresh fruit exports, other than general credit and technical assistance programs. Under the new Comisión Nacional de Desarrollo Agroindustrial and the export promotion programs of the Mexican Institute of Foreign Commerce (IMCE) and CONAFRUT, Mexico has encouraged increases in citrus cultivation, especially for processing before export.[59] The Mexican citrus industry has indeed tended to increase production for processing, especially in the 1970s. The most obvious case involves the production of lime oil from Mexican (key) limes, which skyrocketed in the late 1970s (see Table 2.3) and resulted in Mexico's becoming the world's largest producer of essential oil of lime. Mexico exports 90 percent of lime oil production, almost exclusively to the United States.[60]

Other citrus production has also gravitated toward the agribusiness processing element of the industry. The use of grapefruit and oranges for sections, for example, increased from 3,000 tons in 1976/77 to 25,000 tons in 1979/80.[61] Likewise, exports of frozen orange juice concentrate blossomed from 808 metric tons in 1970 to 9,821 tons in 1979.[62] We shall see that similar trends exist in other fruits and vegetables.

The Mexican government has focused on increasing production and consumption of citrus crops for a number of important policy reasons. Citrus is, as mentioned, a crop cul-

[58] Interviews with officials of CONAFRUT, August 1981; director of winter vegetable packing house in Guasave, Sinaloa, November 1981; USDA, *Citrus in Mexico*, 23.

[59] Interviews with directors of the Agroindustrial Development division of the Comisión Nacional de Desarrollo Agroindustrial, Mexico City, August 1981; interviews with CONAFRUT, IMCE.

[60] USDA, *Citrus in Mexico*, 30.

[61] Ibid., Table 22.

[62] Ibid., Table 20.

TABLE 2.3
Estimated Production and Processing of Mexican Limes,
1970/71-1979/80 (metric tons)

	Produced	Processed
1970-71	330,000	80,000
1971-72	310,000	70,000
1972-73	270,000	90,000
1973-74	270,000	100,000
1974-75	300,000	120,000
1975-76	300,000	110,000
1976-77	320,000	90,000
1977-78	361,000	170,000
1978-79	415,000	180,000
1979-80	430,000	200,000

SOURCE: USDA, *Citrus in Mexico*, Table 23.

tivated on a broad regional basis with heavy participation by small- and medium-scale producers, including *ejidos*. Fruits also number among the twenty-five food groups targeted for production increases under the Sistema Alimentario Mexicano and the Plan Nacional de Desarrollo Agroindustrial.[63]

The export initiatives of the Mexican government and private sector have extended to the field promotion of small-scale juice extractors for citrus growers, an industry still heavily influenced by small-scale and ejidal production. Additionally, the government has increased investment in the Montemorelos, Nuevo León, area to increase orange juice concentrate production and fruit-sectioning facilities. These efforts are particularly important to note in citrus because of the growing domestic demand for fresh fruit, the government's desire to increase domestic suppliers of such produce under the "basic

[63] Mexico, SARH, Comisión Nacional de Desarrollo Agroindustrial, *Plan nacional de desarrollo agroindustrial* (Mexico: SARH, 1980), 33; Mexico, Oficina de Asesores del C. Presidente, SINE-SAM, *El Sistema Alimentario Mexicano*, 12.

foodbasket" plan of the Sistema Alimentario Mexicano and its successor Programa Nacional de Alimentación, and the stiff competition faced by Mexico in attempting to export frozen juice concentrate to a highly selective international market already provisioned by Israel, Brazil, and the United States.

The plan to popularize juice extraction through small-scale plant facilities also satisfies the political requirement that more agroindustry be devoted to small-scale production, in order to wrest control of agroindustry from large corporations, 2 percent of which control 75 percent of value-added in agroindustry.[64] At the international level, the prospect of selling processed fruits instead of fresh produce promises to deliver more value-added to the Mexican economy and to counter the historical tendency of Latin American societies to provide primary goods to the international system for finishing elsewhere. It may be that such a policy attempt to avoid the old international division of labor unwittingly leads into greater, but no less difficult, paths to international integration.

There are important problems with such an agroindustrial strategy, however, at both local and international levels. First, the citrus industry internationally has been a highly irregular one through the years, now favoring fresh fruit prices over processing, now shifting to frozen concentrate over fresh fruit.[65] The international market for citrus products has varied widely because of freezes in Brazil and Florida, contamination in Israel, high land prices in California, and other factors well out of the control of a single producer. The most recent perturbations affecting the Mexican market include the citrus canker scare that interdicted citrus exports to the United States in 1982 and 1983, and the 1984 U.S. restrictions on imports of EDB-contaminated fruit. Interestingly, EDB was applied to Mexican fruit as a packing house fumigant according to USDA regulations.

[64] Mexico, SARH, Comisión Nacional de Desarrollo Agroindustrial, *Plan nacional de desarrollo agroindustrial*, 17.

[65] For an interesting narrative, see Arthur M. Louis, "Squeezing Gold Out of Oranges," *Fortune* 103:2 (January 26, 1981), 78-82.

Mexico, though it is the sixth-largest producer of citrus, has a relatively weak position in frozen juice concentrate and processed fruit sections, areas in which the government has decided, at least momentarily, to concentrate its attention. Such a weak position is hardly enhanced by the dislocations caused by geographic shifts in production troubling the Mexican fresh fruit industry in recent years. Likewise, the frozen concentrate industry has increasingly required imports of certain blends of citrus juice to Mexico. The value of U.S. frozen orange juice concentrate exports to the Mexican border zone increased from U.S. $19,000 to U.S. $261,000 over the period 1975-1980.[66] U.S. officials have argued that Mexican entry into the frozen juice concentrate industry will mean increasing imports of such inputs, because of the inability of the Mexican citrus sector to regularly produce the required amounts of all the varieties of fruit necessary for a palatable international blend of concentrate.[67]

In citrus and winter vegetables, agribusiness is difficult to characterize, for its diversity and its widely varying levels of sophistication. In both crop complexes small producers abound, and agribusiness activities take place at very humble levels, in the lively brokerage between *ejidatario* or *minifundista* and a local packing house or distributor, in the provision of credit to certain producers according to expectations in local or international markets, and in the universal patron-client networks of rural Mexico. Agribusiness at all levels of fresh produce has played important personal and corporate roles in the allocation and appropriation of value.

In winter vegetables, we have described the patterns of credit, contracts, and consignment prevalent in the export trade. But the social relations of export vegetable production and processing in the countryside have more profound implications in the lives of residents within the productive radius of the packing shed. Packing sheds often employ ejidal and

[66] USDA, *Citrus in Mexico*, 33.

[67] Interviews with John Montel, U.S. Agricultural Counselor, Mexico City, August 1981.

village labor, and the *empaques* generally prefer women and adolescents. In contrast to the migrant labor force so active in the winter vegetable harvest of the Northwest, the packing shed employees local laborers to ensure a secure labor force during the hectic months of December through April. At the same time, of course, the packing shed actively encourages a new mode of labor integration, in which the ejidal or small-farmer family enters the wage labor scene in ways not contemplated before the appearance of the *empaques*. While data are not available to make a more systematic evaluation of the effects of agribusiness processing on the labor market in agriculture, the likely hypothesis is that the *empaques* free migrant labor for picking by using local female labor for packing. Such patterns of production also increase the output of household labor and, one suspects, hold down the price of labor itself. Of course, such changing local relations of production both respond to the exigencies of international competition *and* act to change the character of competition itself by introducing new modes of incorporating rural workers into the wage labor force.

In citrus and vegetables for processing, agribusiness activities are even more complex than in fresh produce, as are their effects. We shall treat the idea of rural industries (e.g., the portable juicers, or small cotton gins) in Chapter 5. Contradictory effects of the international market include the reorientation of production itself for "industrialization" or agribusiness processing as well as labor effects similar to those just discussed. Likewise, the internationalization of the demand side of the citrus and processing vegetable markets generates more labor in nonfarm rural occupations. That assumption must be examined in more detail in Chapter 5 as well.

Another effect of internationalization, the internalization of international consumer tastes in processed fruits and vegetables, generates certain specialized benefits in the countryside. In Sinaloa, for example, *ejidatarios* and small farmers join large landowners in garnering large profits through potato production.[68] That production, which at a national level has increased from 43,000 hectares in 1960 to more than 71,000 in 1980,[69] responds in great part to demand from potato chip producers who process the crop for consumption as a fast-food variant of traditional *chicharrón* and vegetables with *salsa* and spices. But industrializing popular snack foods in such ways diverts crops from fresh consumption, increases the price of the good itself, and homogenizes tastes in the style of the productive facility and not necessarily the local culture.

On the domestic side, Mexican per capita consumption of citrus fruit has not grown in line with the hopes of the Mexican government, as shown in Table 2.4. Although output staggered generally upward in the 1970s (see Table 2.5), much of that increase has gone to the export market (Table 2.6) or to industrial processing. Such lack of success in increasing the amount of fresh fruit available to the mass of Mexican consumers has been attributed to a combination of high prices, selective marketing practices, and low incomes. To those difficulties we might add the diversion of fresh fruit away from immediate consumption to processing into a form not accessible to the bulk of the Mexican population. Thus, the internationalization process creates supply- and demand-side constraints on national policy goals in nutrition and food distribution.

At the local level, problems abound in delivering fresh and processed citrus products to more of the Mexican population. First, the question of rural mediation in marketing is critical. The Merced—the Mexico City wholesale produce market—was, until its recent demise and resurrection as the Mercado de Abastos on the outskirts of Mexico City, the central clearing house for produce coming from the North and coastal zones of the country for consumption in the main markets of the Mesa Central. As a result, a large part of Mexican citrus

[68] Interviews with Asociación de Agricultores Productores de Hortalizas de Sinaloa, Los Mochis, Sinaloa, November 1981.

[69] Mexico, SPP, *El sector alimentario en México*; Mexico, SARH, "Valorización de la producción agrícola, año agrícola 1980."

TABLE 2.4
Estimated Per Capita Consumption of Fresh Citrus in Mexico
1970/71-1979/80 (kilograms per capita)

	Oranges	Tangerines	Grapefruit	Limes
1970-71	22.6	2.9	0.7	4.9
1971-72	18.4	1.8	0.6	4.6
1972-73	21.2	2.7	0.9	3.3
1973-74	18.2	2.2	1.0	2.9
1974-75	17.1	2.6	1.2	3.2
1975-76	22.0	1.5	1.4	3.2
1976-77	21.9	2.4	1.7	3.8
1977-78	15.5	1.3	1.3	3.1
1978-79	14.5	1.4	1.1	3.8
1979-80	19.1	2.3	1.2	3.8

SOURCE: USDA, *Citrus in Mexico*, Table 9.

production for domestic use somehow passed through the
Merced and continues to arrive at its successor market outside
Mexico City. In interviews with fresh fruit and vegetable
growers and government officials and in selected literature on
rural crop commercialization, it is universally recognized that
small- and medium-scale producers, or marketing agents without "connections" in the highly organized and closed networks of the Merced, encounter great obstacles to marketing
their produce.[70]

In formal recognition of this marketing *caciquismo*, which,
in effect, closes many producers out of the wholesale market
and cuts off their goods from the consumer, the government
instituted in 1980 a state marketing stall in the Merced called
FRUTIMESA. It was intended to circumvent the strangle hold
of Merced operators on the commercialization of fresh fruit
in Mexico. Given the inefficiency generally associated with
such government enterprises and the widespread corruption

[70] Interview with CONAFRUT officials, August 1981.

TABLE 2.5
Citrus Production in Mexico, 1970-1982 (thousands of metric tons)

	Oranges	Tange-rines	Grape-fruit	Persian Limes	Mexican Limes	Total
1970-71	1,310	170	54	10	330	1,874
1971-72	1,130	104	48	10	310	1,602
1972-73	1,410	177	70	10	270	1,937
1973-74	1,280	147	77	12	270	1,786
1974-75	1,230	177	100	14	300	1,820
1975-76	1,280	107	110	15	300	1,812
1976-77	1,710	185	140	18	320	2,373
1977-78	1,290	105	125	26	361	1,907
1978-79	1,280	118	145	39	415	1,997
1979-80	1,630	180	170	52	430	2,463
1980-81	1,600	120	163	61	469	2,416
1981-82						

SOURCE: USDA, *Citrus in Mexico*, Table 2.

and *politiquería* (petty politics) in government food marketing particularly, many producers described the concept of FRU-TIMESA as "trading one *cacique* for another."[71] Since allegations are far from unwarranted—private agriculturalists and *ejidatarios* alike share a uniform hostility toward government intervention in agriculture—the government has a negative marketing tradition of its own to overcome before enterprises such as FRUTIMESA perform properly. This, of course, relates more to government incapacity than to internationalization per se. But, in fact, one of the difficulties encountered in agricultural modernization involves the syncretic adaptation of traditional marketing to modern markets.

On the consumer's side of the marketing problem arises the issue of which targeted populations might benefit from in-

[71] This became a constant theme in interviews with various agricultural producers and agribusiness entrepreneurs in Michoácan, Querétaro, Sinaloa, and Sonora throughout 1981.

TABLE 2.6
Mexican Exports of Fresh Citrus to the United States, 1970/71-1979/80

	Oranges and Tangerines*†		Grapefruit†		Limes‡	
	(metric tons)	($1,000)	(metric tons)	($1,000)	(metric tons)	($1,000)
1970-71	37,769	—	1,707	—	1,902	—
1971-72	34,460	—	1,732	—	1,557	—
1972-73	41,654	5,984	3,275	972	1,574	301
1973-74	38,237	6,122	3,470	1,034	2,259	493
1974-75	27,412	5,449	2,531	799	3,331	937
1975-76	20,501	3,753	1,667	631	3,759	1,252
1976-77	41,651	10,041	5,298	1,496	5,188	1,808
1977-78	26,525	6,024	2,410	664	9,443	2,764
1978-79	41,507	8,951	1,432	363	11,602	2,990
1979-80	33,218	7,529	4,260	1,251	15,148	4,796

SOURCE: USDA, Citrus in Mexico, Table 12.
* Data on Oranges and tangerines are not available separately before 1978.
† October-September.
‡ April-March.

creased citrus production under the current model. If the Mexican citrus industry is inclined to devote much of its new investment to integrating itself into the international citrus concentrate market, there are limited spinoff possibilities for the Mexican consumer, none of which benefit the rural poor. While more value-added in production attracts *ejidal* cooperatives and rural agroindustries to try such a program of citrus processing, prices to the consumer prohibit rural dwellers from participating in the market. As Table 2.7 shows, even fresh citrus is not consumed in balanced amounts by the rural poor and the urban lower-income strata. The high prices and private marketing of juices and canned goods from citrus

TABLE 2.7
Mexican Domestic Consumption of Fresh Oranges, Lemons, and Bananas, 1975

Income Category (pesos/month)	National (kg/month)	Urban (kg/month)	Rural (kg/month)
0	4.6	14.6	3.0
1-300	2.3	3.6	2.1
301-400	3.3	7.3	2.3
401-530	4.8	7.3	4.4
531-700	5.4	6.4	5.2
701-950	6.0	6.8	5.8
951-1,250	8.3	7.1	8.9
1,251-1,700	8.7	10.4	7.1
1,701-2,200	11.1	11.7	10.3
2,201-3,000	14.4	14.0	14.9
3,001-4,000	15.7	18.5	10.0
4,001-5,200	16.3	17.2	14.1
5,201-7,500	19.7	18.6	22.7
7,501 and above	22.0	24.5	12.7
Total	11.4	15.4	7.8

SOURCE: Mexico, SPP, *La población de México, su ocupación, y sus niveles de bienestar*, Tables 4A.5-4A.7, 199-201.

clearly exaggerate this imbalance, showing little benefit to the "basic foodbasket" strategy of the SAM and like-minded programs.

Of course, the more obvious point is that frozen juice concentrate and other perishable products of the citrus industry are not consumed in the countryside for the simple lack of uniform refrigeration—in transport, in retail establishments, and in homes. That Mexico might have, in the short term, delivered frozen or perishable fresh fruits to the *zonas marginales* of the country in the spirit of food redistribution under the SAM was a highly unlikely, if laudable, prospect. In that respect citrus is similar to other fresh and processed vegetables that have supplanted basic foodstuffs and feedgrains for the sake of providing high-quality luxury comestibles for the urban dining rooms of Mexico City and the distributors of the far northern frontier. For that matter, citrus is the least intrusive of the fruits under examination for the theft of traditional cropping.

For some time, in fact, Mexican analysts have concentrated attention, not on citrus and winter vegetables as targets for a critique of agribusiness, but on the rapid and startling transformations taking place in traditional areas of cultivation, thanks to the agribusiness processing of vegetables, strawberries, and pineapple. There is little puzzle in such attention, because certain canning vegetables and frozen berries in the Bajío region of central Mexico (Michoacán, Guanajuato, and Querétaro) have literally seized the breadbasket of colonial Mexico and appropriated its fertile soil for the industrialization of crops in a form foreign to the palates of the Mexican *campo*.

While strawberries and processing vegetables in the Bajío have captured the attention of many analysts of Mexican agribusiness,[72] such activities are only the most important and

[72] Burbach and Flynn; Ruth Rama and Raúl Vigorito, *El complejo de frutas y legumbres en México* (Mexico: Nueva Imagen, 1979); Ernest Feder, *El imperialismo fresa* (Mexico: Editorial Campesina, 1977).

visible of a set of changing rural relationships involving a variety of Mexican fruits and vegetables. Frozen strawberries for export have been, over the past two decades, a top foreign exchange earner for the Mexican economy. In 1980, Mexico exported nearly 25 million dollars worth of frozen strawberries to the United States,[73] which placed them third as a crop for export, behind coffee and tomatoes. In addition, fresh strawberry exports—which together with their frozen counterparts involve the exportation of over half the Mexican strawberry crop—add another important element to U.S. agricultural imports from Mexico. As in citrus and winter vegetables, women clean and strip the berries before shipping and processing; also similar are the increasing danger posed by the irrational use of water resources in strawberry cultivation and the overwhelming reliance on labor-intensive technologies and U.S. cultivation practices. Mexican strawberry growers use imported plants and export their crops to the north.[74] Unlike winter vegetables and citrus, however, transnational corporations dominate the processing industries related to strawberry cultivation, whether in freezing (Birdseye/General Foods, Pet, Inc.)[75] or in processing for jellies, marmalades, and preserves (McCormick, Del Monte, Gerber, Clemente Jacques).[76]

THE ASCENDANCE OF THE STRAWBERRY SYNDROME

In strawberry production, increasing amounts of agricultural land and labor are devoted to a crop that is consumed elsewhere with little side-benefit for the rural population. That "strawberry syndrome" prevails also in asparagus, peas, sweet

[73] Heimpel, 4.

[74] L. P. Bill Emerson, Jr., "Mexican Strawberry Industry Strong Despite Problems," *Foreign Agriculture* 16:7 (July 31, 1978), 2-4.

[75] Feder, *El imperialismo fresa*, 29ff.

[76] U.N. Comisión Económica para América Latina (CEPAL), "Las empresas transnacionales en la agroindustria mexicana" (May 1981, mimeo.), 100.

corn for canning, and in other fruits and vegetables throughout Mexico. While much of the fruit and vegetable agribusiness complex in Mexico is no longer dominated by transnational corporations, the exigencies of production are not changed by the domestic content of capital. Nor does the federal government steer the quantity or location of such fruit and vegetable production through the management of federal irrigation district resources. While in winter vegetables and some fruits the federal districts are essential to production, an increasing share of national fruit production has come, in recent years, from private irrigated areas (*unidades de riego*), subsidized but not controlled by the federal government. Such is the case with grape production.[77] Likewise, as we shall see in more detail in Chapter 5, the federal government has little leverage in rain-fed areas, or with producers not requiring federal credit or inputs. Willy-nilly, then, fruit production takes an increasing share of acreage in federal irrigation districts and also significantly affects the prospects for food production in private irrigated lands. Even if the federal government were inclined to divert resources of *unidades de riego* to greater food production, state power is much more modest than in the federal irrigation districts. Noncitrus fruit production—especially pineapple and grapes—is one of the leading growth areas in Mexican export agriculture, as Table 2.8 demonstrates. Those fruits are grown increasingly in uncontrolled irrigation zones.

Grapes have proved particularly intrusive on lands previously used for basic grain cultivation. They are the classic boom commodity, following in the grand tradition of strawberries but with even less potential linkage to the domestic market. On the coast of Hermosillo, a key beneficiary of federal irrigation and colonization projects in the 1950s and one of the largest pump irrigation districts in the Northwest (consistently over 100,000 hectares), grape harvests have nearly quintupled in area and increased their output sixfold. Total

[77] Mexico, SARH, *Estudio de mercado de la uva* (Mexico: SARH, 1974).

TABLE 2.8
Production of Grapes and Pineapple in Mexico and Their Export to the United States, 1970-1980 (metric tons)

	Grapes		Fresh Pineapple		Canned Pineapple	
	Production	Export	Production	Export	Production	Export
1970	178,467	595	248,800	9,000	27,400	22,383
1971	182,280	783	297,300	10,000	33,060	25,408
1972	190,977	978	218,200	16,000	27,420	21,760
1973	217,619	2,215	268,300	14,000	27,450	20,332
1974	237,744	3,127	397,800	13,000	43,480	18,034
1975	247,072	1,683	371,300	17,000	42,660	14,417
1976	282,669	3,087	442,000	19,000	48,330	22,634
1977	296,604	4,848	510,000	27,000	61,950	29,842
1978	350,000	6,662	568,300	37,800	63,650	33,492
1979	450,000	5,613	632,100	44,000	70,700	26,843
1980	—	—	604,600	47,000	72,350	30,000

SOURCES: Pineapple production and export figures come from USDA, "Mexico: Pineapple Report" (MX-1015). Grape production and export figures are from USDA, *Mexico's Grape Industry: Table Grapes, Raisins, and Wine*, Foreign Agricultural Service, November 1979.

nominal revenues from grapes in that district increased from 7.9 million pesos in 1970 to 202.5 million in 1977, despite recession, high energy requirements, and land tenure problems in the area.[78] During that same period, wheat production declined by more than 100,000 tons in the district, despite strong government pressure and incentives to maintain traditionally high levels of wheat production. Cotton, safflower, sorghum, soya, and beans—other major products of the region—all either stagnated or declined radically. The Laguna region of Durango-Coahuila experienced similar changes, with grape cultivation increasing in pump irrigation areas but yielding variable results in harvest tonnage.

With grape production, it is clear that the market has changed in the past fifteen years, with more production de-

[78] Mexico, SARH, *Anuario estadístico: año agrícola 1977-1978*.

voted to export and new producers appearing mainly in the northern irrigation districts and private pump irrigation areas. Sonora alone has some 20,000 hectares devoted to existing vineyards with an equivalent amount due to be planted in the near future. According to a 1979 USDA report, Sonoran production of grapes, raisins, and wine will likely double by the mid-1980s.[79] According to that same report, Mexican table grape exports may grow to represent more than half of U.S. grape imports and 10 percent of annual U.S. consumption. While the effects of Mexico's current crisis on such projections is unclear, the dynamic of northwestern grape production has clearly tended toward more international links.

Currently, of the four largest producers of grapes in Mexico, three states (Durango, Coahuila, and Sonora) are northern parvenus, with only Aguascalientes, a traditional producer of grapes, representing old viniculture.[80] The geographic center of the industry has moved northward, in response not only to the lure of new irrigation and better weather but also to the attraction of better export markets for fresh grapes. As we shall see, such developments are particularly disturbing to U.S. competitors in California during hard economic times for grape and raisin producers.

Finally, pineapple offers further insights into the "strawberry syndrome." From 1974 to 1980 total production of pineapple increased by half, and exports as a proportion of total production increased from 8 to 13 percent.[81] In addition, more pineapple was "industrialized" or processed before export. Despite slight export setbacks in 1979, world demand

[79] L. P. Bill Emerson, Jr., "Grape Output in Mexico Rising Rapidly," *Foreign Agriculture* 18:9 (September 1979).

[80] Mexico, SARH, *Estadística agrícola en los distritos y unidades de riego* (1979).

[81] USDA, "Canned Pineapple," FAS Report MX-0020, American Embassy in Mexico, 1980; "Mexico: Pineapple Report," FAS Report, MX-1015, American Embassy in Mexico, 1981; and USDA, "Pineapple Voluntary Report," FAS Report MX-1037, American Embassy in Mexico; Banco Nacional de Comercio Exterior (BNCE), "Piña enlatada," *Comercio exterior* (April 1980).

for fresh pineapple is burgeoning,[82] and the export market for pineapple seems greater than the capacity of the Mexican agricultural system to satisfy it.

Pineapples appear to be following the general sectoral trend of rising proportions going toward an industrialized product for domestic consumption and export, as opposed to fresh produce. This does not imply greater control locally, since many processors are large international firms that use production contracts in Mexico to broaden their food processing investment. But, whether agribusiness processors are transnational or national, fresh produce disappears from rural markets and reappears in cities or in foreign countries at a higher price, transformed into a commodity beyond the price and local market range of the rural poor. Little discretion is left to the producer regarding market destination or price, though generally prices have been high.

The increase in fresh exports seems to compete directly with canneries and exporters of processed pineapple. Such competition has the potential of making the rationalization of fresh pineapple supplies to canners more difficult, as the fresh export industry grows. In 1981 canners had some difficulty keeping their canneries open throughout the season, precisely for lack of secure supplies. This aspect of the industry—which also finds its analogs in grapes for raisins and wine, and strawberries for freezing and preserves—creates two tendencies: the rural work force dependent on the industry is made more vulnerable as a product of the poor articulation among producers and processors, and the industry itself seeks contracts and vertical coordination or integration in order to rid itself of uncertainties created by variable supplies. In Mexico, such difficulties, in the context of an export surge and official export promotion plans combined with official dedication to rural employment, have resulted in the state's intervention in production contracts and its stimulation of new pineapple growing areas such as Loma Bonita, Oaxaca. Thus the surge

[82] USDA, "Canned Pineapple."

113

in pineapple also encourages a model of fruit production based on agribusiness needs rather than a more general consumer orientation. And, finally, more of the product is consumed outside the country, further adding to our list of crops disarticulated from the Mexican economy.

THE HIGH POLITICS OF PRODUCE

The historical development of the Mexican fruit and vegetable complex has generated a set of political relationships that are the subject of bitter domestic conflicts and high politics at the international level. Here we will briefly consider produce as an important political arena in three distinct spheres: international trade, allocative politics, and the control of economic property. In-depth consideration of each of these areas will follow in Chapters 5 and 6. For now, our purpose is to set the political agenda of internationalized produce.

First, and most obvious, has been the international conflict over the trade of agricultural produce from Mexico. The most important instance of that conflict has come in the Florida tomato war, which was labeled as an explosive issue by all parties to the battle. At one level, the tomato war and other trade disputes governed by U.S. antidumping statutes[83] have now become historical cases in a rapidly changing international agricultural complex that focuses its integration, not on commodity circulation, but on *productive* integration from farm to market. As we have seen in this chapter for various crops, the production of Mexican fruits and vegetables for export and processing cannot be governed by trade arrangements simply designed in another epoch for the regulation of "predatory pricing."[84]

---

[83] For a convenient summary, see A. Paul Victor, "United States Antidumping Rules," in Harvey Applebaum and A. Paul Victor, eds., *Basics of Antidumping and Other Import Relief Laws: Multilateral Trade Negotiations Update* (New York: Practicing Law Institute, 1979). The current regulations are updated in the Trade Act of 1979.

[84] Predatory pricing is defined here as "the act of charging a lower price

The first weakness in such anachronistic legislation is that it fails to take into account the political and economic importance of the trade to principal partners in the industry, on both sides of the national border. In this sense, at least, the idea of a Mexican producer or a U.S. distributor has been made obsolete by the high level of productive coordination of the industry. In such circumstances, no unilateral action to govern trade will fairly represent the interests of the sector, however conceived. To restrict Mexican exports of tomatoes to the United States offends U.S. distributors, Mexican growers, and the Mexican government, for the sake of pleasing an intractable Florida competition. To continue an open trade environment is to theoretically penalize Florida producers for the lack of producer subsidies guaranteeing their position in the market (though their position has not yet really been threatened), as well as to encourage a productive system resulting in the misallocation of national resources in Mexican federal irrigation districts. In a word, the transnational character of the produce trade and production complex in Mexico has precluded government by one country.

Extrapolating this point, the more international agriculture tends to govern its own production through the coordination of various phases of cultivation, distribution, exchange, and consumption, the less governments' attempts to steer the sector's trade according to simple principles of commodity exchange will fit the proper function of the agricultural sector. Such political inadequacy has appeared in graphic relief in various trade disputes recently, in which certain interests have argued that Mexican producers of pineapple are somehow improperly competing with Hawaiian producers, when the contractor for both their services is the same global corporation: Del Monte. Similarly, it is contended that Mexican producers are "dumping" their crops on U.S. markets, when

than is warranted by profit considerations alone in order to increase the monopoly power of the firm." See William A. Wares, *The Theory of Dumping and American Commercial Policy* (Lexington, Mass.: D. C. Heath, 1977), 84.

price of sale and destination are both out of their hands, transferred to the control of U.S. distributors not liable for dumping duties. And, of course, the logic of such arguments is strained to the limit when domestic U.S. producers complain of cheap Mexican labor and its challenge to their competitive position, while in their fields Mexican migrants labor under similar circumstances. Humanitarian concerns for the exploitation of the Mexican agricultural labor force shrink in the face of the issue of whom to exploit: Mexicans in Mexico or Mexicans in Florida and California? Such questions are not amenable to easy unilateral answers.

A number of state-based solutions to immediate production problems in the produce industry have been tried in recent years, as have trade remedies for import injury to domestic industries in the United States. In Chapter 5, we will examine in more detail the possibilities of such political solutions to the various problems of the produce complex, beginning with plans to ameliorate conflicts at the international level and ending with mechanisms for shifting production among crops for policy reasons.

In that second realm—the allocation of value and resources in the Mexican countryside—the political conflicts and issues make even the complexities of modern international trade disputes pale by comparison. Here again we face the explicit political dimension of agricultural transformation, whether in the form of credit levels, crop insurance, commercialization incentives, state intervention in production or marketing, or the subsidization of consumer goods. Of course, as we shall see in Chapter 5, price and credit incentives have not proved any more convincing as instruments of public policy than the doctrine of comparative advantage. Neither has yielded the right mix of agricultural and traded goods for the Mexican economy. But, apart from the general indictment of public policy failures in the produce area or critiques of the shortsightedness of producing goods that have no national market potential in the short term, two outstanding features of the politics of produce recommend it as an interesting sector to study in the Mexican agricultural economy. First, the modern export- and agribusiness-oriented fruit and vegetable complex in Mexico is externally reliant on markets that are not only hostile politically but fickle economically. In the absence of domestic market alternatives, the Mexican production system is often faced with devastating economic losses when plant disease, pesticide residue, or low prices block crops from crossing the northern border. At the same time, these candidates for credit, technical assistance, and input subsidies occupy the best land in Mexico, employ the poorest rural proletarians at abysmally low wages, violate the laws governing limits to land ownership and the disposition of the land, and oppose state intervention in agriculture, except in the instances that serve their interests.

It has been argued, of course, that the produce industries of Mexico employ a great number of the rural poor and improve their ability to survive the general devastation of peasant life. Indeed, the comparative advantage of Mexican produce cultivation shows up in the labor intensity of export crops over import crops. But, if strawberries, grapes, coffee, bananas, and tomatoes lead all Mexican export crops in labor content, the per capita income and personal misery associated with these industries hardly mark them as a labor solution for the marginal rural dweller. In fact, high rates of unemployment continue in Michoacán, Querétaro, Guanajuato, Puebla, and other important export produce states. Field interviews with producers, *ejidatarios*, and agricultural laborers, in addition to government officials, indicate that such unemployment endures partly because the local labor in the canebrake, avocado orchard, berry patch, or onion field is done by the migrant poor from the Mexican South, while local residents stand by, priced out of the market even at the level of the minimum wage. An important study that might systematize such impressions remains to be done. In a similar vein, in agribusiness processing female and adolescent labor often appear to supplant former farmers and marginal peasants, contributing to the exaggerated exploitation of the ejidal household and avoiding the difficulties of sustaining a regular labor force through market incentives. While many producers argue that the problem with export fruits and vegetables is the difficulty of contracting for regular, reliable labor in the migratory circuit, the contrary argument is that the migratory circuit would have little reason to exist if it were not for the planned seasonal push given to the rural proletarian as he bounces from the cane fields of Michoacán to the cotton fields of the Laguna to the grape orchards of Aguascalientes.

This summary of the political issues confronting the daily production of Mexican produce leads to the conclusion that Mexico is not in control of the economic property dedicated to export- and agribusiness-related produce. Whether we consider the distortions of the rural labor force due to land concentration and resource misallocation (from a social viewpoint) or consider instead the external control of markets crucial to the survival and well-being of produce suppliers in general, it is clear that the central problem for Mexico is to reapprehend the national control of its fresh produce complex. The limits and possibilities of such a political orientation—however remote it may be in the current regime—will be addressed in Chapter 5.

CHAPTER THREE

From Cimarron to Feedlot:
The Emergence of the Binational
Frontier Beef Industry

> (Texans are) . . . a bold and hardy race, but
> likely to prove bad subjects and most incon-
> venient neighbors
> —British diplomat in Mexico, 1825

> Send the hunters powder and lead if you will,
> but . . . let them kill, skin, and sell until the
> buffalo are exterminated. Then your prairies
> can be covered with cattle and the cowboy,
> who follows the hunter as a second forerunner
> of an advanced civilization.
> —General Philip Sheridan, U.S. Army

> In the Nueces country, the southern point of
> the Great Plains . . . Mexican cattle came into
> the presence of the mounted Texan armed with
> rope and six-shooter—the cowboy.
> —Walter Prescott Webb, *The Great Plains*

The modern international system for raising, slaughtering, processing, and marketing beef cattle in many respects embodies the general argument made throughout this study. The market for cattle and meat products is global.[1] The forces and

[1] Winrock International; Mexico, Oficina de Asesores del C. Presidente, SINE-SAM, "Sistema integral de carne de ganado bovino," Five Volumes (Mexico, 1980-1981, disscussion document); Anthony S. Rojko and Martin W. Schwartz, "Modeling the World Grain-Oilseeds-Livestock Economy to Assess World Food Prospects," *Agricultural Economics Research* 28:3 (July

relations of production in cattle and meat products have been transformed and "globalized" by international improvements in refrigerated shipping, communications, industrial organization, and technology. Since World War II, in particular, Latin American cattle industries have been inserted into that global framework, not only in sales and procurement (i.e., trade), but in technology, stock lines, and methods of processing cattle products.

Given the long history of Latin American primary commodity exports, the internationalization of cattle industries hardly seems surprising. After all, British and U.S. capital in the nineteenth century paved the way for the modernization of beef export production in Mexico and Argentina. Cattle slaughter for trade with foreign powers such as the United Kingdom and the United States dates back at least to the 1849 gold rush and subsequent westward expansion. Attempts to ship fresh beef from Texas to Europe began after the Civil War, and by 1884 totaled 120 million pounds and 190,000 head of live beef.[2] Likewise, the technology of stock breeding has been dominated by the Western powers, with the universalization of European and North American breeding stock in bovine and hog production and the more recent appearance of U.S.-based turkey operations in poultry raising. Foreign direct investment now identified with Purina, Bayer, Hoechst, Anderson-Clayton, Ciba-Geigy, and other international giants continues the productive legacy born in a long chain of forebears led by the famous robber barons of the American West and succeeded by the huge meat-packing trusts of early twentieth-century America. Their tradition is carried on in the daily workings of modern international and national livestock industries.

The essence of the internationalization of cattle industries in Latin America involves the standardization of producer

1976), 89-98; Donald W. Regier, "Feed Demand in the World GOL Model," *Agricultural Economics Research* 30:2 (April 1978), 16-24.

[2] Edward Everett Dale, *Cow Country* (Norman: University of Oklahoma Press, 1943), 90-93.

technology and social relations along lines that are transnational in scope. For example, such global relationships now commonly involve the use of European antibiotics, U.S. feedlots, and Japanese markets for boxed beef. The product of this standardized livestock system must also approach an international standard for consumption and trade. In most cases, this has meant that cattle should at least display immunity from major contagious diseases, that beef should have certain marbling characteristics attractive to consumer palates in world markets (mainly in developed capitalist countries and the institutional beef market in host countries), and that it should be available in recognizable Western standard cuts that conform to the cultural eating habits of those markets.

Such standardization was inadequate in the "old" beef trade system before the 1870s in Mexico, Argentina, and the southern United States. There, producers and merchants unsuccessfully tried to penetrate European markets with jerked beef, only to find later that the market for fresh, chilled beef was enormous, matched only by Continental disdain for dried beef products.[3] While that particular obstacle to marketing has been overcome by the advent of refrigerated shipping in the intervening century, the internationalization of the beef cattle industry in Latin America still lacks uniform, internationally acceptable standards of hygiene for exports to developed capitalist markets, and still faces a number of occasional nontariff barriers in the form of quotas and standards.

The cattle industry has also "internalized" the norms of international industry, including the substitution of internationally preferred cuts of meat for national or *criollo* cuts, the elimination of traditional pasture-fed lean beef technology in

[3] See H. S. Ferns, *Britain and Argentina in the Nineteenth Century* (London: Cambridge University Press, 1960); James R. Scobie, *Revolution on the Pampas: A Social History of Argentine Wheat, 1860-1910*, Institute for Latin American Studies, Latin American Monographs, No. 1 (Austin: University of Texas Press, 1964); and Peter H. Smith, *Politics and Beef in Argentina: Patterns of Conflict and Change* (New York: Columbia University Press, 1969).

favor of confinement feeding, increases in per capita beef consumption in certain socioeconomic strata, and the abolition of traditional modes of rural mediation in the commercialization of small-scale cattle enterprises. That internalization has not, however, depended exclusively on the presence of the transnational corporation. While such corporations are obviously central to the accumulation of capital in the livestock sector, the nationality of beef cattle enterprises is interesting mainly for its correlation with technological and managerial internationalization. Currently, many national firms in Brazil, Mexico, Colombia, and Argentina all subscribe to the essential principles of international trade promotion and product homogenization. They are as effective as transnationals in the propagation of internationalized cattle products, despite the lesser participation of foreign capital in their firms.

THE POLITICAL NATURE OF CATTLE RAISING IN THIRD WORLD COUNTRIES

Although not necessarily apparent at first glance, the raising and slaughter of cattle is a profoundly political process in Latin America. Such a judgment does not square, of course, with the mainstream of thought emanating from many international development assistance institutions. Developmentalist premises have focused on the technical requirements involved in increasing the yield and dynamism of Latin American cattle herds: improving stock lines, controlling slaughter, increasing carcass weights, and improving reproduction rates. Likewise, there has been substantial enthusiasm for the export potential of Latin American beef cattle and, not incidentally, for the region's growing potential as a consumer of transnational inputs, feedgrains, and medicaments. The improvement of cattle-raising techniques is a proper focus for development, given the traditionally low productivity in Third World animal husbandry and the protein deficiencies of rural populations. Unfortunately, such improvements have changed the character of cattle raising itself, in both location and beneficiaries.

Cattle raising and herd modernization are not inherently bad for an integrated rural development strategy. Under proper conditions, cattle can provide a measure of economic security for the peasant while serving as an efficient, dual-purpose producer of energy and nutrition. Local slaughter of cattle plays an important part in the cultural life of a small community, as well as providing a medium for the social distribution of wealth. Unfortunately, however, in Latin American societies the most frequent counterpoise is between popularly based modes of cattle raising and the international industrialization of the enterprise. From a purely distributive perspective, the development of larger and more scientifically managed cattle herds and products has had little to do with the nutritional exigencies of the rural poor, as animal protein consumption figures from Mexico showed in the Introduction to this study.[4] Per capita consumption of beef in Latin American countries is quite low compared with beef consumption in the United States and Canada (see Table 3.1), with the notable exceptions of Argentina and Uruguay. Additionally, data from national household consumption surveys in Brazil and Mexico show that lower-income groups enjoy little or no animal protein. Although aggregate data (Table 3.2) show increases in the Mexican cattle herd over the past two decades, there is little evidence to suggest that such increases bring more animal protein to the poor and nutritionally deprived. Likewise, in Brazil from 1965 to 1975 the share of a worker's income required to purchase a kilo of meat increased by more than 100 percent, during a time when workers' real incomes declined precipitously.[5] While indirect, these data, combined with the demographic explosion of the poor in Brazil and

[4] Mexico, SPP, *La población de México.*
[5] Charles Wood, "The Political Economy of Infant Mortality in São Paulo, Brazil," *International Journal of Health Services* 12:2 (1982), 225.

TABLE: 3.1
Per Capita Beef and Veal Consumption in Latin America, Canada, and the United States, 1961-1980 (kilograms)

	1961	1970	1980
Argentina	83.2	82.4	88.8
Brazil	18.4	18.6	16.9
Colombia	19.2	19.5	22.7
Costa Rica	11.4	12.1	16.7
Dom. Republic	7.0	6.5	7.0
El Salvador	8.0	5.9	7.3
Guatemala	8.3	7.6	11.1
Honduras	7.2	4.9	5.9
Mexico	9.1	10.6	14.6
Nicaragua	12.9	15.4	11.8
Panama	19.3	22.4	26.0
Uruguay	79.0	77.8	75.2
Canada	35.6	40.9	37.4
United States	42.8	53.3	48.2

SOURCE: USDA, *Livestock and Meat Situation*, various issues.

Mexico, hardly suggest that cattle herd increases per se relate to better nutrition for the poor.

In addition to the obvious distributive inequality in animal protein throughout Latin America, much of the herd increase found in those countries represents export promotion efforts by national governments. While increased cattle herds sometimes mean more domestic beef consumption, herd increases are more closely identified with export expansion, either in fresh or processed beef products. Foreign investors, local merchants, and agents of the state have historically infused the cattle modernization process in Latin America with export promotion efforts, partly in recognition of the irregular or limited domestic market, but mainly in search of more foreign exchange and higher profits abroad. To the extent that do-

Selected Livestock Statistics for Mexico, 1960–1981

	Number of Cattle and Buffalo (1,000 head)	Percent of Herd Slaughtered	Percent of Herd Exported Live	Exports of Beef and Veal (1,000 metric tons)	Total Consumption of Beef and Veal (1,000 metric tons)	Imports of Beef and Veal (1,000 metric tons)
1960	17,413	13.65	2.24	—	—	—
1961	17,668	14.15	3.07	35.7	339.3	—
1962	18,453	13.94	4.07	38.6	357.5	0.1
1963	19,325	14.30	3.03	46.2	381.8	—
1964	20,219	13.95	1.64	32.3	407.7	—
1965	21,078	14.17	2.54	31.0	432.2	0.2
1966	21,975	13.78	2.66	38.8	430.5	0.3
1967	22,965	13.05	2.18	30.2	444.3	0.5
1968	23,294	13.51	3.01	45.7	454.6	0.3
1969	23,627	14.22	3.43	49.5	485.2	0.8
1970	24,876	14.46	3.77	52.1	538.8	0.9
1971	26,053	13.43	2.89	48.6	532.9	0.6
1972	26,371	13.53	3.47	58.3	543.2	0.5
1973	26,830	16.31	2.51	38.5	706.1	0.5
1974	27,512	18.05	1.57	19.6	824.7	0.4
1975	28,400	18.97	0.69	14.0	875.4	0.4
1976	28,800	18.75	1.76	23.3	895.3	0.6
1977	29,333	19.53	1.97	34.3	929.9	—
1978	29,700	20.87	2.74	45.2	1,009.6	0.7
1979	29,300	20.82	1.29	5.7	1,021.1	1.8
1980	29,500	21.35	1.12	2.3	1,054.2	1.5
1981	29,500	21.69	1.09	8.5	1,068.3	1.8

SOURCE: USDA, *Foreign Agriculture Circular: Livestock and Meat*, "Livestock Statistics in Selected Countries." FLM 9-78, 10-78, 2-80, Foreign Agricultural Service, various years.

mestic consumption is also enhanced, demand is skewed away from the countryside to upscale urban consumers.

The political aspects of cattle raising in Latin America also involve the technology of production itself. First, traditional range-fed cattle are land extensive animals, requiring little labor and low levels of capital investment. In countries with an open frontier or low population densities (modern Brazil, Argentina in the nineteenth century, Mexico during the *Porfiriato*, Cuba before the modernization of sugar, and the United States during westward expansion), cattle functioned as productive occupants of the land. The presence of cattle on the land typically generated proprietary claims issued by their owners or tamers. At the extreme, on the Texas longhorn frontier, Samuel Maverick, among others, aspired to control huge expanses of territory—in Maverick's case from San Antonio to El Paso—by virtue of claiming and branding wild cattle.[6] In countries without frontiers and in those with closing frontiers, cattle have tended to push land out of agricultural use and to dispossess peasant farmers and traditional cultivation to a great extent.

In addition to the generous provisions for large cattle holdings in Mexico, the internationalization of the industry threatens traditional agriculture and artisan modes of rural survival in several ways. Most obviously, the export orientation of the Mexican frontier cattle industry combined with the increased urban market for beef require that land previously dedicated to agricultural purposes be usurped by cattle enterprises. One of the most painful examples of such appropriation of public purpose can be found in the execution of the Plan Chontalpa, described in great relief by David Barkin.[7] Other examples

[6] J. Frank Dobie, *The Longhorns* (Austin: University of Texas Press, 1980, reprint), 44-48. For similar social functions played by cattle raising in different circumstances, see Joe Foweraker, *The Struggle for Land: A Political Economy of the Pioneer Frontier in Brazil from 1930 to the Present Day* (Cambridge: Cambridge University Press, 1981); Smith.

[7] David Barkin, *Desarrollo regional y reorganización campesina: La Chon-*

abound, including the current deforestation of Chiapas and Tabasco[8] for the sake of provisioning the domestic beef market.[9] In addition to the awesome ecological devastation left in the wake of the *ganaderización* of many previous agricultural zones and rain forests in southern Mexico and the Brazilian Amazon, there is a real threat to traditional wood gathering and charcoal production carried on by peasants as important market activities.

In slightly more subtle fashion, certain modes of cattle modernization threaten some artisan crafts and the *traspatio* (back yard) mode of cattle rearing. In Mexico, the export of increasing numbers of live cattle during the past two decades has been accompanied by a dramatic increase in imports of cattle hides and by-products.[10] The fact that Mexico's export cattle are processed in the United States differentiates the industry across national boundaries. Consumers of hides, horns, and lard—principally artisans and poor consumers—are required to reimport primary inputs at a price above domestic hides or under supply constraints that limit artisan production.

As it intensifies, the technology of production also requires that more efficient use be made of inputs into the cattle industry, most importantly land and water. In the Mexican case, as we shall see, the government—in league with private landholders—has struggled to protect the use of cattle land against the encroachment of agrarian reform, to extend the use of

---

talpa como reflejo del problema agropecuario mexicano (Mexico: Editorial Nueva Imagen, 1978).

[8] Luis Má. Fernández Ortiz and María Tarrio G. de Fernández, "Ganadería y estructura agraria en Chiapas" (Mexico, 1979, manuscript), and "Cattle Raising, Farmers, and Basic Grain Products: A Study in Chiapas" (Mexico, 1980, manuscript).

[9] U.N. CEPAL, *La industria de la carne de ganado bovino en México* (Mexico: Fondo de Cultura Económica, 1975).

[10] For example, Mexican imports of cattle hides increased fivefold from roughly 2 million to 10.6 million from 1971 to 1979. Feedgrains also experienced enormous increases in import volume. See U.S. Department of Commerce, Commodity Trade Schedule B.

scarce water resources to cattle raising through public policy instruments, and to stimulate the improvement of the industry in ways amenable to its further integration into the global cattle economy.

External technological improvements, of course, also play an important part in the political character of cattle raising. In the Mexican case, the advent of hybrid sorghum in the high plains of Texas transformed the nature of cattle feeding in the United States and permanently affected the role of the northern cattleman in Mexico. The introduction of hybrid sorghum to the Texas high plains in the 1950s has been acclaimed as "one of the monumental achievements in the annals of U.S. agriculture"[11] and, in its aggregate effects, deserves such comment. But, from the Mexican perspective, the changed face of cattle feeding in the United States, as we shall see, also aggravated some severe structural problems of the Mexican cattle economy and its role in rural development. The political aspects of cattle raising extend to the internationalization of control over the agricultural sector itself.

As a corollary to the impact of external technological innovations on domestic cattle raising, the role of increasing herd numbers in a general strategy of food self-sufficiency and independence from grain imports is also important. While beef cattle in Mexico have traditionally played a very modest role in the demand for concentrated feed, plans continue that would divert more cattle from range to feedlot in order to provision the increasing institutional food market and urban palates of Mexico.[12] The bullish market projected for U.S. sheep exporters[13] promises to strain the poorly managed for-

[11] *Texas Agriculture in the 1980s: The Crucial Decade* (College Station: The Texas Agricultural Experiment Station, 1980), 101.

[12] "Plan Would Bring Mexican Cattle to U.S.," *Feedstuffs* 53:14 (April 6, 1981), 14.

[13] "Western Producers Visit Mexico, Report 'Good' Market for U.S. Sheep," *Feedstuffs* 53:47 (November 16, 1981), 16. Winrock International, passim; "Increased World Livestock Needs Will Strengthen U.S. Grain Trade, Study Says," *Feedstuffs* 53:14 (April 6, 1981), 9.

age system of rain-fed Mexico. Likewise, the increasing foreign marketing of food animals raised in Mexico will likely increase Mexican demand for U.S. feedgrains, vertically coordinate livestock production on an international scale, and further strain the feedgrain production system of the country.

The political impact of such changes is severe, whether viewed as a balance of trade issue for the national government, a food self-sufficiency constraint in basic grains, or a loss of national control over key food industries in a country plagued by poor and unbalanced nutrition. Whether such political challenges come in official form via multilateral assistance for livestock improvement and modernization, bilateral credits for grain purchases, or transnational corporate integration in livestock industries, Mexican government and society are forced to confront the effects as a political matter in the short term. Thus, DeKalb AgResearch's creation of local pullet chick distributors in Mexico and the USDA Foreign Agricultural Service's grain export promotion provide implicit challenges to the autonomy of the Mexican food system—challenges universal to the world agricultural system but particularly difficult to manage in a poor Third World country with such vulnerability to the world market and the charms of agribusiness.

The political impact of cattle raising extends beyond the technical and organizational effects of capital on rural development, however. In an agricultural system such as Mexico's, in which arable land is in short supply and the incremental change of cropping carries great significance for the food system as a whole, the political character of cattle raising extends to the question of controlling economic property itself. In the decades following the Cárdenas agrarian reform, cattle raising blossomed at least partly as a result of official decrees of immunity granted to cattlemen to protect them from the agrarian reform enacted during the 1930s. The first *certificados de inafectabilidad ganadera* had their origins in Article 27 of the Constitution, but became reality in a leading counterreform regulation appearing in 1948. The rise of certificates of im-

129

munity thereafter undid many of the reforms undertaken by Cárdenas in the 1930s.[14] Unfortunately for the small cattle operator, however, the law primarily benefited the large cattle enterprise with its generous coefficients of pasturage.

In succeeding years, more concessions were granted to cattlemen, including the right to plant forage as a commercial crop[15]—a privilege previously accorded only agriculturalists engaged in crop production on land classified for such use. In fact, such a concession removed the only clear distinction between those lands immune from agrarian reform as unfit for cropping and those immune for reasons of political or economic privilege. Finally, in an underpublicized "reform" of the agrarian code in 1981,[16] the Mexican government added a provision allowing cattlemen to acquire immunity from agrarian reform provisions limiting land tenure, even if their enterprises were not solely dedicated to cattle but also engaged in the production and sale of forage crops as a primary activity. Thus, the veil finally dropped from a program that gradually favored the use of certain lands for cattle raising over cropping for human consumption and then sanctioned the transformation of cattle land back to crop land without falling under the provisions of Mexico's most durable revolutionary legacy: the agrarian reform.

The evolution of such a political posture by the Mexican government is complex, and interacts in subtle fashion with the international market, with transnational entrepreneurs in Mexico and in other countries, and with conflicting interests in the state apparatus itself. To understand that evolution, it

[14] Mexico, "Reglamento de inafectabilidad agrícola y ganadera del 23 de septiembre de 1948," *Diario oficial*, October 9, 1948.

[15] Mexico, "Ley federal de reforma agraria de 22 de marzo de 1971," *Diario oficial*, May 2, 1971, Article 260.

[16] Reforms of Article 260 cited above appeared in the same legislation that decreed the new *Ley de fomento agropecuario* on December 29, 1980. Those reforms permitted the qualified commercialization of cattle forage crops on immune lands.

is necessary to trace the historical progress of the livestock-feedgrain-foodgrain complex in Mexico.

ORIGINS OF THE MEXICAN-U.S. FRONTIER CATTLE INDUSTRY

It is commonly understood that beef cattle arrived in Mexico almost with the conquest. Coronado and other expeditionaries permanently affected the future of New Spain's far northern frontier by sprinkling *cimarrones* (wild cattle) from Sinaloa to East Texas. Those bovine populations were further stimulated by the development of Brownsville/Matamoros as a port, the landing of beef in San Diego in the eighteenth century, the wild gold rush of 1849, the commerce of the old cotton trail to Monterrey during the Civil War, and, ultimately, the arrival of the "bovine aristocracy" of cattle speculators and barons in the great cattle boom of the 1870s and 1880s.[17]

In Arizona and New Mexico, as well as parts of Texas, Indian "depredations" limited the growth of the beef cattle industry before the Civil War. Nevertheless, trade and settlement around the Santa Fe Trail encouraged more intrepid pioneers to take advantage of a grassland able to "afford a sufficiency to graze cattle for the supply of all the United States," according to the redoubtable Josiah Gregg.[18] Two decades after Gregg's optimistic on-scene assessment, a representative of the U.S. War Department believed "that all the flocks and herds in the world could find ample pasturage on these unoccupied plains and the mountain slopes beyond; and

---

[17] The history of the range cattle industry on the U.S.-Mexican frontier is voluminous and rich in texture. For leading works, see Billington; Dale, *The Range Cattle Industry* and *Cow Country*; Josiah Gregg, *Commerce of the Prairies* (Dallas: Southwest Press, 1933, reprint of 1844 ed.; Webb; Brand; and T. J. Cauley, "Early Business Methods in the Texas Cattle Industry," *Journal of Economic and Business History* 4 (November 1931–August 1932), 461-486.

[18] Gregg, 346.

the time is not far distant when the largest flocks and herds in the world will be found here, where the grass grows and ripens untouched from year to year."[19] Less than twenty years would pass before that prophecy would be fulfilled, only to be dashed in the great blizzard of 1886-1887 and the evaporation of range cattle speculation in the Great Plains.[20]

Precipitous though the rise and fall of the range cattle industry in the United States might have been, it had a number of permanent effects on the border beef cattle industry. The settlement of Arizona and New Mexico took place only in the second half of the nineteenth century.[21] It resulted in the elimination of the Indians from their free territories in the Southwest.[22] Contemporaneous developments included the arrival of barbed wire enclosures, windmill irrigation, transcontinental railroad ties, and a north-south commerce between the remaining border regions of Mexico and its erstwhile northernmost frontier. That frontier was now dotted with ominous outposts of the expansionist United States. The trade with the border states, in particular, served ultimately to supplant earlier links between the Mexican frontier and the interior regions of that country, replacing Mexico City and Veracruz with Santa Fe, San Antonio, Tucson, and San Diego as the entrepôts of economic life in North Mexico.

Despite the depression in range cattle following the blizzard of 1886-1887 in the United States, the industry nevertheless began to rationalize breeding, feeding, shipping, and slaughter somewhat. In the first two decades of the twentieth century, the Southwest range became the breeding ground for improved strains of cattle managed on fenced pasture. Northern Texas became the range for their improvement and maturation

[19] William MacLeod Raine and Will C. Barnes, *Cattle* (Garden City, N.Y.: Doubleday, 1930), 156.

[20] Ebeling; Raine and Barnes; Webb.

[21] Hubert Howe Bancroft, *History of Arizona and New Mexico, 1530-1888* (Albuquerque; Horn and Wallace, 1962, reprint of 1889 ed., 345, 644.

[22] See especially Bancroft and Edward H. Spicer, *Cycles of Conquest: The Impact of Spain, Mexico and the United States on the Indians of the Southwest, 1533-1960* (Tucson: University of Arizona Press, 1962).

prior to departure for the Corn Belt and further feeding before slaughter. Gradually, with the introduction of rail transportation north to the packing centers, the feedlot and railhead became heir to the great legacy of the trail drive, producing and delivering high-quality meat from Texas to the centralized slaughter system serving markets in the East.[23] Likewise, the Corn Belt became the specialized feeding region for cattle and diminished in importance as a cattle-raising area.

No doubt during this time the contemporaneous development of the great cattle hacienda in North Mexico presented opportunities for cattle trade between the two countries. It was not until after World War II, however, that the integration of the U.S.-Mexican cattle complex became enduring fact. Growth in cattle production in Mexico after the revolution followed the rationalization of the U.S. industry in several respects. Such rationalization is best considered in light of the traditional collinearity of the two industries in the nineteenth century. Development of the frontier beef cattle industry in the twentieth century, however, was separated from that earlier common heritage by the disjuncture of the Mexican revolution and the Great Depression, and a subsequent technological revolution that transformed the face of cattle raising on the border.

Generally, during the period following World War II, cattle production grew rapidly in the Mexican North (15 percent in the period 1950-1960) and in the Gulf region (41 percent during the same period), while the central states stagnated (-5.3 percent growth).[24] Whereas Gulf cattle production grew to meet the increasing demand for beef for domestic consumption, the northern states, characterized by open range and low-quality grazing, fell to the control of cattlemen who ran feeder cattle operations for export to the U.S. Southwest, supplying a growing feedlot and meat-packing industry. A small proportion of beef cattle were slaughtered in Mexico for export as fresh beef or tinned beef for U.S. contracts.

[23] Dale, *The Range Cattle Industry*, 128-30.
[24] U.N. CEPAL, *La industria de la carne*, Table IV.

The presence of serious disease among Mexican cattle created an obstacle to such development in the frontier range cattle industry after World War II, delaying the appearance of a secure, stable market of export-quality cattle. During the war years 1942-1945, the frontier cattle industry had blossomed in response to the burgeoning import demand of the U.S. war effort. That boom was cut short by the outbreak of hoof-and-mouth disease (*aftosa*) in 1946, and a six-year quarantine imposed by the United States. While cattlemen suffered short-term losses as a result, the industry response also served to shape the modern beef cattle complex. On the Mexican side, cattle producers created new canning and packing facilities for export to Greece and the United States. And, of course, the 1947-1954 campaign against *aftosa* broke the barriers to an increased exchange of cattle between the Mexican North and the United States, and established the basis for an export platform in chilled beef as well.

The bilateral disease control commission, created by the United States and Mexico for the dual purpose of eliminating disease from the Mexican herd and simultaneously creating a clean buffer zone between the U.S. herd and the contaminated central cattle-raising region of Mexico, supported a program of veterinary and technical assistance designed to eliminate disease in Mexico. It also established contracts for U.S. government purchases of Mexican canned meat processed from contaminated animals and distributed throughout the world through the U.S. Commodity Credit Corporation. Interestingly, such canned meat purchases did not intrude on the U.S. market, because of fears they might interfere with the domestic industry. Nevertheless, this new relationship in meat exports from Mexico generated a new system of border region meat-packing plants, oriented toward export to the United States.[25] The U.S. government, acting through the bi-

[25] USDA, "The Mexican Beef Cattle Industry," 259; USDA, *Mexico's Livestock and Meat Industry* (Washington, D.C.: USDA, FAS Report M27, November 1957), 14.

lateral commission, was repeating an earlier policy of buying low-quality "manufacture beef" for U.S. troops and other consumers from a Mexican industry that did not exist in such form previously.[26] In the earlier experience, the U.S. government was implicated in a scandal related to the purchase of spoiled beef for canning and use by U.S. soldiers in the field. It is said that one of President Theodore Roosevelt's motivations in the passage of the Meat Inspection and Pure Food and Drug acts was the memory of having sampled that tainted meat during the Cuban adventure of the Spanish-American War.[27]

After the elimination of *aftosa* and the recognition of the division of Mexican beef cattle production into two zones— the North, free of disease and free to engage in foreign trade with the United States, and the South, without the permission or opportunity to export—Mexico began in 1955 to export boned, frozen, and fresh beef to the United States. Reacting to a requirement of the U.S. government later embodied in the Meat Inspection Act, Mexico abided by the requirement that foreign plants be "at least equal to U.S. plants" in sanitary standards in order to gain permission to enter U.S. markets. The Mexican government created a special category of meat packers inspected by the Secretariat of Agriculture and Cattle

[26] Manuel A. Machado, Jr., *An Industry in Crisis: Mexican-United States Cooperation in the Control of Foot-and-Mouth Disease*, University of California Publications in History, Volume 80 (Berkeley and Los Angeles: University of California, 1968), and *The North Mexican Cattle Industry, 1910-1975: Ideology, Conflict, and Change* (College Station: Texas A & M Press, 1980). Mexico, Unión Nacional de Empacadoras, T.I.F. (UNE), *Industrialización del ganado en México* (Mexico: UNE, 1970), 13.

[27] A popular verse of the day—publicized by Upton Sinclair's *The Jungle*—went:

> Mary had a little lamb,
> And when she saw it sicken,
> She shipped it off to packingtown,
> And now it's labeled chicken.

From Robert B. Downs, "Afterword" to Upton Sinclair, *The Jungle* (New York: Signet Edition, 1960).

Raising. The packing houses, referred to as T.I.F. (*tipo in-spección federal*), are the only ones licensed for export, and they reacted originally in their production schedules almost exclusively to the export market and to the growing institutional beef industry within Mexico.

It is not surprising, therefore, that the bulk of T.I.F. packing houses are in the border states of the U.S.-Mexican frontier. According to the industry, the first canned beef plants with refrigeration appeared in the northern cities of Juárez, Torreón, Monterrey, Piedras Negras, Magdalena, Agua Prieta, Hermosillo, Gómez Palacios, and Tampico—all of which are either border towns or in border states.[28] Current beef-exporting states include Chihuahua, Sonora, Coahuila, Durango, Tamaulipas, Nuevo León, and Zacatecas.[29]

CURRENT CHARACTERISTICS OF THE FRONTIER BEEF COMPLEX

In the 1970s, *maquila* beef operations—meat-packing plants processing live cattle imports from the United States in the free zone of northern Mexico and shipping the boned meat and offal to Japan—became important centers of economic activity as well. The market for these products in Japan appears secure, and the *maquila* operations provided not only an outlet for exports from the United States but an opportunity for expansion by the Mexican meat-packing industry. *Maquila* beef totaled nearly 2.7 million pounds in its best year (1979),[30] and one of the largest investment groups in Mexico (Grupo Alfa) began to set up a similar integrated operation for pork exports before its devastation and reorganization in the financial crisis of 1981-1983. Since 1979, however, *ma-*

[28] Mexico, UNE, 13.

[29] Mexico, Secretaría de Agricultura y Ganadería (SAG), *Plan nacional ganadero, 1975-1980. Bovinos productores de carne* (Mexico: SAG, 1975), 145.

[30] USDA, "Mexican Government Concerned over Lag in Meat Production," *Foreign Agriculture* 18:4 (April 1980), 10-11.

quila beef operations have been "on hold," due to that year's January embargo on export licenses for chilled beef from Mexico, followed by the economic dislocation of the border region due to the exchange rate crisis of 1982.

The bulk of Mexican cattle and beef exports to the United States in recent years has not taken the form of chilled beef or processed meat, however. Led by Chihuahua and Sonora over the past two decades, Mexico has developed a lucrative feeder cattle export industry in conjunction with some major transformations in the U.S. beef sector. Leaving for the moment the enumeration of those changes in the United States, let us evaluate the historical and structural reasons for the development of that impressive sector in the Mexican North.

First, it is useful to divide the live cattle export industry itself into two sectors: a high-technology, internationalized feeder steer and feeder calf system oriented toward export and dominated by Sonora and Chihuahua, with Tamaulipas as a key new entrant; and a more traditional range cattle industry providing lean beef for export as well as for domestic slaughter and consumption. Coahuila and Chihuahua are, perhaps, the archetypal producers of such range cattle, though zones exist in all the states for such enterprises, given the semiarid land and grazing qualities of the frontier. As is known already, in the past decade Chihuahua and Sonora have dominated the export trade in feeder cattle to the United States, but for different reasons. In the case of Chihuahua, an important element is the lack of alternative feeding, due to the arid nature of the state; in Sonora, high-quality pasture is available, but the investment climate for feedlots and improved pasturage has not matched the demand pull of the frontier market for feeders.

Within the feeder steer and calf element of the live beef export industry, Mexican growth has been impressive. As Table 3.3 shows, feeder calves and steers (200-699 pounds) from Mexico represent the vast bulk of U.S. imports of such cattle. During several years since 1940, Mexico has enjoyed a virtual monopoly of feeder steer exports to the United States. Even

TABLE 3.3
U.S. Imports of Cattle From Mexico, 1940-1981

	Under 200 lbs		200 to 699 lbs		700 lbs and over		Total	
	U.S. Imports (head)	From Mexico (%)	U.S. Imports (head)	From Mexico (%)	U.S. Imports (head)	From Mexico (%)	U.S. Imports (head)	From Mexico (%)
1940	104,602	28.6	346,289	97.1	169,720	26.3	620,611	66.2
1941	102,195	38.9	412,312	97.5	205,488	26.4	719,995	68.9
1942	66,518	20.3	386,495	97.6	180,054	35.9	633,067	71.9
1943	14,269	58.0	502,909	99.7	77,520	99.7	594,698	98.7
1944	5,861	5.3	276,297	99.6	25,696	99.4	307,854	97.8
1945	7,742	13.5	393,672	99.6	41,995	99.8	445,409	97.7
1946	10,053	7.0	413,665	99.2	25,915	99.2	449,633	97.2
1947-51*	-----------	Imports prohibited 12/26/46 to 8/31/52					----------------------------	
1952	810	11.8	82,280	98.6	47,491	91.8	131,031	95.3
1953	4,000	12.1	102,831	99.1	48,320	52.5	155,151	82.3
1954	2,872	—	3,377	—	46,798	—	53,277	—
1955	3,795	14.2	191,849	98.8	73,696	76.2	269,340	91.4
1956	4,419	19.1	97,984	98.5	14,038	79.2	116,441	93.2
1957	18,400	43.0	434,901	65.3	230,272	19.2	683,573	49.1
1958	16,811	19.2	776,837	51.9	311,724	25.8	1,105,732	44.0
1959	31,775	3.2	503,725	62.9	135,956	33.6	671,456	54.2
1960	33,852	5.2	509,584	72.4	80,496	24.4	623,932	66.6
1961	37,620	23.2	835,451	59.6	125,070	29.1	997,781	54.4
1962	66,240	37.6	1,041,564	66.3	108,937	33.7	1,216,741	61.8
1963	63,739	42.5	688,938	78.4	69,163	26.2	821,840	71.2
1964	63,876	20.6	403,375	78.3	47,657	3.7	514,903	64.3
1965	80,991	20.9	863,771	58.4	150,603	9.3	1,095,365	48.8
1966	126,494	17.6	828,128	66.1	105,380	13.7	1,060,002	55.1
1967	97,738	10.8	607,842	79.9	21,920	17.9	727,500	68.8
1968	147,396	8.8	802,547	85.7	58,509	2.3	1,008,452	69.6
1969	159,143	20.4	792,356	97.6	46,679	8.8	998,178	81.2
1970	168,933	26.9	906,992	98.1	31,824	4.1	1,107,749	84.5
1971	158,689	20.4	748,873	95.9	25,583	4.3	933,145	80.6
1972	173,336	24.5	939,163	92.3	31,363	11.9	1,143,867	80.0
1973	143,851	10.6	783,851	80.9	77,417	29.4	1,005,119	66.9
1974	77,602	4.4	413,777	95.7	55,239	63.9	546,618	79.4
1975	9,966	5.9	220,851	86.0	149,459	3.6	380,276	51.5
1976	119,765	3.9	562,707	87.5	266,167	3.8	948,639	53.4
1977	132,317	2.4	718,047	79.5	250,371	1.9	1,100,735	52.6
1978	154,692	7.9	873,542	90.9	209,401	3.8	1,237,735	65.8
1979	146,034	1.3	430,726	87.4	137,320	0.7	714,080	53.1
1980	135,515	3.0	382,325	85.7	148,540	—	666,480	49.7
1981	145,122	0.6	370,056	86.5	130,173	—	645,351	49.7

Source: USDA, *Livestock and Meat Situation*, various issues.

* U.S. imports of beef cattle were prohibited from 1946 to 1952 due to an outbreak ⟨of⟩ foot-and-mouth disease. They were prohibited again from May 23, 1953, to January 1955.

after the "beef crisis" in the Federal District of Mexico City in 1978 called forth a reduction in exports of live cattle to the United States, Mexico maintained its position in the United States, relative to other competitors. Despite its weak position in other categories of live cattle exports to the United States, Mexico has clearly established itself as the single most important provider of live bovine animals in the past four decades, accounting for half or more of total U.S. imports.

Mexico has a rather more curious role in the export of so-called *carne magra*—generously translated as "lean beef"—on the hoof to the United States. Increasing demand from the United States for range cattle or "manufacture beef" appears to have its roots in the disappearance of range beef cattle from the U.S. system combined with contemporaneous changes in beef consumption patterns. Ground beef and beef for processing in fast-food, frozen food, and institutional food markets such as hospitals, cafeterias, and hotels has created demand for lean beef not produced in the U.S. beef system. Though the import content of the ground beef consumption has remained relatively constant over the short term (at 13-15 percent), that may be due to spurious effects caused by an incomplete picture of the overall beef cycle or to stopgap interventions by the Mexican government in the export of cattle. In any event, the U.S. market does exert a strong "pull" attracting Mexico's northern range cattle, whose meat is mixed with fat from U.S. domestic trimmings to offer a cheap quality beef, not only for fresh ground beef consumption, but for the booming fast-food and processed food industries.[31] The introduction of new "lean beef" technologies and the greater acceptance of "blended beef" in the United States might further stimulate such demand, as we shall see momentarily.

Such provisions for the U.S. market have limited Mexico's

[31] Mexico, UNE, p. 43; U.S. Department of Commerce, International Trade Commission (ITC), *Conditions of Competition in U.S. Markets between Domestic and Foreign Live Cattle and Cattle Meat for Human Consumption* (Washington, D.C.: U.S. Government Printing Office, 1977), 12.

ability to build its herd for national consumption in several ways, the most obvious of which is revealed in Table 3.2. For thirteen of the past twenty years (1960-1980), cattle exported to the United States have represented more than 15 percent of the national slaughter rate, diminishing only with major increases in national cattle slaughter in Mexico in the 1970s, which itself reflected increases in gross consumption of meat. As a result, more than one-fifth of the national herd was either exported or slaughtered in Mexico in 1980, as compared with one-sixth in 1960. Such a drain on national cattle numbers— particularly severe in view of the genetic and reproductive superiority of the northern export steer—obviously affects the Mexican government's plans to expand animal protein production throughout the 1980s. Based on 1975 estimates by COPLAMAR, national meat production has to increase at an average annual rate of 3.5 percent in order to satisfy such plans for increases in domestic consumption.[32] While national slaughter accounts for more herd attenuation than exports, a combination of a growing slaughter rate and the export of the best breeds of cattle to the United States serves to undermine herd-building strategies greatly. While the share of the national herd exported to the United States is minor, its contribution toward replenishing the total numbers of cattle liquidated annually would be great if those exported breeds were retained in the country.

Another, less obvious way in which the frontier trade in live cattle perpetuates a divided market for cattle products involves the structure of the industry itself. The Mexican feeder cattle industry fits into an integrated U.S. industry that provides differentiated cattle raising, feeding, finishing, slaughtering, processing, and cutting. Often, the process is so differentiated as to separate the role of broker from the industry altogether, as we shall see later in this chapter. In Mex-

[32] Mexico, Coordinación General de Plan Nacional de Zonas Deprimidas y Grupos Marginales (COPLAMAR), *Mínimos de bienestar*, Vol. II, *Alimentación* (Mexico: Secretaría de la Presidencia, 1979), Table 50.

ico, however, the opportunities for analogous integration of the frontier feeder cattle industry at the national level do not exist on such a grand scale. Such weaknesses fall into three basic areas: feeding, transportation, and marketing. In those important areas, Mexico finds itself a weak competitor for internationally integrated capital: a politically restricted policy of cattle and range development in a context of Third World resource scarcity can hardly hope to compete successfully for secure and lucrative international markets presided over by multinational capital.

Feeding Cattle in Mexico

The inadequacy of the cattle-feeding system has been a major concern in the Mexican North, due to the rapid rise in the cattle herd regionally, the overgrazing of already marginal pasture, the irregularity of rainfall in semiarid zones, and the general poverty of range management compared with similar areas in the United States. Likewise, in the case of improved strains of feeder cattle destined for export markets or for upper-class tables in Mexico, feeding requirements and technologies are more sophisticated and demanding. In order for Mexico to divert beef cattle production on the frontier to national purposes (a disputed policy to be evaluated later), clearly the economy has to address the inadequacy of the national feedlot system.

The natural forage of the northern states is simply inadequate to maintain a large herd. To the extent that that herd is a product of the internationalization of cattle production itself, the distortions and resource diversions created by deficiencies in the natural range are attributable to the international system's effects on Mexican agriculture. In the desertic North, cattle lack adequate forage about seven months per year, which is necessarily replaced by crop waste and improved animal feed concentrates.[33] Over the past two dec-

[33] Mexico, SAG, *Plan nacional ganadero*, 17.

ades, the combined influences of diminishing range land and growing integration into an international complex of beef cattle raising have diverted significant amounts of crop land to forage cultivation. That land has become an essential ingredient in the northern frontier beef cattle industry and has challenged other, more basic food crops in the region. Table 3.4 clearly shows the increases in land area dedicated to cattle raising since 1940.

Particularly interesting are the increase in oilseed cultivation for cattle consumption and the dramatic increase in cultivated forage. More significantly, such crop diversion in favor of cattle raising has also affected the irrigation districts, especially in the North. In the federal irrigation districts over the past decade, forage crop cultivation has increased as a proportion of total crop cultivation (Table 1.6), so that the latest published data of the Agriculture and Water Resource Ministry show an increase of 127,084 hectares of forage cropping from 1970 to 1978. Similarly, oleaginous crops—a major contributor to improved livestock feed—increased 190,898 hectares over the same period. These crops challenge the cultivation of basic grains in federal irrigation districts, though in the case of many oilseeds they do not directly compete with wheat in the same season.

Feeding beef cattle is still a fairly marginal element of the balanced feed industry. Range cattle are still of overwhelming importance to the Mexican beef system, and the orientation of the most modern sector of the beef industry still points toward exporting the animal live before maturity. So confinement husbandry with improved feed has remained a low priority in the Mexican beef system. As a result, the Mexican balanced feed industry reports that only about 2 percent of the balanced food product in Mexico went to beef cattle for fattening in 1976, and only an additional 9 percent to the dairy industry, as compared with 69 percent to chicken and egg production and 18 percent to hogs.[34] Nevertheless, in the

[34] Mexico, Cámara Nacional de Industrias de Transformación (CANA-

TABLE 3.4
Land Area Dedicated to Cattle Raising in Mexico 1940-1979 (thousands of hectares)

	Natural Grasses	Forages	Oilseeds	Cultivated Grasses	Total
1940	56,172	102	59	—	56,333
1950	67,378	191	171	—	67,740
1960	79,092	366	233	1	79,692
1970	74,497	1,228	561	29	76,315
1971	73,788	1,481	675	19	75,963
1972	69,744	1,725	696	26	72,191
1973	69,869	1,801	765	38	72,473
1974	74,401	1,892	732	65	77,090
1975	74,401	2,124	926	72	77,523
1976	74,401	2,011	555	81	77,048
1977	74,401	1,876	923	513	77,713
1978	74,998	1,886	766	511	77,650
1979	74,998	1,920	1,243	511	78,672

SOURCES: Mexico, SIC, Censos agrícolas, ganaderos y ejidales de 1940, 1950, 1960 y 1970, Dirección General de Estadísticas, SIC. Mexico, SARH, Econotecnia agrícola, Consumos aparentes de productos agrícolas 1925-1978, Dirección General de Economía Agrícola, Vol. III, no. 9, September 1979. Mexico, SPP, Manual de estadísticas básicas del sector agropecuario y forestal, 1979.

most recent fifteen years for which data are available, green alfalfa, forage oats and barley, and cultivated pasturage all grew at rapid rates nationally, as Table 3.5 shows. In addition, sorghum for all livestock feed increased remarkably over the period. Recent changes in legislation that favor the cultivation of animal forage crops by cattlemen, as described above, have furthered that trend, though the extent of the impact on food crops and land tenure will not be understood for some years.

In Mexico, then, there has arisen along with the beef cattle and livestock industries a feedgrain complex that interacts with the basic grains sector, to be outlined later in this study. The feedgrain complex, in turn, partly responds to the need to reorient the beef cattle industry toward the growing consumption of animal protein in Mexico, the high-technology model of poultry and hog raising that has gained ground over traditional animal husbandry, and the urbanization of the market for products from this sector. That urbanization ultimately threatens the ability of the Mexican food system to produce basic foodstuffs for those most nutritionally deprived

TABLE 3.5
Annual Rates of Growth in Area Devoted to Basic Food and Forage Crops in Mexico, 1965-1979

Basic Foods	Growth (%)	Forage	Growth (%)
Corn	− 1.75	Green alfalfa	5.5
Beans	− 6.15	Forage oats	26.5
Wheat	− 2.3	Grain barley	4.0
Rice	0.5	Forage barley	18.8
		Sorghum	14.5
		Seeded pasture	26.8

Source: Mexico, SARH, *Econotecnia agrícola*, 1979.

CINTRA), Sección de Fabricantes de Alimentos para Animales, *La industria alimenticia animal en México (en cifras)* (Mexico: CANACINTRA, 1978), 4, 7.

and, instead, supports the off-farm consumers of the country and the export market.

The first tendency in the rise of that feedgrain complex involves the substitution of feedgrain crops for food crops. As Table 3.5 shows in graphic display, the rise in sorghum cultivation in Mexico accompanies a decline in corn, bean, and wheat cultivation, and virtual stagnation in rice. Leaving rice and wheat aside for the moment—as they are jeopardized by a different dynamic in fruits and winter vegetables— sorghum clearly has displaced corn production throughout Mexico. Known primarily for its great resistance to drought and its absence from the Mexican human foodbasket, sorghum has increasingly offered advantages not available to corn: it is a cash crop in increasingly short supply, and it offers contracts and technological packages from local or multinational feedmills. In addition, as traditional subsistence corn farmers have disappeared from the farm population, sorghum producers have arisen as a group more fully integrated into the market borne by the livestock-feedgrain-foodgrain complex. It is not surprising, then, that the rise of sorghum has been associated with the decline of corn and also with the decline of beans, which are often planted between rows of corn as a complementary crop.

Looking more closely at this relationship, we can associate the rising demand for sorghum with the rapid growth of the poultry industry, most of which is now part of an internationally integrated, high-technology production industry using confinement feeding and the advantages of tremendous scale. Of the twenty-three largest poultry companies in Mexico (all producing over 50,000 birds per cycle), five are vertically integrated from hatchery to processor.[35] The small, rural producer of hens for local use has all but disappeared in the

[35] Agribusiness Associates, Inc., *The Poultry Breeding Industry and Mexican Development* (Wellesley Hills, Mass.: Agribusiness Associates, 1981), 53. This document is a consulting report prepared for the Mexican government's Sistema Alimentario Mexicano.

145

Mexican poultry industry, representing only about 8 percent of total production, according to the best estimates available.[36] Projecting poultry meat output based on current trends, it appears that growth in per capita poultry consumption exceeding 5 percent per annum throughout the 1970s assures a continuing strain on feedgrain supplies for the industry well into the 1980s.[37] Such a projection, of course, is consistent with expectations from other sources about the growth of the livestock-feedgrain complex and the resulting strains on grain production in underdeveloped countries.[38]

Field interviews and aggregate data also suggest that the *traspatio* hog industry is in grave crisis due to overproduction and the combination of high sorghum prices with low pork prices in 1979, and that the trend in that industry is definitely toward the high-technology integrated operations dependent on balanced feed. Likewise, to the extent that the Mexican consumer market for meat is an upper-class market—a point to which we will return later—the institutional consumers (hotels, hospitals, restaurants) catering to the urban and tourist markets will demand more lot-fed beef and international cuts. Prior to the economic crisis of 1982, some cattle were being bred in the Mexican North, fattened in Texas, and returned for slaughter and consumption in Mexico. A number of government and industry reports have recommended increasing the feedlot capacity of the Mexican cattle system, which would necessitate more cropping in basic forage and improved feeds.[39]

[36] Ibid., 57.

[37] Ibid., 48. See also "Broiler Boom in Mexico," *Poultry International* (May 1980).

[38] See especially Winrock International.

[39] Field interviews with officials of the Texas State Department of Agriculture, Austin, Texas, March 1, 1982; Mexico, SAG, *El extensionismo pecuario en la situación actual de la ganadería nacional y en su proyección para 1983* (Mexico: SAG, 1976); Mexico, SAG, *Síntesis de la problemática de la ganadería bovina productora de carne en México* (Mexico: SAG, 1976); Mexico, SAG, *Plan nacional ganadero, 1975-1980*.

Feeding Cattle For Whom?
Nutrition and the Cattle Industry in Mexico

Since 1979—which marked the first Mexican response to beef shortages in the national capital since the 1940s—the role of the beef cattle industry in providing adequate nutrition to the Mexican population has been a major national policy concern. The Sistema Alimentario Mexicano commissioned studies of the national beef cattle system as a part of its mission to improve the nutritional profile of the rural poor.[40] In parallel efforts, the COPLAMAR launched studies of marginal economic zones in Mexico, based on the 1975 national household expenditure study.[41] Part of the effort to reintegrate meat consumption into the national diet clearly recognized the role of the Mexican food system in the international market. As will be seen later, the general lines of policy included limits on live cattle exports, increases in productivity in the domestic industry, and attempts to deliver meat to the poorest populations in volumes and networks never before available in Mexico.

As mentioned in the Introduction, the 1975 household consumption survey showed that fully one-third of the rural population never consumed meat of any kind; roughly that same number never ate eggs; and 59 percent never consumed milk. Other data showing spending patterns by income category suggest that meat in general (and beef especially) is underconsumed by nearly 60 percent of Mexican families.[42] Likewise, studies stratifying the Mexican population by income level show that agricultural families are overwhelmingly represented among the poorest income categories (Table 3.6). As

[40] Mexico, SPP, *La población de México*. Some of the data in this source actually come from Mexico, Secretaría de Industria y Comercio (SIC), Dirección General de Estadística, *IX Censo general de población, 1970* (Mexico: SIC, 1972).

[41] Mexico, COPLAMAR, *Mínimos de bienestar*, Vol. II, *Alimentación*.

[42] Mexico, Oficina de Asesores del C. Presidente, SINE-SAM, "Sistema integral de carne bovina," I, 133.

147

we shall see in closer detail, both the structure of cattle and meat production and the consumer market preclude the rural poor from benefiting from an improved beef cattle system unless fundamental changes occur in both income and production. Though Mexican per capita consumption of beef has increased over recent years (Table 3.1), quite clearly that has not meant increases in meat consumption among those populations for whom the Mexican SAM and COPLAMAR were ostensibly designed. Again, the search for reasons begins with agricultural and cattle production at the local level.

The problem of food underconsumption in the countryside is not simply a problem of the maldistribution of income. If that were the case, a "cheap food" policy for the countryside would presumably eradicate hunger in Mexico. In fact, however, an important corollary to the poverty thesis of rural hunger is the less-recognized dynamic created by the rationalization of food systems themselves. In the case of the cattle industry, the production, distribution, exchange, and consumption of beef and beef products have become regionally

TABLE 3.6
Proportion of Low-income Earners in Mexican Agriculture, 1968

Monthly Family Income (pesos)	Agricultural Families (%)	Non-agricultural Families (%)	Total Number
0-300	72.6	27.4	438,063
301-600	70.7	29.3	1,256,517
601-1,000	50.0	50.0	1,628,266
1,001-3,000	26.8	73.2	3,324,888
3,001-6,000	10.0	90.0	1,060,668
6,001-10,000	8.0	92.0	275,618
10,000 and above	10.7	89.3	166,952
All families	37.5	62.5	8,150,792

SOURCE: Banco de México, S.A., *La distribución del ingreso en México* (1974). Cited in Montañez and Aburto, *Maíz: política institucional y crisis agrícola* (Mexico: Nueva Imagen, 1979), elaborated from Table XXXII.

centralized to the detriment of local consumers. Clearly the leading role in that process of rural social change has been shared by the forces of internationalization via the live cattle and chilled beef trade and the urbanization of beef consumption in general.

The SAM reported in its first wave of studies of the Mexican cattle industry that "on-site" and non-T.I.F. slaughter both declined over the period 1960-1979 (See Table 3.7). While domestic consumption accounts for an increasing proportion of the national slaughter in export-capable meat-packing plants (*empacadoras* T.I.F.),[43] the importance of the displacement of local slaughter facilities in favor of regional and municipal plants cannot be overestimated. In the first place, the number of local slaughter facilities has fluctuated radically throughout recent years, indicating the fragile nature of their

TABLE 3.7
The Structure of Bovine Meat Supply in Mexico for Selected Years (percentage)

	Regular Slaughter	Slaughter in TIF Plants	TIF Slaughter for Domestic Consumption	TIF Slaughter for Export	On-site Slaughter
1960	81.1	11.2	—	—	7.7
1970	74.8	18.9	36.6	63.4	6.3
1971	76.9	16.7	23.6	76.4	6.4
1972	73.7	20.0	33.7	66.3	6.3
1973	70.4	22.9	60.7	39.3	6.7
1974	71.0	22.5	76.8	23.2	6.5
1975	74.3	18.1	81.0	19.0	7.6
1976	75.3	18.1	70.2	29.8	6.6
1977	74.7	19.6	69.1	30.9	5.7
1978	74.6	19.8	70.6	29.4	5.6

SOURCE: Mexico, SAM, "La exportación de becerros y sus alternativas de engorda," 42 and 133.

[43] Ibid., 123.

existence and their relationship with the major forces in the market. The total number of slaughter facilities reported in the industrial census from 1965 to 1975 varied from 563 in 1965 to 882 in 1970 to 721 in 1975.[44] The most likely movement in the industry comes at the low end, of course, where slaughter facilities are little more than hammer, hoist, and saw. The smallest enterprises in the Mexican beef cattle slaughter network are able to process less than three head of cattle per day, whereas the largest slaughterhouses can yield such slaughter in a single man-hour of activity.[45] It goes without saying that the farther removed the slaughter facility from the point of production, the greater the necessity for intermediaries in transportation, brokerage, and other services, all of which add to the cost of the final product. Likewise, the regional concentration of packing facilities in the major cities and export areas reduces employment opportunities in local slaughter facilities that are more labor-intensive. In every respect—in income generation, price, and locus of consumption—the regional rationalization of the meat industry has removed beef consumption from the countryside and transferred it either to the city or across the border.

INTERNATIONAL INFLUENCES ON THE CHARACTER OF BEEF PRODUCTION

From the international side, it may be argued that the influence of the United States has recently diminished in its power to divert Mexican beef cattle from domestic consumers. Presumably, one would cite the relative decline in meat packing for export as a proportion of total national slaughter and the decline in total numbers of live cattle crossing the U.S.-Mexican border since 1979. Nevertheless, important changes in the United States meat system continue to act as a significant "pull" factor in the future of the Mexican livestock-feedgrain

[44] Ibid., 125.
[45] Ibid.

sector. For instance, there has been a shift in the feedlot industry in the United States in both geography and structure of production. In the 1950s and 1960s almost all cattle not used for herd replacement were destined for feedlots, in response to the burgeoning demand for high-quality beef in the United States.[46] Much of the growth in the feedlot industry took place in the high plains of Texas and the Southwest. As Table 3.8 shows, between 1964 and 1981 the total number of feedlots in the principal cattle-feeding states was sharply reduced, from 220,886 to 104,409, at the same time that total numbers of cattle fed and marketed increased from 17.1 million in 1964 to 23.0 million in 1981. Of those lots feeding cattle in 1964, the four U.S. border states with Mexico marketed over half the cattle fed on lots having over 1,000 head capacity, with 40 percent of the nation's 1,000-plus capacity lots within their borders. In 1981, as total lots over 1,000 head decreased in the Southwest in general, these four states still marketed 34.6 percent of all U.S. cattle fed on such lots, using only 12.6 percent of the U.S. lots of that category. Simultaneously, the proportion of cattle marketed from lots of over 1,000 head capacity steadily climbed from 1964, until in 1981 cattle marketed from such lots made up 99 percent of the total marketed in the four border states, up from 94 percent in 1964. While the small feedlot is still an important producer in the United States, the feedlot industry has experienced an undeniable regional and resource concentration in the past decade.[47]

Feedlot size increased dramatically in the 1960s, and the

---

[46] Dyer and O'Mary; J. McCoy, *Livestock and Meat Marketing* (Westport, Conn.: AVI Publishers, 1979); "Beef Extra: The Changing Face of Cattle Feeding," *Farm Journal* 106:1 (January 1982); USDA, *Livestock and Meat Situation*, various years.

[47] 1964-1965 data from USDA, Economics, Statistics, and Cooperatives Service (ESCS), *U.S. Fed Beef Production Costs, 1976-77, and Industry Structure*, Agricultural Economic Report No. 424 (Washington, D.C.: USDA, June 1979); 1981 data from USDA, Statistical Reporting Service (SRS), *Cattle on Feed* (Washington, D.C.: USDA, January 18, 1982).

TABLE 3.8
Number of U.S. Cattle Feedlots, Fed Cattle Marketed, and Feedlot Capacity for Selected States and Years

	Total All Feedlots		Under 1,000 head		Over 1,000 Head	
	Lots	Cattle Marketed (thousands)	Lots	% Cattle Marketed	Lots	% Cattle Marketed
1964						
Texas	1,734	971	1,527	12.6	207	87.4
Arizona	135	166	27	11.2	35	89.8
New Mexico	109	600	100	1.2	82	98.8
California	604	2,061	281	2.4	323	97.6
Total 32 States	220,886	17,058	219,251	59.5	1,635	40.5
1971						
Texas	1,525	3,663	1,300	2.7	225	97.3
Arizona	61	901	8	0.2	53	99.8
New Mexico	68	340	22	0.9	46	99.1
California	410	1,990	139	0.7	271	99.3
Total 23 States	165,237	25,281	163,032	41.6	2,204	58.4
1981						
Texas	1,100	3,960	955	1.3	145	98.7
Arizona	27	519	4	0.6	24	99.4
New Mexico	34	280	2	0.4	32	99.6
California	103	1,139	21	0.4	103	99.6
Total 23 States	104,409	23,014	102,168	26.7	2,241	73.3

SOURCE: USDA, *Cattle on Feed*. U.S. Crop Reporting Board, Statistical Reporting Service; various issues.

industry became vertically integrated and coordinated to a greater degree. The feedlot industry concentrated within only a few of the twenty-three producer states, and the larger producers (over 16,000 head capacity) were increasingly found in the U.S. Southwest and in Washington, Kansas, and Nebraska. Western states became responsible for 75 percent of all cattle fed in the United States.[48] This geographic shift and concentration was related to changes in the international division of labor, since it came on the heels of improvements in refrigeration, transportation, and communication that permitted the deconcentration of meat packing to the benefit of new entrants, such as feedlot owners. The significance of this shift for Mexico has become apparent since the 1974 recession, which began a period of unstable domestic growth in beef supplies, matched by undue dependence on an unreliable (viz., the beef boycott) U.S. consumer market.

A related phenomenon, already mentioned, has been the disappearance of range beef from the U.S. cattle system, mentioned earlier. "Manufacture beef," low-quality beef for processing, has experienced a slight boom in recent years. U.S. consumers, themselves beset by inflation, appear to be stimulating supplies of manufacture beef and live range cattle through changes in their beef consumption patterns. Ground beef consumption as a proportion of total beef consumption has crept up since 1970, as Table 3.9 shows. Given the difficulties experienced by cow-calf operators and the increasing cost of inputs and land, one can hardly expect the U.S. cattle system to produce higher amounts of range beef in the short-term future, notwithstanding the interest in new lean beef technology.[49] The increasing concentration of the feedlot industry and the integration of cattle fodder production, balanced feed, meat-packing, and retail operations mark a new and different level of internationalization in this sector. The

[48] USDA, *Livestock and Meat Situation*, various issues.

[49] Interviews with officials in the Texas State Department of Agriculture, March 2, 1982.

TABLE 3.9
Ground Beef as a Proportion of Total U.S. Beef Supply,
1970-1977 (pounds per capita)

	Ground-processed Beef	All Beef	Percentage Ground-processed Beef
1970	46.6	114.6	40.7
1971	46.5	113.6	40.9
1972	46.8	115.8	40.4
1973	45.2	108.5	41.6
1974	49.3	114.7	43.0
1975	57.9	118.2	48.9
1976	59.3	127.5	46.5
1977	55.2	122.8	45.0

SOURCE: James R. Simpson, "The Cattle Cycle."

increased use of soybeans and other grain additives in "blended beef" may also pose a future pricing problem for Mexican importers of basic grains.

In beef cattle production, as in other export agriculture, we return to the recurring theme of the divided market. That is not to say that the Mexican market is divided in any strict sense, with one section of the country being a part of a separate structure of production and a separate policy environment. Rather, it is the integration of a national system into the international capitalist system that permits the bifurcation of the Mexican market. In the case of beef cattle, the northern frontier states (Baja California, Sonora, Chihuahua, Coahuila, Nuevo León, Tamaulipas, Sinaloa), with more than 27 percent of the national census of beef cattle and less than 20 percent of the population,[50] generally serve markets to the north of the border, not the concentrated consumer population of the

[50] Mexico, SPP, *México: estadística económica y social por entidad federativa.*

Mexican Mesa Central. This assertion is not unambiguous, however. First, in recent years growers assert that a significant proportion of northern Mexican cattle products have gone to the institutional food market in Mexico, though adequate data are not available.[51] Cattlemen in the most sophisticated operations of Sonora, Tamaulipas, and Durango regularly provide high-quality beef and international cuts to the tourist hotels and restaurants of Mexico City and national resorts. The recent peso devaluations would seem likely to give impetus to that trend, given the relative price structure. The common but often clandestine practice of exporting feeder steers to the United States for fattening and return to Mexico for slaughter will likely suffer as a result of the recent peso crisis, however. Disparities in national grain prices might encourage such practices to resume in the future.

U.S. demand for cattle imports has varied widely over the past forty years, as has Mexico's participation in the U.S. import market. As Table 3.3 shows, other than 1946-1955—years affected by disease control campaigns—U.S. imports varied from 116,441 head in 1956 to 1,237,735 in 1978. Mexico provided between 48.8 percent (1965) and 98.7 percent (1943) of that total import figure. Clearly, Mexico's most important role in U.S. imports has been to provide cattle of the "feeder steer" class, between 200 and 699 pounds, ready for U.S. feedlots. Contrary to common understanding, and distinguishing the Mexican from the U.S. feeder calf industry, Mexico does not provide a large proportion of newly weaned calves under 200 pounds.

Despite the great potential importance of Mexican cattle exports to the national slaughter numbers (Table 3.4), Mexico's contribution to the U.S. beef cattle industry has been modest. Mexican exports of cattle to the United States have generally represented less than 2 percent of the U.S. slaughter

[51] It is reasonable to assume that Mexican providers would respond to alternative markets, were they available on a regular basis. Some evidence supporting that assumption appears in the hotel beef trade, which is growing internally in Mexico.

over the past two decades (Table 3.10). It appears that the low levels of Mexican exports of live cattle to the United States respond less to the U.S. cattle cycle than to domestically imposed cattle quotas in Mexico. That is not to say that there is no structural synchrony between Mexican export cattle production and the U.S. cattle cycle. But Mexican exports do not seem to correspond evenly to the U.S. cattle cycle, as described in Figure 3.1. A direct correspondence would entail increases in exports during low slaughter years and decreases in exports during the liquidation phase of the U.S. cycle, a relationship which is not clearly demonstrated. This inference, of course, is incomplete without a more careful study of the origins, ports of entry, and destinations of Mexican cattle exports.

In beef and veal, Mexico's record of exports is also modest (Table 3.11). The proportion of total U.S. beef and veal imports entering from Mexico has steadily declined since 1950. Gross volume has also decreased in more or less steady fashion over the past decade, owing probably to increased demand in Mexico as well as to the poor investment climate and weather conditions experienced in the North during the mid-1970s. Mexico has exported no veal to the United States since 1974.[52]

Regarding the Mexican contribution to the U.S. market, the conclusion must be that Mexico's export opportunities in beef cattle are tremendous but that so far they have represented only a small increment to the U.S. national slaughter. Mexico's integration into the U.S. market is clear from the import data just presented. An adequate understanding of that integration is difficult, however, owing to the inadequacy of current representations of the two beef cycles. More refined models might account for the relative prices and supplies of feedgrains, the composition of beef output from custom feeders, the regional availability of feeder steers, domestic cattle prices for comparable stock, weather variability in feeder cattle regions, and similar factors. One can hypothesize without such a model

[52] U.S. Department of Commerce, *U.S. Imports for Consumption and General Imports* (Washington, D.C.: Bureau of the Census, various years).

TABLE 3.10
U.S. Slaughter, Number of Cattle Imported from Mexico, and
Mexican Cattle Imports as a Percentage of U.S. Slaughter,
1960-1980

	U.S. Slaughter* (1,000 head)	Cattle Imported from Mexico† (number)	% from Mexico
1960	34,644	390,517	1.13
1961	34,581	543,064	1.57
1962	34,768	751,885	2.16
1963	35,274	585,342	1.66
1964	39,310	330,901	0.84
1965	40,959	535,260	1.31
1966	41,036	584,085	1.42
1967	40,407	500,418	1.24
1968	41,030	702,308	1.71
1969	40,584	810,387	2.00
1970	39,557	936,583	2.37
1971	39,716	752,209	1.89
1972	39,267	915,767	2.33
1973	36,403	672,654	1.85
1974	40,499	434,092	1.07
1975	46,870	196,039	0.41
1976	48,726	507,361	1.04
1977	48,073	579,370	1.20
1978	44,272	814,821	1.84
1979	36,932	379,499	1.02
1980	36,830‡	331,830	0.90

* Data were compiled from USDA, *Foreign Agricultural Circular: Livestock and Meat*, "Livestock Statistics in Selected Countries 1960-1981," Foreign Agricultural Service, FLM 10-78, September 1978.

† Figures were taken from U.S. Department of Commerce, *U.S. Imports for Consumption and General Imports*, Table 1.

‡ Preliminary.

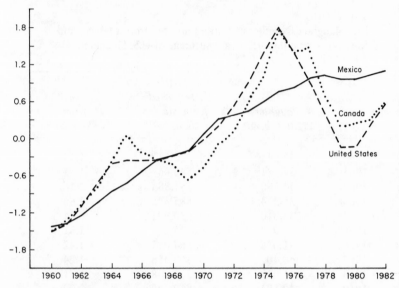

FIG. 3.1   The Cattle Cycle Movement for Canada, Mexico, and the United States, 1960-1982

SOURCE: Plots are based on standardized z-scores computed from data from USDA, *Livestock and Meat Situation*, various years.

only that the U.S. demand pull for Mexican feeder cattle is stronger in times of relatively low feedgrain prices in the United States, if initial feeder cattle prices are not excessively high. In this relatively small regional market, it is possible that buying decisions are made with criteria similar to the hog-corn ratio: in such a scenario a relatively high ratio dictates increased slaughter rates and lower inventories; a low ratio dictates decreased slaughter rates and higher inventories. Naturally, the longer lag in beef cattle breeding complicates this scenario, as does the international scope of the market.

THE ROLE OF MEXICO IN THE U.S. CATTLE CYCLE

On a more general plane, it appears that Mexico is integrated in a complex way into the U.S. cattle cycle. On the one hand,

158

TABLE 3.11
Total U.S. Imports of Beef and Veal and Imports from Mexico,
1950-1980

	Total Imports (millions of lbs.)	From Mexico (millions of lbs.)	% of Imports from Mexico
1950	348	—	—
1951	484	48.6	10.0
1952	429	56.4	13.1
1953	271	25.0	9.2
1954	232	18.1	7.8
1955	229	10.4	4.5
1956	211	6.5	3.0
1957	395	12.9	3.2
1958	909	75.0	8.2
1959	1,063	48.9	4.6
1960	775	39.1	5.0
1961	1,037	53.4	5.1
1962	1,445	59.3	4.1
1963	1,667	73.0	4.4
1964	1,085	48.9	4.5
1965	941.8	46.3	4.9
1966	1,204.2	57.1	4.7
1967	1,327.7	47.8	3.6
1968	1,518.0	65.6	4.3
1969	1,640.5	66.5	4.0
1970	1,815.7	78.6	4.3
1971	1,755.5	79.1	4.5
1972	1,996.3	81.9	4.1
1973	2,022.0	67.0	3.3
1974	1,646.3	38.8	2.3
1975	1,781.8	29.8	1.7
1976	2,100.7	52.3	2.5
1977	1,962.7	59.8	3.0
1978	2,321	63.3	2.7
1979	2,431	5.3	0.2
1980	2,085	0.5	0.02

SOURCE: USDA, *Livestock and Meat Situation*, various issues.

159

Mexican cattle exports do not react directly to the oscillations of the U.S. beef cycle and probably respond more to the factors cited above. On the other hand, the frontier beef cattle industry has been directed for a century or more to the U.S. consumer market and really has no consistent alternative. This assertion must be qualified in light of the rapid growth of local markets, such as Monterrey, and the institutional food market mentioned earlier. But the basic observation is valid: the frontier beef cattle industry is responsive, not to the simple fluctuations of U.S. cattle numbers and slaughter rates, but to the absence of a domestic alternative. That absence, in turn, is a direct product of the internationalization of the industry itself, led by U.S. influence. The lack of a domestic market is also influenced by the oligopsony in U.S. cattle buying.[53]

Cattle cycles involve a dynamic disjuncture in the marketplace involving price, supply, and demand. A cattle cycle is defined as the period from one low point in cattle numbers to the next low point.[54] Cattle cycles are conventionally described by a lagged response in cattle numbers to market prices. Low prices cause producers to increase slaughter rates and reduce inventories or leave the business. Initially, then, increases in slaughter lower prices that are already falling. After the initial "liquidation" phase of the cycle, supply begins to shorten and prices begin to increase. With better prices, cattlemen begin to rebuild herds by holding back breeding

[53] That contract purchases of Mexican cattle are the norm has been known since the first USDA studies of the frontier beef cattle industry. A recent study commissioned by the SAM contends that only fifteen "introducers" of cattle handle all exports of live cattle from Mexico to the United States. See Mexico, Oficina de Asesores del C. Presidente, SINE-SAM, "La exportación de becerros y sus alternativas de engorda," (November 1980, mimeo.), I, 126-129.

[54] James R. Simpson, "The Cattle Cycle: A Guide for Cattlemen," Food and Resource Economics Staff Paper, Institute for Food and Agricultural Sciences (IFAS), University of Florida, 1978, and "World Cattle Cycles and the Latin American Beef Industry," Food and Resource Economics Department Staff Paper, IFAS, 1979; USDA, *Livestock and Meat Situation*, September 1978; Wonyoung Choi, "The Cattle Cycle," *European Review of Agricultural Economics* 4:2 (1977), 119-136; McCoy.

stock, which further stimulates prices. This "building" phase of the cycle continues until the price response induces the next liquidation. Cattle cycles are, like other market cycles for primary goods, imperfect and variable in duration.

In the United States there have been eight cattle cycles in the past century.[55] At the international level, it is more difficult to associate all productive systems with a single cycle. Nevertheless, some convincing recent evidence has shown the U.S. cycle to be a leading factor in world fluctuations in production. This certainly is the case with the leading exporters of beef and cattle to the United States, including Mexico. Even in such cases, however, the relationship is subtle.

As Table 3.12 shows, cattle numbers in various regions do not fluctuate with U.S. cattle numbers. In fact, as might be expected, the larger the region the less sensitive the numbers to anticipated fluctuations of the cattle cycle. Even in cases intimately associated with the U.S. beef cattle production system, such as Mexico and Australia, the relationship between the U.S. cycle and national herd size is not obvious. Mexico, in particular, has continued to build herd numbers very slowly over the past two decades, without great sensitivity to the U.S. cycle.[56] Nevertheless, the U.S. cattle cycle by its very nature affects the major providers of live cattle and beef imports to the United States, among whom must be counted Mexico and Canada as well as Oceania. It is reasonable to assume that the lagged producer response, which is the essence of the cattle cycle at the national level, is also a factor at the international level, intervening in the association between, say, the United States and Mexico, and making the relationship appear less obvious.

Despite the complexity of the association, however, Figures 3.1 and 3.2 show the great consonance among various na-

[55] USDA, *Livestock and Meat Situation*, September 1978.

[56] Aside from the methodological issues arising from great differences in herd scale, complicating factors in this assessment include the aggregation of production for domestic consumption with production for export and the permeability of the U.S.-Mexican border.

TABLE 3.12
Numbers of Cattle and Buffalo in Selected Countries, 1960-1982 (thousands)

	1960	1965	1970	1975	1980	1981	1982
NORTH AMERICA	131,606	151,001	159,096	186,794	167,474	171,668	176,168
Canada	10,387	12,128	11,626	14,008	12,403	12,468	12,698
Costa Rica	901	1,211	1,496	1,816	2,093	2,263	2,416
Dom. Republic	1,132	1,104	1,100	1,900	2,153	2,155	2,157
El Salvador	1,110	1,271	1,440	1,074	1,289	1,172	1,100
Guatemala	1,062	1,384	1,443	2,031	2,700	2,813	2,950
Honduras	1,394	1,483	1,578	1,689	2,218	2,279	2,414
Mexico	17,413	21,078	24,876	28,400	29,500	29,600	29,900
Nicaragua	1,305	1,373	1,980	2,500	2,401	2,301	2,300
Panama	666	969	1,188	1,348	1,525	1,604	1,759
United States	96,236	109,000	112,369	132,028	111,192	115,013	118,474
SOUTH AMERICA	138,686	156,167	177,229	204,015	205,741	208,519	208,617
Argentina	45,484	49,173	52,260	58,700	58,938	58,684	57,655
Brazil	55,700	66,100	78,448	91,000	91,000	93,000	93,000
Chile	2,913	2,870	2,931	3,606	3,568	3,664	3,785
Colombia	15,000	17,000	20,200	23,222	27,196	27,753	28,720
Ecuador	1,600	1,900	2,200	2,711	2,554	2,451	2,348
Peru	3,132	3,644	4,127	4,200	3,850	3,600	3,500
Uruguay	8,532	8,100	8,564	11,536	10,313	10,974	11,089
Venezuela	6,325	7,380	8,499	9,040	8,322	8,385	8,520
OCEANIA	22,495	25,617	30,939	42,446	34,334	33,470	33,150
Australia	16,503	18,816	22,162	32,793	26,203	25,170	24,700
New Zealand	5,992	6,801	8,777	9,653	8,131	8,300	8,450

SOURCE: USDA, *Foreign Agriculture Circulars*, *Livestock and Meat*, FLM 10-78, FLM 7-81 (1960-1982).

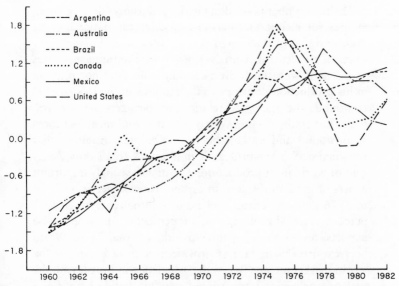

FIG. 3.2   The Cattle Cycle Movement for Canada, Mexico, the United States, Argentina, Brazil, and Australia, 1960-1982

SOURCE: Plots are based on standardized z-scores computed from data from USDA, *Livestock and Meat Situation*, various years.

tional cattle cycles.[57] Cattle producers in developed countries seem to be more sensitive to the world cattle cycle than do their counterparts in underdeveloped countries, as might be expected from the greater market flexibility of producers in developed countries. Thus, Canada and Australia tend to reproduce the U.S. cycle more closely than do Mexico and Brazil. We can hypothesize that if the aggregate cattle numbers were broken down according to destination—domestic or international—the association in the cases of Brazil and Mexico would match that of Canada and Australia more closely for international than for domestic production.

[57] The figures represent standardized fluctuations about a common mean of zero. Such a method is required by the huge differences in scale among herds.

163

The trade imperative, along with agribusiness development, assures some congruity between the Mexican national cattle cycle and that of the United States. Obviously, the small producer of *criollo* cattle who does not control reproduction rates of his herd with much precision and who does not respond in his production decisions to fluctuations in the U.S. market confounds the aggregate relationship between the two systems. But trade in Latin American cattle and meat has roots as profound and unshakable as the colonial tradition that spawned it. While world trade in livestock totals only 7 percent of world meat production, it is an increasingly important aspect of the Latin American cattle-raising scene. From 1974 to 1976 Latin American beef exports alone represented 12.3 percent of world beef exports, 1.0 percent of all merchandise exports, and a stunning three-fourths of total Third World beef exports.[58] The largest providers of chilled beef for the world market include Argentina, Mexico, and Brazil, with the first two achieving international standing beside France and Australia.

Of course, the great cattle-trading economies of Argentina, southern Brazil, Uruguay, and northern Mexico have not developed under the same circumstances. Nor are these "old cattle" systems modal representatives of newer entrants in international cattle and meat trade, such as the Dominican Republic and some Central American countries. Likewise, some nations of Latin America have a highly diversified trade (Argentina, Mexico, and Brazil) with the United States, Europe, and Japan; some are strictly tied to Europe (most notably Uruguay); and some are totally dependent for trade on the United States (the Dominican Republic and Panama). As graphically displayed in a recent report from Winrock International, Latin America's participation in the global cattle and meat trade is split between those countries which essentially serve the European market and those which serve the United

[58] U.N. Centre on Transnational Corporations, *Transnational Corporations in Food and Beverage Processing* (New York: U.N., 1981), 23.

States, with both sets attempting to reach the lucrative Japanese market as well. Naturally, such distinct trading systems create differences in national production systems.

With the trade imperative and the emergence of an international cattle complex comes a shift in the control of cattle production itself. The traditional Latin American model assumes that the producer/rancher controls herd size, reproduction rates, and slaughter according to a calculus of land resources, weather conditions, and prices available in the market (to the extent that he participates in a market). Due to the internationalization of cattle production in the late twentieth century, however, that producer control—if it ever really existed in peasant-scale production—has eroded. This is most obvious in advanced capitalist agricultural systems such as that of the United States, where feedmills lease sows for farrow in order to create future markets for their feed and additives.[59] Similar situations are found in contract providers of feeder cattle for feedlots. The traditional cow-calf operator of the high plains of Texas, for example, has become more integrated into a feedlot-centered beef system and raises more feeders for "order buyers" who may provide only finance capital to "custom feed" calves for future sale.[60] The rancher has, in some circumstances, joined the poultry farmer as a wage laborer for the feedlot and its intermediary customers.

In Latin America, because of the relatively recent appearance of such levels of integration, the decline of producer control is not yet as prevalent. But there are signs in the Mexican case particularly to indicate that the integration of the cattle complex increasingly emanates from the slaughterhouse and the feedmill, or in some cases from the stock-breed-

[59] Hillard Jackson and Lewis D. Malphrus, *The South's Hog-Pork Industry and Vertical Coordination*, Southern Cooperative Series Bulletin #179 (September 1973), 20-22.

[60] See especially R. A. Dietrich, J. R. Martin, and P. W. Ljungdahl, *The Capital Structure and Financial Management Practices of the Texas Cattle Feeding Industry* (College Station: Texas Agricultural Experiment Station, 1972).

ing company and the feedlot. A central impetus for this relationship—in addition to the roles of the feedmill, feedlot, and slaughterhouse as providers of capital and technology—is the producer contract, which has increasingly come to dominate market relationships in cattle as in other commodities, such as tobacco, tomatoes, and canning goods.

The effects of feedlot concentration in the U.S. Southwest have included a tendency to shift feeder cattle operations away from marginal U.S. providers, the group who benefited most from the growth between 1950 and 1970 but who now suffer a cost-price squeeze. Production has shifted geographically to the benefit of Mexican contract providers who have advantages in size, transportation costs, and capacity to produce a large-frame, fast-growing steer for the U.S. market.

Across the industry, vertical coordination and integration have accompanied regional and capital concentration. Mexican providers are no exception. From the 1950s Mexican suppliers of feeder cattle to the U.S. market faced the unique problems of transborder traffic: export permits, sanitation and hygiene standards, and other barriers to regular commerce among nations. Partly as a response to the irregular connections between buyer and seller and partly as a "natural" consequence of the industry's organization, Mexican providers began to deal almost exclusively through order buyers, dealers, and custom feeders.[61] Such relationships fulfilled the expectations of both provider and buyer and reduced uncertainty in the low-margin, high-risk cattle-raising industry. From the Mexican perspective, they fulfilled the need to find regular and reliable buyers in the United States who would bid for Mexican cattle in a competitive market. Because of the expanding nature of the Southwest feedlot industry, most Mexicans apparently enjoyed more than one bidder and an environment of competitive pricing.[62]

[61] For early evidence, see USDA, "The Mexican Beef Cattle Industry," 259.

[62] Although the evidence for this comes mainly from the historical studies of the Mexican frontier cattle industry conducted by the USDA Foreign Agricultural Service, it is not inconsistent with the earlier assertion that a small

From the U.S. feedlot's perspective, of course, the regional advantages of finding Mexican providers of quality cattle were enormous. Particularly in later years, such relationships would graphically display regional superiority in costs of transportation, weight loss to livestock, stock losses, and predictability in delivery. But even in the 1950s the feedlots were able to cement the relationship between themselves and the North Mexican cattle industry via the contract-for-sale and other, more elaborate linkages.

Currently, Mexican providers operate either through order buyers acting on behalf of stockers or feedlots or through dealers acting as brokers for third parties. The tradition of auction markets for Mexican cattle seems to have waned, primarily due to the characteristics of the Texas and southwestern industry, rather than the initiative of the Mexican providers. Specifically, feedlots of tremendous size have found it necessary to plan production more rationally than the traditional farmer-rancher, who fed cattle seasonally. Custom feeding—the practice of finishing cattle for specific customers instead of the open market for fed cattle—has come to dominate the large-scale feedlot. Custom feeding with the assistance of the order buyer or dealer provides the feedlot with the flexibility to avoid high-risk futures markets, by contracting for purchase ahead of time, and to link backward to the Mexican feeder operation for supplies *without having to engage in the riskiest aspect of the enterprise—breeding and raising calves.* While the feedlot typically offers contracts-for-purchase to Mexican cattlemen, the production contract that dominates other forms of agricultural trade is not common. In the competitive and oscillating environment of cattle raising, it is rare to see a buyer contract for production not already underway.

---

number of buyers dominate the trade. The cattle-feeding business is a highly competitive one, concentrated in a small area, which accommodates both lively market bidding among different buyers and oligopsony power over the producer. As contracts are remade regularly, one would assume transborder relationships to be flexible.

U.S. feedlots and order buyers contract for Mexican feeder cattle purchases in order to achieve a greater vertical coordination among phases of the industry and to avoid the painful possibilities of ownership in the more volatile aspects of cattle production: stock raising.[63] Finances, breeding stock, resources for artificial insemination, antibiotics—even whole feedlot facilities—are readily available from international companies specializing in such services. One need only visit a state cattle fair in Mexico to meet representatives of U.S., European, and Canadian firms selling their technologically advanced wares to the enterprising Mexican cattleman.

But producer contracts have their difficulties from a standpoint of rural development: they specify the quality, breed, and delivery date—among other conditions—to be adhered to by the producer. Industry advocates contend that such insistence on U.S. quality enhances the modernization process, as do the confinement feeding and other technological "packages" that are the necessary concomitants to a successful international beef or feeder calf operation. And, indeed, from the standpoint of increased carcass weights that generally also mean better reproduction rates and higher-quality meat, high-technology feeding has meant an improvement in the most modern and capital intensive part of the Mexican beef cattle industry.

THE INSERTION OF THE FRONTIER BEEF CATTLE INDUSTRY INTO THE INTERNATIONAL MARKET

Even if one concedes a complex and indirect relationship between the frontier beef cattle industry and the U.S. cattle cycle, the fundamental datum guiding projections for the Mexican industry must be the growth of cattle raising in the United States. The dependent variable in that relationship, of course, is the future Mexican cattle and beef market itself.

[63] Dietrich et al.; "Beef Extra" argues that cattle feeding is profitable even on occasions when fed cattle are not.

Projections, like other products of future studies, are perilous and imprecise. In this case, however, the inferences to be drawn for Mexico from projections for the U.S. cattle cycle are relatively unambiguous. A recent study has projected two scenarios for the U.S. system of beef and veal production, and cattle inventory, until the year 1990 (Table 3.13). Under the first scenario, previous cycles are replicated, with herd building taking place through 1986, followed by liquidation through 1990. The second scenario, one of slow growth, assumes a change in the basic U.S. cattle cycle, with gradual increases in numbers throughout the 1980s.[64]

There is no question that the most recent cattle cycle has been a severe one in the United States, characterized by large fluctuations in production and sharp curtailing of consumption due to such influences as the oil crises of 1974-1975 and 1979-1980, a possible consumer shift away from beef for dietary and health reasons, and the insensitivity of retail prices to decreases in prices at the farm level. All of these factors, to the extent they affect the U.S. cattle cycle, also will continue to have impact on Mexican export production under relatively low government intervention scenarios. Particularly interesting is the projection for hamburger production. Two countervailing trends seem apparent: on the one hand, the depth and durability of the recent recession dampened the growth of the institutional and fast-food markets, both of which are primary consumers of U.S. ground beef production. On the other hand, as a hedge against inflation, consumers have increasingly turned to hamburger beef in recent years and away from more expensive choice cuts. According to the *Farmer's Digest*, by the mid-1980s Americans will consume 60 percent of their beef ground.[65] In 1978, the institutional food market accounted for 45 percent of all beef consumed in the United

---

[64] See James R. Simpson, "An Assessment of the United States' Meat Import Act of 1979," University of Florida 1979, manuscript.

[65] Lee Schwanz, "Your Customers Demand the Hamburger Steer," *The Farmer's Digest* 41:10 (April 1978), 12.

TABLE 3.13

U.S. Beef and Veal Production and Cattle Inventory, 1959-1980, with Two
Cattle Inventory Scenarios, 1981-1990

	Beef and Veal Production* (million lbs.)	Historical (1,000 head)	Inventory if Similar to Previous Cycle (1,000 head)	Inventory if Slow Increase (1,000 head)
1959	14,162	93,322		
1960	15,399	96,236		
1961	15,890	97,700		
1962	15,867	100,369		
1963	16,896	104,488		
1964	18,965	107,903		
1965	19,261	109,000		
1966	20,355	108,862		
1967	20,740	108,783		
1968	21,358	109,371		
1969	21,600	110,015		
1970	22,030	112,369		
1971	22,213	114,578		
1972	22,647	117,862		
1973	21,413	121,539		
1974	23,286	127,788		
1975	24,500	132,028		
1976	26,480	127,980		
1977	25,780	122,810		
1978	24,610	116,375		
1979	21,553	110,864		
1980	21,245	110,961		
1981			112,000	112,000
1982			115,000	114,000
1983			118,000	116,000
1984			122,000	118,000
1985			128,000	120,000
1986			132,000	122,000
1987			128,000	124,000
1988			123,000	126,000
1989			116,000	127,000
1990			111,000	128,000

* SOURCE: *Livestock and Meat Statistics* and ESCS/USDA estimates, cited in James
R. Simpson, "An Assessment of the United States' Meat Import Act of 1979."

States.[66] When complemented by shifts away from red meat to poultry and shifts from beef to pork, ground beef projections look relatively bright when compared with other beef. Ground beef production in the United States is a crucial indicator for Mexican frontier cattle exports, as "processing beef" (all beef which is ground, cured, or cooked) originates to a great extent in imported beef and live cattle. Mexican frontier beef cattle fit the requirements of the U.S. ground beef market by yielding precisely that tall, rangy, muscular, quick-growing feeder steer which is not produced domestically.

A concomitant factor affecting the Mexican export situation is the environmental cost of producing and feeding some 5 million beef cattle in Texas annually. Texas, as can be seen in the SAM data on ports of entry into the United States for Mexican cattle, handles well over half of Mexican cattle exports.[67] Texas is the point of origin for about 17 percent of all beef cattle and beef carcasses marketed in the United States, at tremendous resource cost.[68] Recent scholarship has indicated that high fuel costs and depletion of underground aquifers raise serious doubts as to the feasibility of continuing the level and pace of cattle raising and feeding in Texas. Some analysts even project a movement in the cattle-feeding industry away from Texas to the North in the 1980s.[69] Such a geographic shift in the feedlot industry away from the Southwest would have a serious negative impact on Mexican feeder cattle exports, even without disincentives from the Mexican government. Regional comparative advantage, which figures large in the frontier cattle industry, would be diminished as transportation costs from grower to finisher increase and as climatological differences widen.

One of the hedges against such a shift away from Texas

[66] Ibid.

[67] Mexico, Oficina de Asesores del C. Presidente, SINE-SAM, "Sistema integral de carne de ganado bovino."

[68] *Texas Agriculture in the 1980s*, 66.

[69] "Beef Extra"; also Allan W. McGhee, "A Comeback in Cornbelt Cattle Feeding?" *Farmer's Digest* 44:4 (October 1980), 60-61.

has received much attention in U.S. farm circles: the elaboration of a new "lean beef" technology, emphasizing more range "backgrounding" before cattle are put on feed as well as genetic and technological improvements to produce a high-quality lean beef for U.S. palates and ground beef buyers.[70] In this light, Mexico might actually benefit in its own domestic beef-finishing program from technical exchanges with the Southwest on topics of improved range management, integrated pasturage, and other elements of modern lean beef technology. Potential for such exchanges can be found in the willingness of producers on both sides of the border to engage in alternative technologies for better range management, leaner beef, and cheaper inputs into the industry. Such cooperation is largely in the future, however, especially in view of the fractionalized character of the industry and differing state policies toward cattle raising.

Much of the validity of projections for the 1980s in Mexico and the United States hinges on the question of feedgrains, their price and availability. Currently, many cattle operations and feedlots are substituting wheat for other feedgrains in the United States, as they are substituting corn for pasturage in Mexico.[71] Likewise, in the United States, hog farmers are to some extent substituting wheat for corn, due to the ready availability and low cost of wheat. The United States is responsible for over 40 percent of world exports of wheat and soymeal and approximately one-third of world exports of coarse grains (excluding corn) and soya oil. The United States fed 6 million tons of wheat and 119 million tons of coarse

[70] *Texas Agriculture in the 1980s*; also "You're a Winner—If You Can Raise Lean Beef," *Progressive Farmer* 96:9 (September 1981), 18-20, and "Look for More Forage Fed Cattle," *The Farmer's Digest* 41:9 (March 1978), 81-84; J. Richard Conner and Robert W. Rogers, "Ground Beef: Implications for the Southeastern U.S. Beef Industry," *Southern Journal of Agricultural Economics* 11:2 (December 1979), 21-26.

[71] This, of course, may be true only when wheat prices are lower than corn, and when shortages in corn occur.

grain to livestock in 1977-1978.[72] The viability of both the U.S. and Mexican modern pork and poultry industries depends to a great extent on low feedgrain prices, especially since the *traspatio* livestock industry has diminished in Mexico and alternative feeding possibilities have disappeared.

Bearing directly on Mexico's situation is its position, according to most international analysts of feedgrain trade and production, as one of the growing consumers of feedgrains for livestock.[73] Certainly, recent data on poultry and hog feeding in Mexico bear that analysis out, as does the increasing amount of irrigated and rain-fed land dedicated to improved pasturage and forage cropping. The point here involves the relation between feedgrain availability in the United States and the future of the frontier beef cattle industry. Some directions are clear. First, it seems that a serious increase in the price of feedgrains in the United States in the 1980s would have a deleterious effect on the capacity of U.S. feedlots to custom feed animals in the current grain-intensive mode. Even with low feedgrain prices, it is not clear that the future of the U.S. feedlot lies with long feeding periods. New studies indicate that the marginal returns in quality of meat are, perhaps, insufficient to justify additional feeding time in lots for most cattle.

Second, a countervailing effect of high feedgrain prices might be a short-term pull in the U.S. market for feeder steers in the 200-699 pound category, as they feed quickly and efficiently. Nevertheless, such an effect would almost certainly validate the current U.S. search for an alternative lean beef system to ultimately challenge the market position of Mexican exports. Third, high feedgrain prices would have a serious effect on current Mexican import levels of sorghum, cattle hides and by-products, wheat, and oilseeds. The most obvious prospect arising from such a price shock would involve more agricultural land being devoted to feedgrain production, prob-

[72] Winrock International.
[73] Ibid.

ably in regions currently an integral part of the Mexican basic foodstuff production system. Quite apart from the foreign exchange damage done by higher feedgrain prices, the potential exists for serious policy problems in the area of basic grain production.

Another contributor to the shift in control of livestock raising away from the producer toward intermediaries, feedlots, and feedmills originates in the organizational character of transnational corporations. Transnational beef corporations have affiliates in at least a dozen Latin American countries and several in each of the largest markets (Argentina, Brazil, Mexico, and Venezuela).[74] In addition to the famous Ludwig venture in Brazil, Volkswagen, Gulf and Western, and the King Ranch all hold beef production and processing enterprises in Latin America. It is interesting to note that, over the century, direct foreign investment in the industry has tended to diminish as local holders supplant the former giants (such as Swift and Wilson in Argentina and Mexico). That in itself does not affect the nature of internationalization in the industry. Whether the agent is Swift or Wilson in the Argentine industry of the late nineteenth century or Bremer and Grupo Alfa in Mexican pork processing in the 1970s, internationalization remains a product of the standardization of production, the reproduction of the labor process, and the valorization of capital. In slaughterhouses, as we have seen, the tendency is to standardize the kind of meat being produced to the detriment of rural consumers of meat; to gear production for export and the exotic institutional food market and tourist trade; and to centralize and industrialize the slaughter of cattle, removing the locus of production from ranch to urban abattoir.

In addition to those growing enterprises specializing in export processing and urban demands for fresh meat, and in addition to the direct foreign investment still found in meatpacking and processing, the feedmills have had an important impact on the generation of new cattle activities as well as

[74] U.N. Centre on Transnational Corporations, 21.

the change in cropping patterns accompanying livestock development throughout Latin America. From Purina to Quaker Oats to Anderson Clayton, livestock feed in Latin America has provided an indirect impetus to the cattle industry. In some cases, the connection between the two is more direct.

In Mexico, in particular, transnational agribusinesses affect the improved feed industry greatly. Anderson Clayton and Purina share over 40 percent of the national production of balanced feed in Mexico.[75] Their influence, along with that of other balanced feed manufacturers, can be measured in the general increase of the two main crops for animal feed concentrate: soya and sorghum. In Mexico, about 60 percent of the volume of animal feed concentrate comes from sorghum. Although it made its appearance in official statistics only in 1958, the rise of sorghum cultivation has been meteoric, from 209,000 tons in 1960 to 4.8 million tons in 1980.[76] Likewise, soya has become a boom crop in Mexico since 1960, when it first appeared in official statistics. Production in that first year was slightly less than 5,000 tons, but by 1980 it had skyrocketed to over 300,000 tons, well down from a 1975 high of nearly 700,000 tons.[77] The two crops together compose the leading primary grain materials (sorghum) and oleaginous paste (soya) found in improved livestock rations. Along with smaller contributions from cottonseed, safflower, and sesame, soya contributes the bulk of the rations' protein, complemented by fish or other animal protein meal.[78]

Interestingly, the limits on balanced feed production in Mexico are similar to the limits on pasturage in principal cattle-raising areas: the capricious rainfall which is the bane

[75] Mexico, Oficina de Asesores del C. Presidente, SINE-SAM, "Sistema global de alimentos para ganado" (Mexico, September 1981, discussion document), 87.

[76] Mexico, SARH, *Econotecnia agrícola*, 1980; Mexico, SPP, *México: estadística económica y social por entidad federativa.*

[77] SPP, ibid.

[78] Mexico, Oficina de Asesores del C. Presidente, SINE-SAM, "Sistema global de alimentos para ganado," 91.

of agriculturalists throughout Mexico. Sonora and Sinaloa are the principal soya-producing states, yielding roughly 70 percent of the total national crop in 1980.[79] Soya is dependent on irrigation and has arisen in the great irrigation districts of the Pacific Northwest as a second crop in the spring-summer cycle, supplementing wheat and winter vegetable farmers' incomes. In recent years, particularly since 1975, soya production has fallen because of the degeneration of groundwater reserves in the region, particularly in areas dependent upon pump irrigation from underground aquifers. In the areas irrigated by dams—especially the Río Fuerte, Río Mayo, and Río Yaqui districts—rainfall has been unable to replenish the storage capacity of the major irrigation dams serving the region.[80] In addition to such great burdens, the Sonora and Sinaloa coastline, rich in farmland and soya cultivation, is also a principal area of attack for the devastating autumn hurricanes of the Pacific.

Sorghum cultivation is less susceptible to drought and groundwater availability. In fact, in Tamaulipas, where about 30 percent of the national sorghum crop grows,[81] the federal government has developed the now-famous Federal Rain-fed Districts (*distritos de temporal*) as part of the recent emphasis on improving nonirrigated cultivation. The south of Tamaulipas became available for sorghum and soya cultivation after the collapse of cotton and its replacement by pasturage, cattle raising, and petty commodity production in the 1970s. The high guaranteed price for soya and the commercial prospects of sorghum resulted in Tamaulipas's dedication to those two crops by the end of the last decade.[82] In the irrigated cultivation of soya in Sonora and Sinaloa and the rain-fed cultivation of soya and sorghum in Tamaulipas, Jalisco, Michoa-

[79] Mexico, SPP, *México: estadística económica y social por entidad federativa.*

[80] Mexico, NAFINSA, *La economía en cifras, 1981.*

[81] Mexico, SPP, *México: estadística económica por entidad federativa.*

[82] Ruth Rama and Fernando Rello, *El estado y la estrategia del agronegocio transnacional: el sistema soya en México* (Mexico, 1980, mimeo.), 50ff.

cán, and Guanajuato, the rise of these crops has displaced basic grains and pulses, to the detriment of rural nutrition and the survival of the peasantry.

THE POLITICS OF THE LIVESTOCK-FEEDGRAIN-FOODGRAIN COMPLEX IN THE 1980s

Once again, our attention must return to the concrete political issues involved in the Mexican livestock-feedgrain-foodgrain complex, seen through the particular lens of the frontier beef cattle industry. The political significance of the industry is great. The international cattle complex does not develop agricultural growth patterns and institutions necessary for rural development and genuinely responsive to domestic needs, whether those needs be conceived as increasing the popular consumption of cheap animal protein, establishing a broader base of cattle-raising enterprises, improving nutrition for the rural poor, or satisfying the basic consumer needs of the urban population (excepting, of course, the upper strata of that population, who are relatively well served by the current system). Beef production tends to serve a small proportion of the Latin American population in most countries. It reduces the amount of land available for food production in countries without expanding frontiers of agriculture. It dispossesses marginal peasants or changes their livelihood from one based on food production to one dependent on feedgrain production for mills and other intermediaries. And it does not generate ecologically sound technologies amenable to small-scale production. Although these are *tendencies*, not *laws* of modern cattle production, when we speak of changes in any of these elements, we are in effect speaking of profound changes in the character of agricultural internationalization and agribusiness accumulation.

Regarding the generation of employment in agriculture or nonurban occupations, modern cattle raising and slaughter tend to be profoundly capital-intensive and labor saving, even in the collateral feedgrain production industry. While traditional cattle enterprises have never been particularly labor-intensive, the modern cattle enterprises reduce that contribution further, via the ascendance of boxed beef (which removes the bulk of skilled meat cutting from farm to retail outlet), the regional concentration of slaughter in urban centers (cutting out previously important local *rastros*), and confinement feeding (eliminating the range hands and petty commodity producers, who were previously the only claim to labor generation available to cattle raising).

Finally, in ways too similar to other internationalized commodities under examination here—citrus, winter vegetables, food grains—the state in Latin America has less "policy space" (not relative autonomy) to maneuver against the vicissitudes of the international market in cattle and feedgrains when the system of production extends beyond the realm of its control. For reasons of foreign exchange needed by the national economy, political power wielded by cattlemen, and cultural suasion enjoyed by urban elites, the political possibilities of controlling or limiting cattle herd modernization are reduced as the international dimensions of its development are extended. But, in the case of the collapse of external markets or their prices, the availability of boxed beef and T-bone steaks is not likely to assuage the hunger of the population marginalized by the modern beef cattle industry.

The problems facing Mexico as it attempts to govern the nature of cattle raising fall into four basic areas. The first and most important matter is to control the national livestock-feedgrain-foodgrain complex, with an eye toward regulating the amount of scarce agricultural wealth to be devoted to animal proteins. Second is the matter of reorienting the frontier cattle industry to serve national markets, once the state "decides" that increasing beef production is a central priority. Third, the related matter of providing enough feed for animals in an expanding livestock system, not only in beef cattle but in poultry and hogs as well. Finally, the central question of the Mexican food system since the revolution has been and continues to be the survival of the peasantry as an economic producer and social class element. The current mode of live-stock production and processing threatens that survival in fundamental ways, through the direct displacement of peasants from their land in Oaxaca, Veracruz, Chiapas, and Tabasco and through the indirect transformation of peasant life with the market and state preference for commercial feedgrains over traditional foodgrains.

This last matter—the survival of the peasantry—will appear most fully in the next chapter and in the treatment of state agricultural policy, and is but mentioned here. The other areas of political concern, however, deserve some initial voice in this chapter, as they are fundamental products of the modernization of cattle raising in Mexico. In a sense, the need for national control of the livestock-feedgrain complex contradicts the need to provide adequate balanced protein for a modern livestock industry. On the one hand, it is necessary for the state to exert more control over national production in feedgrains and cattle in order to allocate agricultural resources more carefully. On the other hand, once the state comes to the conclusion that increased beef cattle, poultry, and hog production are essential to agricultural modernization and consumer tastes, the mandate in Mexico is clearly to increase the insufficient production of feedgrains for those livestock occupying such a lofty position in the food chain, to the detriment of a fairer allocation of resources.

Of course, for a number of reasons the state has opted to increase animal protein cultivation. The state has relented to the mandates of technical modernization in the global agricultural system, the integration of agricultural production across borders, the influence of urban markets on state policy, the power of cattle interests in Mexico, and perhaps even the much-labored epiphenomenon of "demonstration effect" in a Third World country vying for economic growth and modernization. In any event, such policies of livestock improvement are fraught with difficulties. Of the livestock considered here, poultry and hogs appear more attractive as an area of expansion because they are not land-intensive, they do not

179

suffer long reproductive cycles, their transport and slaughter are somewhat easier, and their prices are more responsive to scale. Yet poultry and hogs account for most of the balanced feed industry in Mexico. They are responsible for ecologically questionable practices including heavy infusion with antibiotics in a high-technology confinement feeding program. And they are most tightly linked to transnational enterprises vastly removed from the peasantry and rural consumers in general. Focusing on poultry and hog production without first changing production technologies is likely to aggravate the feedgrain shortage and to threaten the peasantry even further, without necessarily enhancing national control over livestock production.

Returning to the problem of reorienting the frontier beef cattle industry toward domestic production—a problem much studied by the Mexican government—we once again find political conflict. Producers, already accustomed to dealing with the frontier merchants of the United States and facing an inadequate feedlot market in their own country, are disinclined to cooperate with Mexican government plans to shift production to the interior of the country. The government itself, faced with a fiscal crisis of the first order, cannot subsidize such endeavors with any degree of commitment. And the agricultural and cattle systems themselves are ill equipped to provide the increasing supplies of balanced feed, not to mention the antibiotics, intermediate goods, and technological advances, implied by a reorientation of the modern beef sector toward domestic consumption.

Most important from the viewpoint of rural development, such a reorientation of the beef system would have little to do with improving rural nutrition or stemming the deforestation of rural lands in the Center and South. It would likely subsidize the consumers of the upper urban strata in their increasing desire for high-quality beef.

So the Mexican food system, from the governmental or producer viewpoint, is faced at every level with a steering dilemma brought on by the internationalization of a key element of rural life in the North. While the impact of the beef complex on basic nutrition throughout Mexico is great, the state finds itself with relatively little power to influence the industry in positive directions and with a growing mandate to change beef production in ways detrimental to the survival of its rural charges. Attempts to address this dilemma will be sorted out in Chapter 5.

CHAPTER FOUR

Not By Bread Alone: The Future of the Mexican Basic Grains Complex

> A country struggling to industrialize . . . cannot enjoy the luxury of maintaining full granaries in the expectation of some unforseeable event that may reduce the ample margins of security of an agricultural system programmed on a national scale.
>
> —CONASUPO Annual Report, 1968

> It is important to consider in the current agricultural crisis two key aspects for the nation: the growing erosion of food security and the brutal assault against the poorest peasantry and his traditional economy.
>
> —Cassio Luiselli, Director of the Sistema Alimentario Mexicano, August 1980

The basic grains complex is the front line of battle against Mexican food production shortages. Of all the commodity and agribusiness groups we have mentioned until now, basic grains, especially maize and wheat, are most amenable to broad national production and consumption by the poorest groups in Mexican society. To a great extent, maize cultivation is the wellspring of peasant life, and wheat plays a regional role of traditional importance as well as acting as the harbinger of the "modern" basic grain sector in an urbanized society.

Yet, in painful paradox, these two basic human foodstuffs have suffered over the 1960s and 1970s as "dependent variables" in the allocation of agricultural resources in Mexico. Wheat cultivation has been vulnerable to foreign markets' luring irrigated areas to produce other, less basic agricultural commodities. Likewise, wheat production has depended on progressive pricing policies by the Mexican government. Maize, in its turn, has waxed and waned in tandem with sorghum cultivation for feedstuffs, as well as the availability of credit and inputs for the peasant sector of Mexican agriculture. In many ways, Green Revolution techniques for the cultivation of superior strains of maize and wheat have either been cut short by local productive conditions militating against the expansion of basic grains or fallen victim to inferior prices and markets at both international and national levels. As we shall see in the next chapter, these problems in the basic grains sector have not been solely "market phenomena" but have links to specific government price and purchase policies as well.

The thesis of this chapter is that the basic grains sector is no less internationalized than winter vegetables and fruits, or cattle and beef. But clearly the mode of internationalization is different: Mexican basic grains, with the exception of some startlingly successful years in the 1960s, have not been traded in international markets. There is no real international market for beans, and maize has never moved in great volume outside the Mexican border. Wheat, the only real exception, appeared momentarily in international markets as the Mexican agricultural economy resorted to trade policies emphasizing comparative advantage in the heyday of the highest per capita wheat production in federal irrigation districts. Nevertheless, Mexico has not historically used wheat as an export staple crop, in the manner of Canada, Australia, the United States, or Argentina.

But, even without the obvious trade impulse that has led the internationalization of other crops we have considered, the basic grains sector has been truly internationalized in more subtle ways. First, the reorientation of the federal irrigation districts away from basic grains in the 1960s and 1970s responded, in great measure, to an international dynamic, as we have already seen in Chapter 2. To the extent that federal irrigation districts moved away from wheat cultivation to other cash crops for processing or export, the basic grains sector became vulnerable to the forces of the international market. More seriously, wheat and other improved basic grains came to depend on a small set of international seed manufacturers who affected the strains and technologies accompanying the cultivation of improved wheat varieties in Mexico. As we shall note briefly, such internationalization through seed stock companies has seriously affected the government's ability to control the dissemination of improved seed for its own policy objectives. Attributing malefic intentions to the international seed companies is unnecessary. Regardless of their motivations, they have undoubtedly shaped the alternatives for wheat cultivation in Mexico for decades. In that sense, at least, the constraints binding wheat production at the national level are a product of the internationalization of key farm inputs at the level of production.

Wheat cultivation has also been internationalized through the modes of agribusiness processing that characterize the sector. Food-processing industries using wheat flour have taken an increasing share of national production, only to yield products of dubious nutritive value at an inflated price for a market far removed from the countryside where the wheat is produced. Through the transnational penetration of the food-processing industry in wheat products a significant proportion of basic grain production has gone to internationally recognizable confections and snack foods, such as Doni Donas, Ding Dongs, Twinkies, and, of course, the redoubtable veteran Pan Bimbo. In other production perhaps less susceptible to obvious criticisms of taste and food value—pasta, crackers, wheat tortillas, wheat flour itself—wheat products have become one of the more obvious elements in the Mexican government's "cheap food" policy for urban workers. Heavily state-subsidized, price-controlled at the market, and moved, stored, distributed, and sold under state aegis, wheat has become not only one of the most obvious elements of the internationalization of Mexican agriculture but a bellwether of national food policy as well.

For purposes of analysis, wheat must be separated from maize and beans, however deeply they are all internationalized in the basic grains complex. Wheat is a success story of the modernization of Mexican agriculture.[1] Maize and beans are the archetypal remnants of Mexican rural life, anthropological and economic links to modes and relations of production rarely enhanced by capitalist agriculture. They are the crops of the peasantry, of the marginal zones, and of the *minifundista* and *ejidatario*. While wheat enjoys the regular benefits of irrigation, maize and beans are still largely dependent on capricious Mexican rainfall. Wheat farmers who regularly manage sizable plots of land and machinery contrast sharply with the maize and bean cultivator, who typically uses little wage labor, less machinery, and draft animals for heavy work. Whereas wheat productivity in Mexico has increased most impressively since 1950, productivity in maize and beans has stayed low, giving rise to the traditional denigration of peasant farming and calling forth the old, if not venerable, clichés of agricultural modernization: that the market, machinery, better inputs, and technical assistance are remedies for the sloth, primitiveness, and anticapitalist mentality of the subsistence farmer.

But, for all their differences in cultivation practices, in regional concentration, and in relation to agribusiness activities, basic foodstuffs from maize to wheat do share a specific and important role in the Mexican food system: they are the crops around which the most recent and serious agricultural policy has hovered. Basic foodgrains by definition also provide more of the low-income population's food than do the winter vegetables, cattle, oilseeds, and fruit against which those grains compete. And, particularly in the case of maize and beans,

[1] Hewitt de Alcantara; David Barkin and Timothy King, *Regional Economic Development: The River Basin Approach in Mexico* (Cambridge: Cambridge University Press, 1970).

basic grain cultivation may literally determine the livelihoods of the most miserably deprived rural populations in Mexico.

THE ORIGINS AND FUTURE
OF WHEAT CULTIVATION IN MEXICO

Wheat made its appearance in the first official agricultural statistics kept after the Mexican revolution, affirming its early importance in national production. On a rain-fed basis, wheat cultivation was common, if not plentiful, even in the nineteenth century. In the northern and Yucatecan extremities, wheat has been a staple food, though it was never a traditional cash crop competing significantly with the boom crops henequen and garbanzo during the Porfiriato. As a popular national foodstuff, wheat clearly did not challenge maize until well into the twentieth century.

Clearly, the revolutionary increases in wheat cultivation came about as a result of the great irrigation districts in the 1940s and 1950s, and the creation of the colonization areas and *unidades de riego* such as the Coast of Hermosillo. As Table 4.1 shows, national wheat production in Mexico stayed at or below 500,000 tons until the late 1940s. In the aftermath of the creation of the first federal irrigation districts, however, total wheat production skyrocketed in the mid 1950s to achieve levels exceeding 2.5 million tons two decades later (1976 being a record anomaly at 3.3 million tons). Productivity also improved remarkably during that period, reaching nearly four metric tons per hectare on a national basis by the end of the 1970s. As expected, by the end of the 1970s irrigated districts dominated wheat production, accounting for some 68 percent of wheat acreage and 80 percent of volume.[2]

Regionally, wheat production is even more amazingly concentrated relative to other crops in the Mexican food production system. Four states—Sonora, Sinaloa, Baja California, and Guanajuato—produce roughly three-fourths of the na-

[2] Mexico, SPP, *El sector alimentario en México*, 97.

tional Mexican wheat crop; Sonora alone accounts for over 40 percent.[3] But even these data give a falsely broad impression of the cultivation of wheat in Mexico. A handful of irrigation districts in the states mentioned account for the vast bulk of national wheat production. In the Yaqui River irrigation district alone, wheat cultivation regularly exceeded 100,000 hectares per season throughout the 1970s, reaching a peak in 1976 with 165,000 hectares. The Coast of Hermosillo, one of the newest irrigation districts, planted up to 90,000 of its 110,000 hectares in winter wheat in the 1970s. And, in the upper Lerma River districts in Guanajuato, upward of 40,000 hectares were regularly devoted to wheat cultivation in the 1970s.[4]

In sum, a few of the largest and most sophisticated federal irrigation districts in Mexico virtually determine the level of wheat cultivation in the entire country. As we shall see in this chapter, that concentration of wheat production leaves the Mexican granaries vulnerable, not only to the caprice of rainfall that determines cropping to some extent in the irrigation districts, but also to the pull of northern markets and agribusiness processors, eager to compete for the favors of the cultivators of the richest land in Mexico.

MEXICAN WHEAT PRODUCTION AND POPULATION

In recent years, it has become apparent that the Mexican wheat production system is deficient neither in improving yields per hectare nor in maintaining acreage devoted to wheat cultivation. Recent criticism that the Mexican agricultural system has shifted out of wheat production on a large scale has not proved correct. In fact, given the market and government stimuli to agricultural production in general, the Mexican food system has responded admirably, especially in light of

[3] Mexico, SPP, *México: estadística económica y social por entidad federativa*, 64.

[4] Mexico, SARH, Dirección General de Distritos de Riego, *Estadística agrícola*, various years.

187

the negative terms of trade toward agriculture throughout the 1970s and the low official price for wheat in particular. Aggregate wheat output actually increased over 1960s averages during the 1970s, and wheat output in 1980 totaled 2.78 million tons, even before the implementation of the Sistema Alimentario Mexicano. Even in the worst years of agrarian unrest in the mid-1970s, wheat cultivation survived strong until the López Portillo administration began, and even then it maintained a relatively high level at more than 2.5 million tons of grain per year.

But aggregate output is too simple a measure of the adequacy of wheat production in Mexico. The reality of Mexican agricultural life hinges, not only on production statistics, but on the growth of the consumer population in the countryside as well as in the growing urban centers of the nation. As examination of Tables 4.1 and 4.2 shows, the critical shortfall in Mexican grain production has not come in aggregate output but in the inability of the federal irrigation district system to sustain great increases in production to meet the burgeoning needs of the Mexican population. In the first place, average annual output per capita peaked in the 1960s and with the exception of three record years, never reached 50 kilograms per person again. After 1976, per capita wheat production slumped to figures more typical of the late 1950s, even with the spectacular subventions of the SAM, to be considered shortly. But, once again, we can see that aggregate area planted remained high over the 1970s, and yield per hectare reached its peak in the late 1970s. It is clear that the rapid growth of the Mexican population, the slowing expansion in the federal irrigation districts, and the limits of water availability together explain the gross grain shortfalls better than simple allegations of decline in the sector.

But per capita output is only part of the story. The social profile of wheat consumption in Mexico is exactly the opposite of maize and bean consumption. While the latter play an essential role in supplying protein to the poorest populations, wheat plays almost no role, accounting for less than 2 percent

TABLE 4.1
Wheat Production in Mexico, 1925-1983

	Area (1,000 ha)	Volume (1,000 tons)	Yield (kg/ha)	Output (kg/capita)
1925	455	298	655	19.35
1930	490	370	756	22.16
1935	460	347	753	19.07
1940	601	464	772	23.32
1945	468	347	740	16.42
1950	644	587	911	22.40
1955	800	850	1,063	27.87
annual avg.				
1950-59	780	927	1,154	30.12
1960	840	1,190	1,417	33.43
1965	858	2,150	2,505	51.07
annual avg.				
1960-69	806	1,828	2,267	43.62
1970	886	2,676	3,020	53.73
1971	614	1,831	2,981	35.62
1972	687	1,809	2,634	34.07
1973	640	2,091	3,264	38.16
1974	774	2,789	3,602	49.27
1975	778	2,798	3,596	47.83
1976	894	3,363	3,761	55.68
1977	709	2,456	3,464	39.36
1978	760	2,785	3,666	43.25
1979	599	2,339	3,907	35.17
annual avg.				
1970-79	734	2,494	3,389	43.21
1980*	738	2,785	3,771	40.60
1981†	850	3,050	3,529	42.14
1982†	950	4,200	4,420	59.81
1983‡	840	3,200	3,810	n/a

SOURCE: Mexico, NAFINSA, *La economía mexicana en cifras.*
* Mexico, SARH, "Valorización de la producción agrícola," 1980.
† USDA estimates, "Mexico: Annual Feed and Grain Report," 1981.
‡ USDA forecast.

TABLE 4.2
Wheat Production in Mexican Federal Irrigation Districts for
Selected Years

	Fed. Irrigation Districts Area (ha)	Irrigated Wheat as % of Total Wheat Area	Irrigation District Acreage Devoted to Wheat (% of total)
1945	123,355	26.3	19.2
1950	145,795	22.6	16.9
1955	342,439	42.8	22.3
1960	354,885	42.2	20.2
1965	552,552	64.4	25.5
1970	512,650	57.8	20.6
1975	502,959	64.6	16.3
1978	516,583	68.0	—

SOURCE: Mexico, SPP, *El sector alimentario en México*.

of the protein intake of the poorest income categories.[5] Wheat has never achieved status as a basic foodstuff of the poor, who are, as we know, also mostly rural dwellers. In 1970 an estimated 37 percent of the rural population in Mexico never ate wheat bread.[6] In fact, this stratification of wheat consumption separates wheat from maize and beans in a basic way: wheat is a basic food for the urban industrial workforce and the middle- and upper-strata consumer in Mexico. It plays a much less important role as a foodstuff in the countryside or as a source of livelihood for small farmers. In effect, the vast federal irrigation system devoted to wheat production has become a life support system for the industrializing Mexican economy and its population. The enormous capital and infrastructure investments in such production have had little

[5] Mexico, SPP, *El sector alimentario en México*, 632. The 1968 household expenditure survey indicated that 1.2 percent of protein consumption in the bottom income category (less than 300 pesos per month) came from wheat and its products; the 1975 survey showed a similar proportion.

[6] Mexico, SPP, *La población de México*, 207.

to do with rural development in the broad sense of the term or with improving the nutritional profile of the poor. At present, something over 800,000 hectares of the best agricultural land in Mexico is devoted to a crop too expensive, rare, foreign, and processed to satisfy the food needs of the nutritionally deprived Mexican rural population.

While the obvious consequence of such emphasis on wheat is the diversion of current agricultural resources away from traditional rural foods, such a case is difficult to make in light of the historical development of wheat land from desert to river valley oases in the Northwest. Nevertheless, two important points do remain. First, wheat production in Mexico is fundamentally a crop of the postwar economic miracle, not only because of the advent of the Green Revolution in wheat cultivation, but in the destination of wheat for national consumption. If maize and beans are the heart of the traditional diet, wheat is the heart of the new diet—of the industrializing, urbanizing, modernizing Mexican population, who have in large part abandoned traditional foodstuffs for wheat products. Any plan to increase wheat cultivation at the expense of other crops, whether oilseeds or winter vegetables, must attend to this limited and specific consumer market for wheat.

Second, such a relationship between wheat cultivation and industrialization and urbanization in Mexico shows another, more subtle face of internationalization. Not only do the production, processing, milling, and consumption of wheat products increasingly conform to the internationally recognizable forms already mentioned, but the creation of such a crop complex to sustain the changing Mexican working population is part of the general response of the Mexican state to its own insertion in the international division of labor. That is, wheat in the broadest sense is a support structure for the transformation of the Mexican economy after World War II, from a primary good exporting economy to an import-substituting industrialization model of growth. That industrialization sought to escape the international vulnerability of primary good export dependency in the prewar era, and wheat became

191

the linchpin of the first "self-sufficiency" drive—not a food self-sufficiency drive, however, but an industrial self-sufficiency drive. Wheat's critical position as an adjunct to the "cheap food" policies of the Mexican government and as a principal wage good for the newly transformed urban industrial workforce mark it as an element in any future self-sufficiency drive in food, but not in the same way as maize and beans.

The growing significance of wheat as a wage good, and the resulting imbalance between production and consumption, manifests itself in Mexico's annual appearance in the international market as a major consumer of imported wheat. As Table 4.3 demonstrates so graphically, Mexican wheat production since the early 1970s has been in a race with consumption demands and has fallen ever further behind in its ability to satisfy the demand of the Mexican population. The bitter penalty for losing this race appears in total imports, which began as incidental volumes to support the basically self-sufficient Mexican wheat sector in the 1960s and which have ultimately resulted in three successive years (1978-1980) of importing more than a million tons, almost exclusively from the United States. Even these data are possibly understated, given the high figures attributed to Mexican production by the U.S. Department of Agriculture compared with official Mexican government statistics.

In any event, the important phenomenon—the increasing external reliance of the Mexican wheat sector—shows itself in two ways: the structural incapacity of the Mexican wheat system to expand production much beyond current yields and, perhaps more disturbingly in light of the current financial crisis of the Mexican economy, the shift in the externally oriented irrigated agriculture system from a net producer of foreign exchange in the 1940s and 1950s to a consumer in the late 1970s and 1980s. Each of these major tendencies in the wheat sector deserves individual attention, both for their immediate impact on the Mexican farmer and consumer and for their

TABLE: 4.3

Wheat Supply, Distribution, and Imports for Mexico, 1960-1983 (thousands of metric tons)

	Pro-duction*	Total Imports	Total Exports†	Domestic for Feed	Con-sumption Total	Imports from U.S.†
1960	1,190	7	—	33	1,253	—
1961	1,402	20	—	34	1,305	1
1962	1,435	36	—	37	1,435	20
1963	1,703	54	282	38	1,469	36
1964	1,800	31	406	37	1,553	49
1965	2,058	7	477	35	1,600	25
1966	1,612	1	30	40	1,650	1
1967	2,061	1	175	40	1,750	4
1968	1,780	1	—	40	1,800	—
1969	1,915	49	262	40	1,850	3
1970	2,148	5	40	50	2,100	3
1971	2,019	409	65	125	2,342	4
1972	1,700	650	16	189	2,390	402
1973	2,000	790	10	150	2,729	650
1974	2,400	832	34	133	2,893	705
1975	2,900	1	31	120	2,990	832
1976	3,350	1	40	200	3,180	1
1977	2,300	625	17	105	3,155	—
1978	2,350	1,055	15	250	3,400	580
1979	2,280	1,020	15	150	3,400	750
1980	2,650	1,100	10	100	3,500	981
1981‡	3,050	938	5	700	4,000	747
1982‡	4,200	50	10	600	4,100	35
1983‡	3,200	900	10	650	4,150	—

SOURCE: USDA, *Foreign Agriculture Circular*, "Reference Tables on Wheat, Corn, and Total Coarse Grains Supply-Distribution for Individual Countries," Foreign Agricultural Service, various issues.

* Note that USDA production figures often differ from SARH data in Table 4.1. This problem is universal among contending data sets in Mexico.

† Calculated July-June.

‡ USDA, *Annual Feed and Grain Report*, 1983.

implicit influence on state intervention in Mexican basic grain production.

CONTENTIONS ABOUT THE NATURE OF MEXICAN WHEAT SHORTFALLS IN THE 1970s

Even in the brief two years of the Sistema Alimentario Mexicano (1980-1982), a fundamental argument emerged among analysts of the Mexican basic grains system. The first skirmish in that argument revolved around the nature of the flagging production in basic foodstuffs. To isolate wheat for the moment, the argument centered on the nature of the declining self-sufficiency in wheat and the prospects for rectifying that decline, which became important issues in the mid-1970s as Mexico entered the international market as a full-fledged, large-scale consumer of imported wheat. In Chapter 5, we will assess the more fundamental question of food self-sufficiency as a policy goal, but for the moment the descriptive dispute over the decline in wheat production must take priority, unconfused by the politics of *autosuficiencia*, however conceived.

Two points are critical to the assessment of the decline in national wheat self-sufficiency. First, it has to be made clear that the main element in declining wheat production per capita is not to be found in reduced wheat acreage per se but rather in the saturation of the possible irrigated wheat cultivation area, combined with competition from other, more lucrative cash crops. The prospects for increasing wheat cultivation for the sake of self-sufficiency hinge on the nature of wheat production itself. If production is, in fact, limited by the finite expanse of the federal irrigation districts—as some have argued—only two options exist for the Mexican wheat system: either increasing productivity in existing wheat zones or increasing the nonirrigated wheat areas of the country as a supplement to current production. We will treat each of these possibilities momentarily.

The second aspect of the wheat production problem involves the matter of arresting the decline that has already occurred in the area devoted to wheat. Such political problems involve an analysis of crops competing with wheat in the federally irrigated districts and an assessment of their importance to the national agricultural system. In this aspect we again find the conventional forces of industrialization at work, in ways intimately related to our concerns in Chapters 2 and 3. As we shall see shortly, wheat has given way to crops with little immediate relation to the Mexican need for foodstuffs but with substantial and durable connections to the international trade and agribusiness system we are interested in analyzing.

On the first matter, it is doubtful that reliable alternatives exist for increasing the area devoted to wheat. The principal obstacle to such expansion is the lack of water available for cultivation. In the federal irrigation districts, it has been clear for some years that the fundamental arbiter of agricultural expansion has been the gross deficiency in rainfall needed to replenish the major storage reservoirs of the great Northwest. As Table 4.4 shows, for most of the past two decades water reserves in the federal irrigation districts have been stretched closer and closer to full use every year; that is, a smaller

TABLE 4.4
Water Availability in Mexican Federal Irrigation Districts
1946-1979 (millions of cubic meters)

	Storage Capacity	Maximum Storage Level	Storage Capacity Used (%)
1946	16,980	5,694	33.5
1950	18,923	4,801	25.4
1955	25,022	14,555	58.2
1960	28,429	23,268	81.8
1965	35,311	22,450	63.6
1970	36,344	26,972	74.2
1975	43,045	35,593	82.7
1979	45,479	34,526	75.9

NOTE: Annual fluctuations actually overstate available water supplies.
SOURCE: Mexico, NAFINSA, *La economía mexicana en cifras*, 63.

195

proportion is being reserved against possible drought. The bulk of the burden imposed by inadequate rainfall has fallen on "second-cycle" crops, such as soya, maize, and cotton, which do not directly compete with wheat in the winter cycle. In many years cultivators with claims to water use rights in the federal irrigation districts have had to forgo second plantings or to sharply reduce such areas under cultivation. The scarcity of rainfall has also clearly limited the expansion of existing acreage in federally irrigated districts, and much potential wheat land lies unirrigated for lack of water.[7]

More serious, however, is the destruction of subterranean water reserves in wheat cultivation areas. Since the 1950s the opening of major irrigation districts served by storage dams—the Yaqui, Mayo, Fuerte, Laguna, and Lerma, among others—has been accompanied by the equally critical expansion of pump-fed irrigation districts in the semiarid zones of the northwestern and north central economic regions. In the Coast of Hermosillo, Baja California, Altar, and Caborca, pump irrigation has not only expanded the acreage under federal irrigation district aegis but has been devoted in large measure to the cultivation of wheat. It has been clear for over two decades, however, that the rate of water use in the pump irrigation districts has far outstripped nature's capacity to replenish the underground aquifers on which they depend. Recent studies in Guaymas and the Coast of Hermosillo indicate that those two important pump irrigation districts are on the verge of irretrievable saline infiltration caused by over-pumping.[8] Once the principal aquifers are contaminated by

[7] For some analysis of such problems, see Sanderson, *Agrarian Populism and the Mexican State*; José Luis Jardines Moreno, "Los distritos de riego por bombeo del centro y norte de Sonora," *Recursos hidráulicos* 5:1 (1976), 8-25; Ángel Jiménez Villalobos, "Condiciones de las aguas subterráneas en el Distrito de Riego #51, Costa de Hermosillo, Sonora," *Ingeniería hidráulica en México* 19:3 (1965), 65-80.

[8] Based on interviews with SARH officials in the Dirección General de Distritos y Unidades de Riego, in Mexico City, Navojoa and Hermosillo, Sonora, and El Carrizo, Sinaloa, in August and November 1981 and February 1982. According to their estimates and unpublished documents of the min-

saltwater—whether from coastal intrusion or residual salts in the ground—they are lost forever to productive use. In that event, the desert may be expected to reclaim those rare but important oases now forced into bloom by overexploitation of the earth's underground water.

An increasingly important but relatively unnoticed challenge to wheat and other crop cultivation comes from agroindustry. Currently, one of the most difficult battles in the Northwest comes in the form of water use for agricultural versus industrial purposes. While the federal water law clearly specifies priorities—favoring agricultural over industrial use[9]—the concerted efforts of the federal government to create jobs in the countryside through incentives to agribusiness have required that businesses and farms compete for the same scarce water resources in irrigated areas. In the Yaqui, Mayo, Fuerte, and Guaymas areas in particular, water resource experts cite the difficulties embodied in the urbanization and industrialization of agricultural areas. In support industries, such as paper carton and packing, water use directly competes with agricultural uses in areas not governed by the federal irrigation system. If this is the "national water resource problem of the 1980s" in Sonora,[10] it clearly has direct impact on the flexibility of the wheat production and processing industries now.

The implication of these water resource problems—which deserve a separate, baseline study that still does not exist—is that the wheat production system in Mexico cannot expand in a way that will satisfy the increasing demand for basic foodstuffs. If in the best years (as was the case in 1981-1982)

---

istry, Guaymas appears to be in the worst shape, and some argue that its southern half may be lost to agricultural production in this decade.

[9] Mexico, SARH, *Ley federal de aguas*, Article 27.

[10] As cited by SARH officials in the Mayo River Valley Irrigation District Headquarters in the city of Navojoa, Sonora, during interviews and field discussions in November 1981. Their impression of the severity of the problem was reinforced in interviews with private sector leaders and farmers in the area at the same time.

the Mexican agricultural system can enjoy relative food self-sufficiency with generous rainfall and unheard-of subsidies, it is nonetheless true that the government of wheat production still lies with Tlaloc and not the carrying capacity of federal irrigation systems.[11]

The Mexican wheat production system is thus left with very few political options: it may nationalize productive resources under the control of the federal irrigation system in order to prorogue the influence of alternative crops on the deterioration of wheat production; it may open new rain-fed districts to wheat cultivation; or it may continue to plan for purchases on the international wheat market. As we shall see in the course of this and the succeeding chapter, the Mexican government should probably combine a strategy incorporating all three of these principles in a certain mix.

One of the most unambiguous arguments for such land use planning in the federal irrigation districts emanated from the official price incentives programs of the Sistema Alimentario Mexicano itself. In Sinaloa and Sonora, two important areas producing basic foods for granaries and other crops for export, economic stimuli in basic grains resulted in greater acreage being planted in wheat, corn, and rice, generally at the expense of oleaginous crops and winter vegetables, depending on the region. USDA information, combined with anecdotal evidence from interviews and informal estimates of the CAADES, indicates that in 1981-1982 Mexican agriculturalists in the federal irrigation districts of the Northwest shifted significantly away from export crops toward rice especially, and toward corn and beans as second-cycle crops. Wheat production was projected to increase in Sonora and Sinaloa by 35,000 hectares to yield an estimated 50,000 tons of wheat alone.[12]

Obviously, a concerted national policy to favor basic grains over other crops in the irrigation districts would demand bet-

[11] Tlaloc was the Aztec god of rain.

[12] USDA, "Mexico: Annual Feed and Grain Report," Foreign Agricultural Service Report MX-1028 (American Embassy in Mexico, June 9, 1981).

ter information about farmer decision making than is currently available, but at a minimum the 1981-1982 experience suggests that the Mexican irrigation district farmer is responsive in some degree to policy incentives and amenable to changes in production on a year-to-year basis. Of course, the presumption behind such a strategy—which will be treated in more detail in Chapter 5—is that the productive structure of the irrigation districts actually leaves some significant amount of land open for conversion to basic foodstuff cultivation. If the amount of agricultural land devoted to other, less strategic crops is insignificant or tied up in fixed capital investment through perennial crops, the argument for federal intervention is moot.

In fact, the irrigation districts have shifted away from basic foodstuff cultivation in such a way as to leave open the prospect of reorienting their production in more positive directions, according to the declared interests of the government and Mexican society. As was outlined in Chapter 1, wheat cultivation has maintained relatively steady levels throughout the 1960s and 1970s, in spite of the tendency in federal irrigation districts to reduce the proportion of total cultivation dedicated to foodgrains. Such a deterioration in relative position is due to the overwhelming increases in other crops grown on newly irrigated lands and in second-cycle cultivation. As Table 1.6 showed, the federal irrigation districts in the 1970s devoted less of their area to basic foods than to other, more remunerative crops with little importance to the "basic foodbasket" of the average Mexican consumer. Particularly important in their increases during the 1970s were winter vegetables, cattle fodder and forage crops, feedgrains for poultry and hogs, and some agricultural commodities for processing (i.e., strawberries, peas, oleaginous crops).

STATE INTERVENTION IN WHEAT PRODUCTION

Throughout the postwar years, wheat has been one of the most heavily state-influenced crops in the Mexican agricultural economy. Obviously, the national state influences wheat

199

production through the irrigation infrastructure and the subsidization of water resource users' fees in the federal irrigation districts.[13] Additionally, however, the Mexican state has a long history of price, credit, input, and insurance interventions in wheat production, all of which are important to our consideration of the future of wheat cultivation in Mexico. Although the bulk of our analysis in this regard will come in Chapter 5, it is necessary to sketch the nature of state intervention here in order to frame the context of wheat production at the farm level.

As other studies have shown,[14] the Mexican state has governed wheat prices and markets in some fashion since 1938, through the CONASUPO (Compañía Nacional de Subsistencias Populares) and its predecessors CEIMSA (Compañía Exportadora e Importadora de México, S.A.) and the original Comité Regulador del Mercado de Subsistencias (Subsistence Goods Market Regulatory Committee). As Chapter 5 will show, the logic of that public intervention in agriculture has shifted over the years, as befits the transformation of Mexican agriculture itself. General lines of pricing policy do suggest themselves, however. First, it must be said that the price policy of the Mexican state has concentrated on two contradictory goals: basic food price controls as a nonwage benefit for the industrial working class, on the one hand, and the subsidization of agricultural prices as a producer incentive, on the

[13] Miguel Wionczek, "La aportación de la política hidráulica entre 1925 y 1970 a la actual crisis agrícola mexicana," *Comercio exterior* 37:4 (April 1982), 394-409; interviews with officials in the SARH, Office of Legal Affairs, Dirección General de Distritos y Unidades de Riego, August 1981.

[14] Some interesting sources on the origins of Mexican state price intervention include the important study by Barkin and Esteva; Gustavo Esteva, "La experiencia de la intervención estatal reguladora en la comercialización agropecuaria de 1970 a 1978," in Ursula Oswald, ed., *Mercado y dependencia* (Mexico: Editorial Nueva Imagen, 1979), 207-246; Merilee Serrill Grindle, *Bureaucrats, Politicians and Peasants in Mexico: A Case Study in Public Policy* (Berkeley and Los Angeles: University of California Press, 1977); Kenneth Shwedel, "Los precios agrícolas: una perspectiva histórica" (Mexico, November 1982, manuscript); and chapters in Yates and CDIA.

other. As Barkin and Esteva have pointed out, that contradictory tendency has encouraged the moderation of profits in wheat cultivation (as well as other basic goods) and a structural shift away from basic product cultivation to more remunerative products.

The state response to such a destructive dynamic (from the viewpoint of cheap food policy and grain self-sufficiency) has tended to involve *more* state intervention to correct the disequilibria that have ensued.[15] Such state intervention has included ensuring that consumer prices do not accelerate too quickly, that producer prices remain profitable, and that the import-export trade be the source of equilibrium in basic grains. Under a model of expanding agricultural resources, modest population growth, a labor-absorptive industrialization drive, and moderate levels of external reliance, such a set of economic circuits might prove a viable strategy to combine agricultural modernization with relative food self-sufficiency. Unfortunately, as we know, the Mexican economy exhibits none of those necessary traits for the success of such a model.

As the cheap production of wage goods became increasingly important to industrializing Mexico, the producer aspect of agricultural price intervention became secondary.[16] During the heyday of import substitution industrialization the Mexican economy transferred capital away from the agricultural sector to industry and commerce, and one of the principal mechanisms was negative terms of trade between agriculture and industry. This experience, of course, has not been unique in Mexico but has transpired in Brazil, Venezuela, and Argentina as well. In any event, the price system, governed to a great extent by the official floor price set by CONASUPO, transferred income and investment capital away from the very sector expected to produce cheap wage goods for the industrializing workforce. At the same time, other mechanisms (e.g., the banking system, input subsidies) transferred resources

[15] Barkin and Esteva, 4.
[16] Ibid., 9.

back into the agricultural sector from 1970 to 1981,[17] but not necessarily for the sake of basic foodstuff production.

In the beginning of heavy price intervention by the state, wheat producers of the Northwest benefited from large-scale purchases by CONASUPO at the official price dictated annually by that agency. Throughout the 1960s and 1970s the proportion of wheat production bought by CONASUPO increased, though the official price level did not improve in real terms. As the quote introducing this chapter might suggest, the enormous improvements in the techniques of wheat cultivation, the opening of vast new territories to wheat cultivation, and the large surpluses of wheat in the Mexican market caused CONASUPO to concentrate on the disposition of excess wheat rather than the guarantee of future wheat self-sufficiency through price incentives. The logic of wheat price intervention seemed to focus on enhancing short-term producer profits in the 1960s, while in maize and bean programs the focus was on maintaining adequate supplies of popular foodstuffs in the central markets of Mexico.[18]

In the 1970s the mission of CONASUPO changed, according to the new realities of Mexican agriculture. Now the Mexican state was unable to produce price incentives sufficient to maintain output in wheat and other basic products at levels commensurate with domestic demand. CONASUPO's role also shifted toward the exterior, as it came to control all foreign purchases of basic grains. But the price mechanism originally designed to enhance the production of basic goods and to protect the position of northwestern wheat farmers did not respond in a consistent fashion. As Shwedel's recent study of real price behavior in Mexican agriculture shows, the price index for basic commodities (maize, wheat, rice, and beans) exceeded 1960 levels in only seven of the past twenty-one years.[19] In fact, as the price data show convincingly, the 1960s

[17] Kenneth Shwedel, "El sector agropecuario mexicano versus el resto de la economía: un análisis de transferencias" (Mexico, 1982 manuscript).

[18] Barkin and Esteva, 11.

[19] Shwedel, "Los precios agrícolas," Graph 2.

were an anomalous period of high agricultural price supports, not repeated even under the high price subventions of the Sistema Alimentario Mexicano (see Table 4.5).

But, if price incentives in basic foodstuffs were not the source of producer subsidies as commonly supposed, other social capital investment, input subsidies, and credit facilities

TABLE 4.5
Guaranteed Agricultural Prices in Constant 1970 Pesos, 1960-1982

	Wheat	Beans	Maize
1960	1290	2119	1130
1961	1247	2391	1093
1962	1211	2321	1061
1963	1173	2249	1208
1964	1111	2129	1144
1965	951	2081	1118
1966	915	2002	1076
1967	890	1947	1046
1968	869	1900	1021
1969	836	1829	982
1970	800	1750	940
1971	755	1652	888
1972	711	1556	836
1973	686	1694	946
1974	834	3851	963
1975	971	2634	1054
1976	812	2319	1085
1977	729	1778	1031
1978	792	1904	884
1979	760	1964	882
1980	699	2362	876
1981	704	2447	1002
1982	552	1581	706

NOTE: Deflated using implicit GNP deflator; base 1970.
SOURCE: Mexico, SARH, *Determinación de los precios de garantía para los productos del campo*, 1984.

provided analogous benefits to the large-scale farmer. We have already mentioned the role of the federal irrigation infrastructure in the development of wheat cultivation. Other important infrastructure developments, including rural roads, the national crop warehousing agency (Almacenes Nacionales de Depósito, S.A., or ANDSA), agricultural extension and research centers, and the growing rural school system, all served to provide important supports to the wheat production system. Direct input subsidies also encouraged agricultural production in the federal irrigation system as well as the important rain-fed areas of Mexico. In the irrigation districts an important subsidy has come in the form of low users' fees, which fall well below the mandate of the federal water law to recover the cost of maintenance and conservation from each district's water users. Estimates have concluded that as little as 40 percent of irrigation district costs are recovered through users' fees.[20] Energy subsidies have also provided important agricultural incentives, which have naturally gone to those farmers employing farm machinery, fertilizer, and irrigation pumps and apparatus, all of which conform to the well-known diversion of resources to the benefit of large-scale irrigated farming in the Mexican North.

Input subsidies are difficult to calculate, especially prior to the oil boom, when Mexico was not self-sufficient in fertilizer production and was unable to provide limitless petroleum products to the farms without recourse to large-scale imports. But, in the late 1970s, Shwedel estimates that input subsidies skyrocketed over the López Portillo years, from 1.6 billion pesos in 1977 to an amazing 65 billion pesos in 1982.[21] The difficulty with direct input subsidies has been that they have not been crop specific. That is, for example, the water users' subsidy cannot be targeted only to producers of basic grains or pulses and, therefore, is less viable as a subsidy for certain kinds of production than as a general impulse to agricultural

[20] Wionczek, 403.
[21] Shwedel, "El sector agropecuario."

activity. Likewise, energy and fertilizer subsidies have not been very sensitive policy tools for guiding the priorities of production in the farms to which they are commended.

Banking and crop insurance incentives have been more successful as programs targeted to certain crops, though the logic of that targeting policy has certainly shifted in cumbersome and inefficient fashion. In the credit system, the Mexican state has offered three basic incentives applicable to wheat production: preferential credit rates through the FIRA, state-managed agricultural credit facilities not generated by the private banking system, and gross transfers of capital to agriculture through the banking system itself.

On the first point, in recent years the official agricultural banking system has provided credit for certain crops at preferential rates. The FIRA operates on a sliding scale of credit rates according to farm size and capital available to the agriculturalist. It also provides guarantees and discounts to require banks to offer scarce long-term credits, whereas the banking system without such incentives normally emphasizes short-term credit to be liquidated during a single crop season.[22] Likewise, the official rural credit bank (BANRURAL) offers credit to *ejidatarios* and smallholders who would normally not be considered good subjects for agricultural credit. While the official credit system governed by BANRURAL has in no sense penetrated the vast bulk of smallholders and *ejidatarios* in Mexico, the Northwest—especially peasants and *minifundistas* engaged in irrigation district production—has received a disproportionate amount of credit. In fact, in 1977 irrigated wheat cultivation was second only to safflower (its chief competitor) in the proportion of crop area served by

[22] Information about FIRA comes from an official SPP seminar on the function of FIRA conducted in Hermosillo, Sonora, November 1981. For more general analysis, see Louis W. Goodman and Steven E. Sanderson, *Agricultural Policy Making in Mexico*, Monograph prepared as a part of a Joint Agreement between the Economic Research Service, USDA, and the Latin American Program of the Woodrow Wilson International Center for Scholars, Washington, D.C., 1985.

agricultural credit. Half of irrigated wheat acreage and 54 percent of rain-fed wheat area received agricultural credit, the latter statistic reflecting the small number of rain-fed wheat farmers and their relative prosperity in rain-fed districts.[23]

Finally, the banking system in general has tended, in recent years, to provide more credit facilities to agriculture. The common assertion in the 1970s was that the agricultural sector in Mexico suffered a gross decapitalization in the 1950s and 1960s, partly as a product of banking system transfers of capital to more lucrative sectors of industry and commerce.[24] Such phenomena are not uncommon, of course, in import substitution experiences. Since 1970, however, Shwedel has shown that the agricultural sector has actually benefited from a transfer of capital from other sectors, reversing the trend of the 1950s and 1960s. In the decade 1971 to 1981 the agricultural sector received net transfers of capital from the economy at large through the banking system, with the exception of 1975, 1976, and 1981.[25] If the breakdown of credit distribution is consistent over that period—an assumption that must be qualified to some extent in view of the great bean crisis of 1973-1974 and other episodes of credit transfer—the bulk of agricultural credit will find its way to the irrigation districts, and specifically to the cultivation of wheat, safflower, soya, and sorghum. In the rain-fed districts, wheat, rice, and sorghum have historically been the most important crops accorded official credit.

As we shall see in Chapter 5, the advent of the Sistema Alimentario Mexicano in 1980 changed the character of production subsidies for at least two years, though the future of subsidy programs is currently threatened by the general fiscal

---

[23] Mexico, SPP, *Manual de estadísticas básicas: sector agropecuario y forestal* (Mexico: SPP, 1979), and Mexico, SARH, *Anuario estadístico: año agrícola 1977-1978.*

[24] CDIA, 181. The baseline study cited by both the CDIA study and Shwedel is Leopoldo Solís, "Hacia un análisis general a largo plazo del desarrollo económico de México," *Demografía y economía* 1:1 (1967).

[25] Shwedel, "El sector agropecuario," 5.

crisis. For now, it is important to note that most incentives have not been directed specifically to the benefit of certain basic crops over others, except to the extent that a producer might favor planting a crop guaranteed under federal crop insurance programs over an uninsured crop. The result of general state intervention in wheat cultivation has been to encourage overall agricultural production in the irrigation districts but not necessarily to target wheat cultivation over other commodities. In fact, if we focus for the moment on the Coast of Hermosillo, we find that in an area of great policy concern producers have resisted state incentives for wheat and have gradually reduced wheat cultivation in favor of grapes. In the period from 1970 to 1977, wheat cultivation declined by over 37,000 hectares. Only grape production increased consistently over the same period, from 631 to 4,800 hectares.[26]

CHALLENGES TO WHEAT PRODUCTION IN MEXICO

If it is difficult to assume that new acreage will be opened to wheat cultivation in Mexico, then the problem becomes one of arresting the decline in wheat production as a proportion of total crop cultivation in the federal irrigation districts and the important rain-fed areas of the country. Recent trends in agricultural production in the irrigated districts show an increasing challenge from several directions: winter vegetables and fruits, safflower, barley and garbanzo, and forage crops for animals. While other oleaginous crops (principally soya) have also made much headway in the federal irrigation districts, they are neither winter-cycle crops competing directly with wheat nor perennial crops monopolizing the land year-round.

In irrigation districts, winter vegetables directly challenge winter wheat for a place in the crop profile of the most pro-

[26] Mexico, Secretaría de Agricultura y Recursos Hidráulicos (SRH), Dirección General de Distritos de Riego, *Estadística agrícola*, various years. Title varies slightly by year.

ductive lands in Mexico. As we saw in Chapter 2, winter vegetables have established themselves as the second most important Mexican agricultural export group, after coffee. Their cultivation in the federal irrigation districts displaces land potentially useful for basic grain production, especially for rice and wheat. The official position of the Mexican government has been to ignore the areas devoted to export winter vegetables as potential grain producers, both because of their importance as foreign exchange earners and their substantial political power. Likewise, government officials contend that the acreage devoted to winter vegetables is relatively insignificant for possible wheat and rice cultivation. Such an assertion, of course, merits examination.

In 1980, over 137,000 hectares were devoted to eggplant, onion, cucumber, squash, and tomato cultivation, with nearly 76,000 dedicated to tomato production alone.[27] Of the total area given to tomato production, typically over 80 percent is under some form of irrigation and over half within federal irrigation districts. Cucumber production is virtually all irrigated and, in 1977, 82 percent of onion acreage fell under irrigation.[28] Of that total winter vegetable production, an increasing proportion has been exported in recent years: 45 percent of tomatoes, 80 percent of cucumbers, and 13 percent of onions.

Accepting a few basic assumptions based on past experience, we can calculate a rough dividend that would accrue *hypothetically* from substituting wheat for winter vegetable production. Estimating irrigated production of tomatoes to be 66,800 hectares (based on 88 percent of the 1980 national acreage) and total irrigated yield to be 1.1 million tons (based on historical yields of irrigated tomato fields), replacing export production with wheat fields would yield a dividend of 38,822

[27] Mexico, SARH, "Valorización."

[28] Mexico, SARH, *Econotecnia agrícola: panorama sobre el comportamiento del sector agropecuario nacional, 1977-1979, y algunas consideraciones sobre el mercado internacional* (Mexico: SARH, 1980), 17; Mexico, SPP, *El sector alimentario en México*, 96.

hectares.[29] While it is recognized that yearly movements in tomato cultivation make this figure slightly suspect, it is not out of line with recent export tomato acreage, as shown in Chapter 2.

If, for the sake of argument, we then calculate the wheat production potential of this prime land, using the national average yield of 3.77 tons per hectare in 1980,[30] we can realize—in the abstract at least—an increase in wheat production totaling 146,359 tons per year, without affecting the other winter vegetable figures at all. Such an increase in production would amount to over 10 percent of total imports in the worst year of external agricultural dependence.

Obviously, such a calculation is not an entirely realistic one, given the minimal probabilities of cutting off export tomato production in one fell swoop and the foreign exchange costs involved, as well as the comparative advantage in question. The point of this simple exercise is not to recommend the abandonment of tomato exports (at least for the moment) but simply to call into question the simplistic argument that the potential dividends available from alternative cropping would be insignificant.

If we abandon, for the moment, the idea of shifting winter vegetable production to wheat cultivation because of the importance of such production for foreign exchange or the comparative advantage of trading tomatoes for wheat, that argument certainly does not extend to the challenge posed by new grape and citrus cultivation in the irrigation districts. In the 1977 crop year, Sonora was the only state with greater than 50,000 tons of grape production. Ninety-seven percent of total national grape acreage fell in irrigation areas,[31] and, as already mentioned, largely at the expense of wheat pro-

[29] Assumptions are based on data from the latest crop analysis of the SARH published for the crop year 1977 and on estimates of the SARH regarding the proportion of total vegetable production dedicated to exports.

[30] Mexico, SARH, "Valorización."

[31] Mexico, SARH, *Anuario estadístico de la producción agrícola de los Estados Unidos Mexicanos, 1977* (Mexico: SARH, 1979).

duction in the Coast of Hermosillo irrigation district and the surrounding *unidades de riego*. By the 1980 crop year, total national acreage had increased from 20,000 hectares in 1970[32] to 37,290 hectares.[33] Grapes play little part in the generation of foreign exchange in the Mexican economy, however. Nor do they enjoy the year-to-year crop flexibility of winter vegetables and other export crops. Other crops challenging wheat production further raise questions as to the validity of market incentives for growth in the federal irrigation system, particularly under the state-supervised and funded model which has made high-technology agriculture a reality in modern Mexico. In addition to grapes, two others stand out, for different reasons.

The first crop challenging wheat production is garbanzo, one of the most traditional export crops in the Mexican North, still dominated by the commercial agents of the major entrepôts of Sonora and Sinaloa, and linked to worldwide trade through Spanish brokers (Table 4.6). While garbanzo has been an important export crop since the Porfiriato, it has never been a major consumer crop in Mexico, and per capita consumption has declined in recent years.[34] In addition to its export orientation, fully two-thirds of the 1980 crop included garbanzo for animal consumption.[35] When production for animals is added to export tonnage, garbanzo appears both as a major challenger to a basic foodstuff and a marginal provider of protein to the Mexican population. As the increase in wheat output during the 1970s shows, garbanzo does not displace wheat output directly. Nevertheless, in an era of limited water and land resources, with a growing need for new sources of rural employment and a burgeoning demand for basic foodstuffs displaced by export enclave crops, the social benefit of growing garbanzo must be questioned. Given the slowing expansion of the agricultural frontier, the same-sea-

[32] Mexico, NAFINSA, 115.
[33] Mexico, SARH, "Valorización."
[34] Mexico, SPP, *El sector alimentario en México*, 605-607.
[35] Mexico, SARH, "Valorización."

son cultivation of garbanzo in the prime wheat lands of the country issues as direct a challenge to food production as sorghum poses for maize.

The second, and most important, challenger to wheat is *carthamus* (safflower), or bastard saffron. Safflower is another of the boom crops of the 1970s, emerging for the first time in official agricultural statistics alongside soya, in 1960, and rising to a peak in the late 1970s (Table 4.6). Over 90 percent of the 1980 crop came from Sinaloa, Sonora, and Tamaulipas, produced in overwhelming proportion in federal irrigation districts.[36] In the main federal irrigation districts of those three key states, safflower directly competes with wheat acreage in the winter crop cycle. In addition, safflower oil carries a much higher price than soya oil in the Mexican market and sustains mainly the middle- and upper-income strata of the consuming population, who favor it over soya and other vegetable oils.[37]

Safflower is a crop that shows the double marginalization of the rural producer. We have already mentioned that the producer is marginalized once by the cultivation of crops (mainly wheat) remote from the farmer's basic foodbasket. And safflower shows that he can be further marginalized by the stratification of wage good production for the urban market. If the first step in the urbanization of cropping patterns in Mexico was the emphasis put on wheat, the second step must be the income stratification of the crops produced. Wheat does not play the same social role as maize, the traditional staple of the peasantry; safflower plays little social role at all for the bulk of its relatively well-to-do Mexican consumers. In this light, the logic of agricultural production in the Mexican food system shifts from one emphasizing basic foodstuff production to one deemphasizing the social responsibility of agriculture in favor of market incentives and profitability.

Barley presents a third challenge to wheat, different in its

[36] Mexico, SPP, *Estadística económica y social por entidad federativa*. Typically, about 75 percent of safflower production comes from federal irrigation districts. Mexico, SPP, *El sector alimentario en México*, 96.

[37] Mexico, SARH, *Econotecnia agrícola: panorama*, 32.

211

TABLE 4.6
Challengers to Wheat Production in Mexico, 1960-1980

| | Safflower | | Garbanzos | |
	(1,000 ha.)	(1,000 tons)	(1,000 ha.)	(1,000 tons)
1960	26	32	147	115
1961	33	41	156	135
1962	37	47	146	129
1963	36	47	105	97
1964	36	47	137	124
1965	59	80	155	135
1966	165	236	163	152
1967	100	149	193	165
1968	86	102	202	179
1969	145	209	206	183
1970	175	288	208	186
1971	265	410	215	167
1972	199	271	247	228
1973	198	298	216	226
1974	192	272	248	249
1975	363	532	191	195
1976	185	240	106	73
1977	404	518	252	272
1978	429	616	198	215
1979	488	588	297	340
1980*	392	445	237	255

SOURCE: Mexico, NAFINSA, *La economía mexicana en cifras*, 1981.
* Figures for 1980 are from Mexico, SARH, "Valorización de la producción agrícola," 1980.

purpose and more limited in geographic scope. It is estimated that 80 percent of the national barley crop goes to the beer industry annually.[38] As a crop it is geographically very concentrated, with three states (Hidalgo, Puebla, and Tlaxcala) providing more than half the national crop in 1980, and five states (add Baja California and Zacatecas) accounting for

[38] Ibid., 37.

three-fourths of national production.[39] The crop is divided in purpose and in season, according to its productive ecology, that is, whether it is rain-fed or irrigated. Irrigated barley relates in a very specific way to agroindustry, through the powerful oligopsony Impulsora Agrícola, S.A. Created as an agroindustry combine for the beer industry, Impulsora Agrícola dominates the irrigated production of barley in the Bajío and in Hidalgo and Puebla, as well as newer areas of cultivation in Baja California. In field interviews with seed merchants and farmers in the Bajío, barley was revealed to be a crop cultivated according to contract with Impulsora Agrícola. Local seed merchants did not even handle barley seed for the most part, because of the limited market, which was, in turn, determined by Impulsora's disdain for market purchases of its crucial input. Only the largest and best-connected farmers in the Valle de Santiago, Guanajuato, for example, maintained production contracts with Impulsora, and others chose not to cultivate the lucrative crop, for want of a consumer.[40]

In these areas, because of its irrigated cultivation and because it is grown in the winter season, barley competes with wheat production.[41] It has been particularly successful in that competition in Río Colorado, Baja California, and Guanajuato, though the oligopsony Impulsora in effect sets certain limits on barley production according to the beer market in Mexico. Barley as an unrestricted challenger to wheat production, therefore, is limited by the very agribusiness that gives it life. Needless to say, the displacement of a food crop such as wheat by an input for the beer industry violates the essential logic of a food system searching for greater basic crop production. As we shall see shortly, the rain-fed production of

[39] Mexico, SPP, *México: estadística económica y social por entidad federativa*, 61.

[40] Field interviews conducted with David Barkin in the Valle de Santiago, November 1981.

[41] Barkin and Suárez, *El fin de autosuficiencia*, 72.

barley also changes the face of other basic foodstuff production in the peasant economy.

Another challenger to irrigated wheat production is cultivated cattle feed, mainly in the form of forage. As Chapter 3 indicated, many cattlemen have become able to irrigate their lands made exempt from land reform limits under the government's certificates of cattle immunity. In addition, droughts and insufficient natural pasturage have increasingly forced the northern herds onto cultivated pasturage. Sorghum makes occasional inroads into the winter-season crops, though it is principally a challenger to spring and summer second crops, such as maize and soya. Oats, alfalfa, winter rye, and forage barley all compete with wheat throughout the North, as the amount of irrigated land devoted to their cultivation increases at the expense of food crops.

As we shall see in Chapter 5, the national importance of wheat and other basic foodstuff cultivation in the federal irrigation districts depends on the political and economic definitions of the role of the agricultural sector in the Mexican national economy. If, in fact, the Mexican state seriously intends to cultivate basic foodstuffs as a "public good" or "collective good" in the 1980s, it must attend to the productive mechanisms which have challenged wheat as a basic commodity in the Mexican agricultural landscape. The implications of such political attention are severe and complex.

MAIZE AND BEANS

If wheat is the miracle foodstuff of the post–World War II industrialization drive, maize and beans are the traditional, basic foods cultivated for a rural society. Though they hold very different positions in the panorama of basic crops in Mexico, maize and beans exemplify the transformation of traditional cropping through state intervention and agricultural modernization. In contrast to wheat, which came with the first irrigation districts, maize and beans have been sustained by rain-fed agriculture in the heartland of the peasant economy. Cultivated in Mexico since pre-Columbian times, they are truly native crops.

We have already suggested that maize and wheat feed different populations, though both crops satisfy basic food consumption needs. At the level of production maize is, in a profound sense, the polar opposite of wheat. Maize is grown throughout Mexico, a crop spanning the full range of Mexican productive ecologies, from the highlands of Tlaxcala and Puebla to the irrigation districts of Sonora, Aguascalientes, Jalisco, and Michoacán, to the tropical extremes of the Yucatán Peninsula. Among basic crops, the land devoted to maize constituted 59 percent of the total area cultivated in Mexico in 1978, a figure which has undoubtedly increased in the years of the SAM.[42] Maize, more than any other crop in Mexico, pervades the entire countryside and dominates the landed resources of the country, with, unfortunately, less than adequate results. Maize cultivation consumes over 90 percent of the agricultural area of the state of Mexico and over 85 percent of all land cultivated in Chiapas, Oaxaca, Quintana Roo, and Yucatán.[43] As testimony to the broad geographical base of maize production, when considered state by state, only Jalisco, with over 70 percent of its rich, rain-fed areas devoted to maize, produces more than 10 percent of the national crop.[44]

Maize is a crop of the poor. Although nearly 40 percent of all agricultural units in Mexico cultivate it, the importance of the crop declines as the size of the unit of production increases.[45] Among peasant cultivators, 85 percent grow maize, which is reflected in the high proportion of maize cultivation in the poorest Mexican states: Oaxaca, Quintana Roo, and

[42] Mexico, SPP, *México: estadística económica y social por entidad federativa*, 65.

[43] Ibid.

[44] Ibid., 66.

[45] Alejandro Schejtman, "Economía campesina y agricultura empresarial: tipología de productores del agro mexicano" (Mexico, U.N. CEPAL, 1981 limited circulation manuscript), 151.

Chiapas.[46] Nearly half the national maize area is cultivated by below-subsistence or subsistence peasants, who farm an average of less than three hectares each.[47]

This distribution of maize cultivation is in inverse relation to the availability of improved corn seed: the small peasant, who seeds half Mexico's land devoted to maize, rarely has access to improved seed, whereas the agricultural entrepreneur on a larger scale benefits disproportionately. Maize is a crop of the poor in another sense: its consumption has a low income elasticity relative to other foods considered in this study. Projections for maize demand in Mexico include the assumption that, while underconsumption is the norm in the countryside, the rapidly urbanizing Mexican economy has tended to isolate the use of maize by class. Income elasticities in the Mexican population are much higher for foods such as vegetable oil, chicken, and beef.[48] Maize is likely to continue to be a crop produced by the poor for the poor.

Maize cultivation has not expanded greatly in area or productivity since the 1950s. In the mid-1950s the Mexican maize system regularly harvested over 5 million hectares of crop land, not much less than the U.S. government's estimate of land devoted to the 1982 harvest. By 1958, the acreage devoted to maize had exceeded 6 million hectares, and by 1965 it had reached the acreage typical of the mid-1970s (Table 4.7). Although maize yields did improve over the entire postwar period—climbing from an average of 0.7 tons per hectare in 1950 to 1.78 tons in 1980[49]—the improvements came mainly in the federal irrigation districts and on large-scale farms that had access to improved seed, fertilizer, and credit.

Peasant farmers on small plots and *ejidatarios* generally did not improve their yields, and the aggregate output of the maize

[46] Ibid.

[47] Data based on 1970 *Censo agrícola y ejidal*, elaborated in ibid., 154.

[48] See USDA, *Country Market Profile: Mexico* (Washington, D.C.: ERS, 1982).

[49] NAFINSA, 134-135; 1980 data are from Mexico, SARH, "Valorización."

216

Maize Supply, Distribution, and Imports for Mexico, 1960-1983

	Area (1,000 ha)	Production	Total Imports	Total Exports	Domestic for Feed	Consumption Total	Imports from U.S.
1960	5,415	5,386	61	53	18	5,399	—
1961	6,391	5,561	20	3	19	5,497	52
1962	6,400	5,450	450	—	19	5,700	42
1963	6,700	6,690	117	66	20	6,000	227
1964	7,200	7,500	20	1,170	22	6,500	249
1965	7,500	8,000	14	1,105	24	7,010	29
1966	7,500	8,200	15	1,055	25	7,410	12
1967	7,500	8,000	25	921	26	7,520	11
1968	7,600	8,500	18	938	26	7,810	24
1969	7,250	6,500	780	61	25	7,300	15
1970	4,000	8,900	139	293	60	8,300	374
1971	8,000	9,100	37	469	325	9,092	165
1972	7,500	8,100	1,300	96	500	9,254	15
1973	7,900	9,000	1,200	—	450	9,800	433
1974	7,700	7,700	2,279	—	479	9,980	1,462
1975	7,900	9,300	1,450	4	410	10,570	1,426
1976	7,870	9,600	1,500	40	500	10,980	1,043
1977	7,920	9,700	1,690	—	500	11,300	869
1978	8,000	10,200	630	—	300	11,400	1,658
1979	7,600	9,200	3,870	—	1,000	12,700	1,306
1980	8,100	10,000	4,000	—	1,600	12,800	2,756
1981	8,150	12,500	553	—	1,000	13,500	553
1982	6,000	7,000	4,300	—	1,800	12,300	4,300
1983	6,500	9,500	3,500	—	500	12,200	3,500

SOURCE: USDA, *Foreign Agriculture Circular*, "Reference Tables on Wheat, Corn, and Total Coarse Grains Supply-Distribution for Individual Countries," Foreign Agricultural Service, through 1980. Figures for 1981-1983 are from U.S. Embassy in Mexico, *Annual Feed and Grain Report*, various issues.

system did not progress as a result. As the 1970 census pointed out, the peasant cultivation of maize yielded fully 100 kilograms per hectare less than the national average. That difference—actually understating the disparity in yields between the poorest peasant areas in Guanajuato or Querétaro versus the federal irrigation districts of Jalisco or Michoacán—became significant in the 1970s as policy makers recognized finally that the poorest peasant region of Mexico (formalized as the *región fundamental de economía campesina*) accounted for one-fourth of Mexican maize cultivation and 22 percent of production.[50] These peasant cultivators also comprised over 70 percent of the nation's *minifundistas* (cultivators of less than 5 hectares).[51]

Bean production has followed the path of maize to a great extent. Although dry bean cultivation in Mexico has never commanded the territories assigned to maize, beans—along with maize and chiles, are a staple of traditional Mexican diets throughout the country. Bean cultivation has followed maize at least partly because the traditional ecology of these basic staples has involved planting beans and maize in alternating rows in the same field. Beans have been one of the most ignored crops in the Mexican agricultural system, however, for a number of reasons—not the least of which is their rural constituency as a consumer item and the marginalization of their producers.

As Table 4.8 shows, bean cultivation in Mexico has stagnated for the past twenty years, even more profoundly than maize. Productivity has not improved appreciably over the past fifteen years; the land area devoted to beans has not increased even in years of tremendous price leaps, as in 1973-1974. And the low aggregate output has necessitated large volumes of imports from the United States. Nevertheless, beans still occupy an important place in Mexican production,

[50] Guadalupe Sánchez Burgos, *La región fundamental de economía campesina en México* (Mexico: Editorial Nueva Imagen, 1980), 59-60.

[51] Mexico, SIC, *V Censo agrícola, ganadero, y ejidal*, 1970, cited in ibid., 66-67.

TABLE 4.8
Bean Cultivation in Mexico, 1960-1983

	Area (1,000 ha)	Production (1,000 tons)	Yield (kg/ha)	Per Capita Production (kg)
1960	1,326	528	398	14.83
1961	1,617	723	447	19.64
1962	1,674	656	392	17.21
1963	1,711	677	396	17.22
1964	2,091	892	426	21.92
1965	2,117	860	406	20.42
1966	2,240	1,013	452	23.29
1967	1,930	980	508	21.78
1968	1,791	857	479	18.39
1969	1,656	835	504	17.32
1970	1,747	925	530	18.57
1971	1,965	954	485	18.56
1972	1,682	870	515	16.38
1973	1,870	1,009	540	18.41
1974	1,552	972	626	17.17
1975	1,753	1,027	586	17.56
1976	1,316	740	562	12.25
1977	1,631	770	472	12.34
1978	1,580	949	600	14.74
1979	1,054	601	570	9.04
1980*	1,763	971	551	14.15
1981†	2,000	1,300	650	18.26
1982	1,600	817	510	11.20
1983	1,900	1,100	580	n/a

* Data for 1960-1979 from Mexico, NAFINSA; 1980, Mexico, SARH, "Valorización de la producción agrícola."

† Data for 1981-1983 are drawn from U.S. Embassy in Mexico, "Grain and Feed Data Update," December 16, 1983.

taking up roughly 10 percent of the national agricultural acreage and constituting 4 percent of the national value of production, even before the inauguration of the SAM.[52] Like maize, beans have been cultivated overwhelmingly on rain-fed lands in the peasant economy. Nearly 90 percent of bean acreage is classified as rain-fed (much of which is, in fact, scarcely fed). Such lands yield nearly three-fourths of the national bean crop yearly.[53]

MAIZE, BEANS, AND THE MEXICAN POPULATION

The two rural staples, maize and beans, maintain a different relationship with the national population than does wheat. While wheat has been characterized as a crop of modern Mexico—in the sense of both modern consumer staple properly processed and an agricultural commodity enhanced by the Green Revolution—maize and beans, as traditional crops, are not market sensitive in the same fashion. Clearly, in the case of beans as well as maize, national production has not kept up with population growth, resulting in stagnation in output per capita. In maize production, even with improved seeds and fertilizers going to the wealthier producers of the crop, per capita production has not improved markedly over the past two decades, and has shown a serious decline in most years after 1965. In bean production, output has stagnated over that same post-1965 period, and per capita production has not improved at all over the past twenty years (see Tables 4.7 and 4.8).

The implications of this per capita stagnation are more complex than in the case of wheat, however. It has been argued that maize and bean demand is less likely to rise sharply over the 1980s, because the Mexican population is shifting away from subsistence consumption of these basic staples as the urban population grows and its tastes change. According to

[52] Mexico, SARH, *Econotecnia agrícola: panorama*, 26.
[53] Ibid.

the Mexican household expenditure surveys of 1968 and 1975, bean consumption as a proportion of total food consumption tailed off sharply at very modest levels of family income. Beans are clearly most important to those at the lowest levels of income and protein consumption. Maize as a contributor to dietary protein drops at even more modest levels of income than beans.[54] While 84 percent of dietary protein comes from maize and beans for those at the lowest levels of income, that proportion drops to 70 percent even at income levels above 300 pesos per month. The top income category consumes less than 13 percent of its protein in the form of maize, beans, and their products.[55] In the countryside, a typical rural resident will consume three-fourths of his daily calories and 80 percent of his protein in the form of tortillas and beans, demonstrating the overwhelming importance of these crops among the poor of Mexico. In stark contrast, bread plays almost no role in the average rural diet,[56] both for its relative expense (over twice as expensive as tortillas) and for the irrelevance of wheat as a crop in subsistence economies.

The double-edged phenomenon of the leveling demand projected for maize and beans, combined with the absolutely essential role these crops play in the diet and productive structure of the Mexican peasantry, implies that the per capita stagnation of maize and bean production is, in fact, a form of the Mexican food crisis writ large. It is a crisis of production, in the sense that the producers of basic foodstuffs are being marginalized from the mainstream of crop production and its benefits as well as being threatened with extinction for lack of alternative crops and food sources for themselves and their families. The decline in maize and bean production in the 1970s was an aggregate reflection of the decline of the peasantry in Mexico, impelled by the changing role of agri-

[54] Mexico, SPP, *El sector alimentario en México*, 614.

[55] Ibid., 616. This information is based on the 1968 household expenditure survey.

[56] Schejtman, I-28.

culture in the Mexican economy, the standardization of dietary habits in urban Mexico, and the wholesale shift of inputs and labor to the production of goods irrelevant to the needs of the *campesino* economy.

STATE INTERVENTION IN MAIZE AND BEAN PRODUCTION

Maize and bean production have also experienced high levels of state intervention, in fashion similar to public sector activity in wheat, though with different results. Traditionally, as Table 4.5 shows, the Mexican government has supported the price of maize and beans at some level through CONASUPO price guarantees. But, as we have seen, maize and beans do not play the same critical role as wheat in the urban wage sector. Nor do the producers of maize and beans command the same level of personal attention from the state as the wealthy agribusiness interests of the wheat-producing Pacific Northwest. But the basic policy premises in maize and beans have been similar: the simultaneous attempt to stimulate production through price supports and to control grain prices as a subsidy to wage good consumption. In wheat production, the failure of price supports to keep up with rising costs of production and to reduce the attraction of more profitable crops was, to some degree, offset by other, nonprice incentives in inputs. Because of the structure of maize and bean production, however, the vast majority of cultivators have not benefited from similar stimuli through the credit and input system, except in the rather special circumstances of the first two years of the SAM.

The maize support program of CONASUPO has been considered, at least for the past decade, to be the backbone of the institution's commodity price support programs and "one of the principal bulwarks against the disappearance of the peasant economy."[57] The maize support program became

[57] Barkin and Esteva, 5.

identified with the salary of the peasant,[58] which, in harmony with the transformation of Mexican agriculture in general, began to stagnate and deteriorate in the 1970s. Instead of stimulating domestic production, however, CONASUPO shifted its attention toward imports during the period of its emphasis on comparative advantage in agriculture. As CON-ASUPO reduced its proportion of domestic maize purchases, it simultaneously entered the international market to import growing amounts of the crop, and therefore to increase the share of national consumption it managed (see Table 4.9).

As this dynamic occurred in the 1970s, the emphasis of CONASUPO shifted from supporting the "peasant economy's salary" (maize prices) to mediating the internationalization of the maize economy in general, and ignoring the stagnation of rural incomes dependent on maize.[59] That shift meant that with the exception of 1976-1978, CONASUPO-guaranteed prices for maize were actually lower than international prices. In a stunning turnaround, the state in the 1970s shifted its real policy from subsidizing the rural wage (in the form of maize prices) and buying small amounts on the international market to a strategy of increasing international purchases at the expense of the domestic crop.

Not surprisingly, bean purchases followed the same trajectory, though the level of state intervention in beans never achieved the levels experienced in wheat and maize. Bean imports before 1974 were practically unknown to CONA-SUPO, and the management of the price support program seemed erratic. Speculation in beans during the 1970s was rampant, due to local shortages of the commodity. Bean hoarding became a typical response to ineffective CONA-SUPO policies in the sector, as well as being a result of the insensitivity of bean production to market incentives.

[58] Ibid., 17.

[59] For this observation, I am obliged to David Barkin. For fuller treatment of CONASUPO's shift in emphasis, see Barkin and Esteva; Esteva, "La experiencia de la intervención estatal"; and Barkin and Suárez, El fin de autosuficiencia.

TABLE 4.9
CONASUPO Purchases of Basic Grains, 1965–1983

	Internal Purchases (1,000 tons)	Percentage of National Production	Imports* (1,000 tons)	Internal Purchases (1,000 tons)	Percentage of National Production	Imports* (1,000 tons)	Internal Purchases (1,000 tons)	Percentage of National Production	Imports* (1,000 tons)
1965	1,861	20.8	—	94	10.9	—	1,459	67.9	—
1966	1,812	19.5	—	132	13.0	—	859	52.1	—
1967	1,911	22.2	—	100	10.2	—	1,101	51.9	—
1968	1,727	19.6	—	54	6.3	—	827	39.7	—
1969	1,463	17.4	761	61	7.3	—	1,195	51.4	—
1970	1,194	13.4	17	33	3.6	—	1,148	42.9	176
1971	1,536	15.7	191	101	10.6	—	682	37.2	656
1972	1,438	15.6	1,155	136	15.6	—	635	35.1	745
1973	804	9.3	1,318	3	0.3	38	922	44.1	1,073
1974	779	9.9	2,625	230	23.7	105	726	26.0	54
1975	345	4.1	955	364	35.4	—	1,066	38.1	5
1976	968	12.1	1,727	241	32.6	—	1,493	44.4	493
1977	1,430	13.0	1,465	248	32.2	—	479	19.5	508
1978	1,809	13.5	827	170	17.9	5	1,205	43.3	1,423
1979	1,952	19.8	4,232	181	30.1	293	785	34.6	783
1980	863	7.0	2,478	133	13.7	478	1,171	42.0	1,269
1981	2,069	20.0	226	298	39.5	—	1,350	37.2	518
1982	3,272	32.2	3,911	530	48.4	—	2,433	54.4	0
1983	1,607	13.2		547	44.0	132	1,859	53.4	

SOURCE: Mexico, CONASUPO, CONASUPO en cifras, 1982, 1983.
* Import figures prior to 1971 are contradictory and unreliable, even when taken from CONASUPO documents. Therefore, they are not included. CONASUPO imported only small amounts of maize during 1962–1963 and no beans in the period not included.

After years of inattention to the stated purpose of the maize and bean price support program in the countryside, CONA-SUPO under Echeverría reacted to falling national production and local shortfalls with a sudden price increase in 1973, the year of the most aggravated bean shortages at the national level. Nominal support prices jumped from 1,750 to 5,000 pesos per ton in beans and from 940 to 1,200 pesos in maize. Wheat and rice supports followed suit, but wheat lagged behind the other basic grains in subsequent price increases.

True to form, however, CONASUPO overestimated the effectiveness of price incentives in bean and maize, ostensibly assuming that small producers were sensitive in their cropping decisions to fluctuations in market prices. Although data are not available, the common assertion among analysts of rural Mexico is that few maize and bean producers were able to respond to such a market device for stimulating production. Instead, many large-scale producers shifted crops in favor of beans, in response to their suddenly greater profitability (income per hectare more than doubled in one year), while small producers—many of whom were petty speculators in the commodity as a hedge against rising inflation—were left holding beans that cheapened with the artificial glut. Meanwhile large producers diminished the value of individual hoards through increased production for local consumption.

Interestingly, the momentary maize and bean surplus generated by the price increases probably had little effect on the consumption of those commodities in the countryside: the rural poor who count on such commodities for their protein were cash-poor and essentially unable to purchase maize and beans. The surplus generated was a government-held surplus, which ultimately satisfied urban shortfalls in beans but probably had little effect on rural malnutrition or deficiencies in basic grain consumption.[60] In some measure, the SAM in-

[60] This is based on extensive discussions with farmers throughout the states mentioned as part of the research base of this study, as well as interviews and discussions with Gustavo Esteva, David Barkin, Blanca Suárez, Arturo Warman, and other analysts of rural Mexico.

225

tended to stabilize the government's policies toward bean and maize production, with more progressive intentions than had characterized the ad hoc inventions of the mid-1970s. The successes and failures of that goal will be examined in Chapter 5.

CHALLENGERS TO MAIZE AND BEAN PRODUCTION IN THE 1980s

As is the case with wheat and sorghum, the real picture of challengers to maize and bean production in the 1980s is somewhat clouded by the heavy subsidies and producer incentives forwarded by the SAM in 1980-1982. Nevertheless, it is worthwhile to examine the "sustainability" of maize and beans, not only in the technical aspects of production, but in the existential threat to the peasantry in general.

In fact, the first challenge to the maize and bean crop in the 1980s comes from sorghum, which displaced these two traditional crops in many areas in the 1970s. Sorghum—which in Mexico is not used as a human foodstuff—is the principal feedstock of the modern poultry industry and a component in the general balanced feed industry for livestock. As a grain, sorghum competes with maize for acreage; it shares many cultivation characteristics with maize and is extremely drought resistant (despite which fact an increasing proportion of sorghum is cultivated on irrigated land, challenging maize and soya as a second crop). Likewise, sorghum is subsidized by the state, and CONASUPO purchases a significant portion of the national crop at an official guaranteed price. Grain sorghum acreage (not including two other varieties of forage sorghum) appeared in statistics for the first time in 1958 and skyrocketed until in 1977 its acreage actually exceeded that of beans for the first time (Table 4.10).

Sorghum, unlike maize and beans, is a crop of the marketplace, intimately associated with the livestock industry and the balanced feed complex in Mexico, led by such transna-

Table 4.10

Cultivated Area of Sorghum, Beans, and Maize in Mexico,
Selected Years (thousands of hectares)

	Sorghum	Beans	Maize
1955	0	1,187	5,371
1960	116	1,326	5,558
1965	314	2,117	7,718
1970	921	1,747	7,440
1975	1,502	1,552	6,694
1976	1,294	1,753	6,783
1977	1,465	1,316	7,489
1978	1,454	1,631	7,232
1979	1,157	1,580	5,567
1980	1,578	1,763	6,955
1981*	1,400	2,000	8,150
1982	1,100	1,600	6,000
1983	1,400	1,900	6,500

Source: Mexico, NAFINSA, *La economía mexicana en cifras*, 1981.
* Figures for 1981-1983 are from U.S. Embassy in Mexico, "Grain and Feed Data Update," December 16, 1983.

tionals as Purina and Anderson-Clayton. A corollary to the encroachment of sorghum on maize acreage is the capacity of the crop to integrate peasant producers vertically into the balanced feed industry and remove them from basic foodstuff cultivation in their traditional subsistence mode. While market advocates see little harm in removing the *campesino* from a subsistence mode which has been particularly harsh in Mexico, a number of seldom-recognized consequences emerge that threaten the livelihood of the new sorghum producers.

The characteristics of sorghum production in Mexico include an increasing dependence on improved seed made available by the state-run seed company (PRONASE, or Productora Nacional de Semillas). Producing sorghum as a nonfood item also forces the *campesino* into the marketplace as a con-

227

sumer of basic foods. No longer is the *minifundista* or *ejidatario* able to fall back on personal reserves of foodgrains when cash-poor. The chain of local production, distribution, exchange, and consumption is broken by cash crops such as sorghum. In addition, the *campesino* cultivating sorghum is made dependent on the balanced feed company or the state to purchase his crop. As the CONASUPO has increasingly turned to international purchases to sustain national supply and maintained a price policy which slips annually in real terms, the *campesino* producer of sorghum is thrown onto a market but remains ill equipped to respond flexibly to its vicissitudes. In that respect, sorghum not only challenges maize and bean acreage but threatens the viability of small-scale agriculture in peasant Mexico.

Barley exhibits many of the same characteristics as sorghum: its linkage to the livestock industry, the vertical integration of production from farm to agroindustry, and the weakness of the producer against the market. Barley is cultivated in Mexico primarily as either a feedgrain for livestock[61] or, as we have seen, a key input in the beer industry. In the Bajío and in Tlaxcala, Mexico, Hidalgo, and Puebla, barley production typically takes place on rain-fed *minifundios* that are dependent on the livestock industry and are only minimally able to earn the interest of the beer industry. As such, barley lands in rain-fed areas represent a further encroachment of livestock onto traditional food crop lands in central Mexico. Once again, it is not surprising that such encroachment takes place in the poorest zones of the country.

While many crops challenge the production of maize and beans, however, clearly the most serious threat to the future of these most basic crops comes from the combination of peasant marginalization, in which the traditional cultivator fails to survive the transformation of Mexican agriculture, and the complementary changes in tastes and incomes in the

---

[61] Barkin and Suárez, *El fin de autosuficiencia*, 72; Sánchez Burgos, 60-62.

principal markets of Mexico, favoring meat, milk, and other foods to which the peasant has no access and disdaining the traditional devotion to maize and beans. As we shall see in the next chapter, even the state's attempt to reverse the productive undoing of the peasant economy has served to challenge the cultivation of food for the Mexican poor.

CHAPTER FIVE

Markets, Politics, and the Public Economy: The Allocation of Resources in Mexican Agriculture

> Dependency on the importation of food in our time is converted into political ties that Mexico ... cannot accept if it is to assume an increasingly autonomous, responsible and sovereign position.
> —Oficina de Asesores del C. Presidente, Sistema Alimentario Mexicano, August 1979

At the end of 1984, the Mexican agricultural system finds itself unable to provide its population with sufficient food, adequately distributed. At the same time, Mexico has appeared in the past decade as one of the most important agricultural exporters in the world, a crucial provider of certain foodstuffs to U.S., European, and Asian markets. That fundamental contradiction in Mexico is hardly unique in the Third World. It is increasingly the condition of national agricultural systems that are "opened" to the international system through transnational agribusiness investment, trade, and national strategies of development. In such societies, economic theory suggests that agricultural commodities will be produced according to market optima. But the openness of the agricultural system suggests that the power over producing and pricing commodities for domestic consumption is removed to external actors. The importance of the state for development in Third World countries also suggests that the internationalization of productive and pricing decisions—and the implied internationalization of distribution and exchange—dictate that such events will also mandate an expansion of the public economy.[1]

In the case under discussion, the Mexican state, emboldened by its half century of agricultural intervention and agrarian reform, and empowered by Article 27 of its Constitution and various statutory supports such as the federal agrarian reform and water and rural association laws, continues to feel obliged to try to shape the future of the Mexican agricultural landscape. This chapter will treat the evolution of political responses to the emerging food crisis, in the general context of agricultural internationalization. The Mexican response is strongly statist, but the expansion of the public economy shaping the state's response to market failures in basic foods is skewed by a number of complications. The role of agriculture in the economy is shifting to reveal more conflicting interests among food consumers. The industrializing economy is unable to absorb enough of the labor force at a wage level sufficient to incorporate them into modern markets. The public bureaucracy reflects a political system that bids up the price of fiscal intervention in the food system. And the emergence of a coherent state response to food insufficiencies is complicated by the sexennial change in presidents (along with virtually the entire decision-making apparatus) and the appearance since 1978 of the oil boom and bust, with its fiscal consequences.

The political logic of state intervention in Mexican agriculture has changed over the past forty years, due in large part to the increasing internationalization of the Mexican economy in general (and the rural economy in particular). Concomitant changes in political program orientation have resulted in the creation of a state-guided agricultural system in a capitalist country surrounded by the imposing power of the international market. It is a system that seeks to create agricultural commodities as a part of the public economy, in the face of market inadequacy. In many aspects of this strat-

[1] David Cameron, "The Expansion of the Public Economy: A Comparative Analysis," *American Political Science Review* 72:4 (December 1978), 1250.

egy, the state has acted as if basic foods were a "public good."[2] In economic terms, the SAM permitted the state to decide productive and distributive optimality, not the market.[3] Because of the inadequacy and distortions of the market, the state attempted to appropriate control of the agricultural system, at some level, with the purpose of providing a basic level of nutrition and national food security, governed by the economic calculus of state agencies. The embodiment of that shift in state intervention in agricultural growth was the Sistema Alimentario Mexicano, considered less for its successes and failures, or its durability in the fickle political atmospherics of presidential succession, than for its importance as an interlude or phase in the progression of state attitudes toward capital accumulation in agriculture.

The SAM has been reincarnated bureaucratically as the Programa Nacional de Alimentación, though its political power and economic impact are still unclear after almost a year of its existence. What is clear is that the exigencies of the Mexican food crisis in the 1970s and 1980s have led to the creation of the food system bureaucracy as a multiagency apparatus designed to allocate agricultural goods publicly, as if they were a natural part of the realm of public affairs. The SAM goal of publicly intervening in foodstuff production satisfied many of the criteria generally applied to the analysis of public goods, even though food is usually considered a private good. The SAM sought to create a production system in rain-fed agriculture that would not challenge the market's ability to provide other agricultural commodities. The produce of the reclaimed peasantry was not targeted to a specific population but was open to all consumers through CONASUPO. And,

[2] A public good may be defined as any good whose consumption by one does not diminish its availability to others (e.g., clean air, national defense, flood control). Foodstuffs under certain conditions of state-managed abundance are not pure public goods, but collective goods that require similar strategies in the public economy.

[3] James E. Alt and K. Alec Chrystal, *Political Economics* (Berkeley and Los Angeles: University of California Press, 1983), 177.

importantly, the SAM attempted to intervene agricultural resources to a great extent because of the depletion of the "national patrimony," which extends to land and water, through the internationalization of the agricultural system. That is, the SAM responded to the economic externalities of the food system by expanding the public economy. To a great extent, the designs and shortcomings of the SAM may be seen as a product of the conflict of such a concept of agricultural appropriation and intervention with the powerful forces of the private sector, pitched at the international level.

The appropriation of agricultural production as a part of the public realm pointed toward the cultivation of basic foods as a universally available consumer good extending beyond the purview of the market. Such intervention distinguishes itself from the different styles of previous epochs. First, the state explicitly proposes to create food, not as the privatized or semipublic (to include the reform sector) "engine of growth" for the economy in general. Instead, state managers involved in agricultural-food policy conceive of the "food system" as a creator of values to be distributed to a large public which, in the production of private goods, is without access to the fruits of the food system at a level sufficient for basic nutrition. We are here, of course, referring to the basic constituency of a food redistribution plan: the nutritionally deprived (i.e., the rural poor and the marginal urban residents).

Second, the state does not seek to create and manage foodstuffs as part of the public realm primarily from moralistic motivations that might evaporate before the more pressing economic exigencies of an underdeveloped country with scarce resources. Rather, this chapter will attempt to show that the state engages this "new politics" of agriculture in a specific historical conjuncture of the collapse of *agrarismo* (agrarian reform), the devaluation of the peso against the dollar, regular external trade and payments problems, and structural market distortions in agriculture. The state need not be conceived, then, as the neutral arbiter of the commonweal. That would impose a different calculus altogether. If that vision of the state can be sustained, it will not be here. This argument follows a more parsimonious concept allowing the state to follow the economic logic of the age: rational self-interest.

Finally, though the results of the SAM may show the contrary, it is not necessary to assume that the idea of basic food production as an impure public good requires that the consuming "public" be comprised of the entire Mexican population. Indeed, as Mancur Olson and others have argued, the concept of public good allows that what are public goods for some are private goods for others.[4] Here the explicit target populations (or jurisdictions) of the SAM—the poor consumer and the marginal producer—are the intended beneficiaries of the "new politics" of food self-sufficiency and redistribution. And the diversion of the food system from those populations is a product of the internationalization of this particular element of the public realm, which prevents the achievement of the distributive goals of the SAM, if not the production goals in the short term.

Two further qualifications merit our attention from the outset. First, Mexico has a longstanding tradition of state intervention in agriculture. The genesis of the idea of the "statization" of integral agrarian reform (or agricultural productivity with some structural transformation) comes at the end of a long revolutionary ethos of *agrarismo*, with the historic abandonment of agrarian reform altogether and the consolidation of agribusiness as the prime mover of the rural economy. Second, the creation of the agricultural system as a part of the public realm in the 1970s and 1980s is *new* primarily for the absence of a true reform element concerning itself with the central question of agrarian Mexico: the control of economic property. It is the purpose of this chapter, first, to sketch the historical development of the "new" politics in

[4] Mancur Olson, "Introduction," in Todd Sandler, ed., *The Theory and Structures of International Political Economy* (Boulder, Colo.: Westview, 1981), 3-16.

234

agriculture and to pose some of the fundamental conflicts that plague the execution of agricultural policies. The first step in that explanation is to outline the shifting logic of agricultural intervention by the Mexican state. Second, we will treat the internationalization of the agricultural sector as a constraining influence on the state. And, finally, we will treat the origins of the food self-sufficiency program of the SAM as a consequence of agricultural development in an era of internationalization and state intervention.

THE SHIFTING LOGIC OF POSTWAR STATE INTERVENTION IN MEXICAN AGRICULTURE

As we know, the Mexican revolution failed, until the mid-1930s, to rationalize agricultural production in the countryside. The production volume and value indicated in Chapter I declined as an indirect reflection of equivocal state policy toward the reorganization of rural society after the effective demise of the hacienda as the leading institution of rural society under the ancien régime. Under the Cárdenas agrarian reform, however, a number of steps were taken to ensure the future productivity of the Mexican food system through politically progressive land reform measures. Cárdenas redistributed more than 20 million hectares of abandoned, expropriated, and otherwise public lands under Article 27 of the revolutionary Constitution.[5] He created the National Invest-

[5] For some contributions to the vast literature on the Cárdenas agrarian reform, see Arnaldo Córdova, *La política de masas del cardenismo* (Mexico: Ediciones ERA, 1974); Romana Falcón, *El agrarismo en Veracruz: la etapa radical, 1928-1935* (Mexico: El Colegio de México, 1977); Moisés González Navarro, *La Confederación Nacional Campesina: un grupo de presión en la reforma agraria mexicana* (Mexico: Costa-Amic, 1968); Iván Restrepo and Salomón Eckstein, *La agricultura colectiva en México: la experiencia de la Laguna* (Mexico: Siglo XXI, 1975); Sanderson, *Agrarian Populism and the Mexican State*; Eyler Simpson, *The Ejido: Mexico's Way Out* (Chapel Hill: University of North Carolina Press, 1937); and Nathan Whetten, *Rural Mexico* (Chicago: University of Chicago Press, 1948). Of course, virtually every survey of modern Mexico includes a section on the Cárdenas agrarian reform.

ment Finance Bank (NAFINSA) and expanded the rural credit bank networks. And he broadened the organizational mandate of the *ejido*, the *minifundio*, and the agricultural producers' associations that have become the standard-bearers of the "reform sector" of Mexican agriculture.

In his last years in office, Cárdenas encouraged a change in emphasis away from simple reforms in land tenure to a more complex interrelated program of agricultural productivity. That shift, which was realized only under his successors Ávila Camacho and Alemán, became known as "integral agrarian reform."[6] The political cast of integral agrarian reform in the 1940s hardly resembled the *cardenista* reforms put to work, however. Agrarian organizations in succeeding administrations diminished in importance and suffered the regular excoriation of the state and the private sector alike. Those critics, complacent in their enjoyment of an economic boom previously unknown in postrevolutionary Mexico, undermined the viability of the reform sector as a long-term revolutionary asset.

As the state retreated from mobilizing peasant and worker organizations to demand their entitlements under agrarian populist programs, it turned instead to stimulating productivity for the sake of increasing output in an agricultural sector less dedicated to social reform and more interested in perpetuating an "engine of growth" for the industrializing Mexican economy. Organizationally, such changes implied a reduction in agrarian reform grants and their relevant bureaucracies, though the DAAC (Departamento de Asuntos

---

Key legislation in this regard included the first agrarian code (Código Agrario de los Estados Unidos Mexicanos) in 1934; the agrarian credit law of that same year (Ley de crédito agrícola); and important reforms to the agrarian code enacted in 1937 (Decreto que reforma varios artículos del Código Agrario de los Estados Unidos Mexicanos). An understated but important law was the 1934 law of producers associations (Ley de Asociaciones de Productores Agrícolas).

[6] Interestingly, the term "integral agrarian reform" seems to have been coined in Mexico by Calles, a staunch opponent of agrarian reform.

Agrarios y Colonización) and its successor the SRA (Secretaría de Reforma Agraria) continued to play conspicuous roles in national politics. The growing emphasis was the "market," not only as the exchange nexus for Mexican agricultural production but as the new reform metaphor. The deficiencies in Mexican agriculture were now blamed on market insufficiency in marginal zones, rather than the inadequate distribution and control of economic property. The official hope for many rural communities was not their integration into the expanding agricultural system of Mexico but the integration of their individual members into the transforming industrial "labor market." The conscious policy of the state was to increase market networks for the commercialization of Mexican agriculture. The goal of state-led integral agrarian reform became the elimination of the dual system of rural life, in which the vast bulk of *campesinos* were marginal to the integrative benefits of the market.[7]

Of course, this programmatic emphasis on market integration also affected the allocation of resources to agriculture, a change which coincided with the rise of technical ministries in the Mexican agricultural bureaucracy. The first line of agricultural reform under the "integral development" model was the creation of rural infrastructure, especially water control projects. As we have shown throughout this study, the rise of the federal irrigation districts had a profound influence on the distribution of agricultural production and the character of cropping in the Mexican food system. The role of the federal irrigation districts became crucial, as they produced more agricultural export value, contributed most of the nation's wheat, and offered a national example of modernity and progress in a transforming agricultural system. The federal irri-

---

[7] The programmatic emphasis on the market in Mexican agriculture can be seen in CONASUPO's proliferation into a number of decentralized marketing agents, namely ANDSA (Almacenes Nacionales de Depósito, S.A.), BORUCONSA (Bodegas Rurales CONASUPO, S.A.), DICONSA (Distribuidores CONASUPO, S.A.), and the expansive network of CONASUPO retail outlets, or CONASUPERS.

gation system was not created or administered as a "public good," however. The irrigation districts did not afford a solution to growing agrarian unemployment, land concentration, and rural unrest. Nor did the irrigation districts succeed in rationalizing the allocation of rural resources to the general benefit of the Mexican food consumer. To the extent the richest areas of Mexican agriculture did provide products to the consumer, it did so on the basis of market initiatives, realized in self-interested fashion. Likewise, the new food products were consumed as private goods according to the stratified income and property distribution of the Mexican economic miracle. But the irrigated areas created in the postwar period did offer the state a greater potential opportunity to control the yield of the Mexican food system, as would later become so crucial to national food policy under the SAM.

The federal irrigation system, along with other major infrastructure projects such as roads, rural electrification, potable water, and rural storage, came in an epoch of decreasing state commitment to the social reform of Mexican agriculture. As a result, and with the obvious agreement of the private sector, the Mexican state created a broad system of social capital investment in agriculture, without exerting fundamental control over the system's output. Only through indirect incentives to production did the state maintain an avenue to controlling the nature of the Mexican harvest in the federal irrigation districts. Such indirect methods were more substantial in the case of the ejidal sector. With total control over the ejidal credit mechanism through the rural bank, the Mexican state was (and continues to be) able to dictate the terms and conditions of the planting cycle, not simply in cropping decisions but in schedules for the preplanting preparation of the soil, fertilizer application, and the use of harvest machinery (or labor). In the mid-1970s, for example, the state credit mechanisms did not provide short-term loans for bean production on *ejidos* in the irrigation districts. Likewise, participation in the federal crop insurance program, often linked as a prerequisite to credit, was not offered to producers of certain

238

lucrative crops such as potatoes or export tomatoes. Often, the bank would finance only seed purchased from PRONASE or production contracts executed with CONASUPO, using powers unavailable to the state when dealing with private agriculturalists who had greater access to the much-vaunted market in capital and inputs. And, of course, ultimately the state controlled the usufruct under which the ejidal sector managed its land tenure. At any time the state was likely to deprive *ejidatarios* of their land for violating the conditions of agrarian rights, most often for the crime of holding an off-farm job to supplement the subsistence income of the ejidal system. In general, the official state agricultural bureaucracy managed the public sector of farming through its exclusive control of the requisites of farm life: land, capital, and inputs.

But, if the market ideology of the state served the private sector well in the formative period of the great agricultural infrastructure projects, it did not serve the changing consumer market of the Mexican republic itself. As the logic of the Mexican agricultural system shifted from "engine of growth" in the 1940s and early 1950s to "adjunct of industrialization" by the end of the 1950s, the market impetus proved insufficient to the needs of the rural producer and the economic miracle itself. Uncontrolled marketing imperatives fell short in three ways.

First, it was clear that the market alone was insufficient for—and perhaps even hostile to—the survival of the peasantry. This problem made itself manifest in several ways. The peasant economy was unable to "articulate" its production with the market without suffering damage to traditional cropping, ecological practices, and community survival strategies. Peasant producers tended to move in one of two directions: a transition to primitive accumulation and eventually agricultural entrepreneurship on a small scale or, more often, disintegration as a rural producer and reappearance as a rural day laborer or urban migrant. This social problem of agriculture in the minifundio and ejidal system was attributed, variously, to inadequate marketing facilities[8] or the encroach-ment of the market on peasant agriculture.[9] The government agricultural bureaucracy—principally the SAG (Secretariat of Agriculture and Cattle Raising, later changed to SARH, the Secretariat of Agriculture and Water Resources) and CON-ASUPO—took the former position, and sought to intervene in rural society to improve peasant market networks, as we shall see shortly.

The second failure of the market as a sufficient impetus to agricultural production was felt in the diversion of agricultural resources away from production for national consumers. This phenomenon became more important after 1965, as did state responses to it. Clearly, though, the market's early orientation toward generating foreign exchange for import substitution industrialization impelled the long-term association of key Mexican producers with foreign markets, their integration into transnational agribusiness complexes, and their relative independence from national controls or incentives for pro-duction.

The final glaring shortcoming of the marketplace was its incapacity to keep sufficient capital in the agricultural sector. As the famous CDIA (Centro de Investigaciones Agrarias) study of 1970 showed, Mexican agriculture suffered a decap-italization throughout the two decades of the postwar eco-nomic boom (1950-1970). The mechanisms for that decapi-

[8] A number of studies by the SAM and the SARH still maintain that the fundamental problem of commercialization is the lack of markets and the existence of *coyotes* and *caciques* acting as rural intermediaries. Undoubtedly the latter is true, but, as in the cases of cattle raising and slaughter, and the commercialization of maize and bean production among peasants, the advent of the market oftentimes means the effective destruction of fragile rural sur-vival strategies.

[9] For analysis of the effects of market encroachment on peasant lives, see Schejtman; Barkin, *Desarrollo regional*; Ursula Oswald, "El monopolio del centro de abastos y sus efectos en la sociedad campesina," in Oswald, ed., *Mercado y dependencia* (Mexico: Nueva Imagen, 1979), 171-200; Héctor Díaz Polanco, "Estructura de clases y comercialización: un caso mexicano," in Oswald, 125-164.

talization included differential interest rates and profitability in industry over agriculture, inadequate returns of capital to agriculture through the banking system, and poor relative prices in agriculture compared with other sectors of the economy. It was not until the late 1970s that the Mexican agricultural system began to "recapitalize" through these same mechanisms, but largely through state intervention in public investment, not through the virtues of the marketplace.

The combined effect of these three shortcomings of the market was shocking to analysts of the Mexican economy, as well as to politicians who nervously witnessed the almost simultaneous withering of the economic miracle and the rise of social tensions and external economic imbalance in the 1970s. By the end of the 1970s, as many as four million rural dwellers were without land.[10] Meat and bean shortages had become a fact of urban life. Imports of agricultural commodities outstripped exports almost two to one. And the heartland of the technological revolution of Mexican agriculture was producing strawberries and white asparagus for the dining tables of American consumers. At the same time, rumblings were heard that the United States would use food as a diplomatic weapon (confirmed almost immediately by President Carter's abortive Russian grain embargo). The external payments crisis of 1976 was continuing unabated by oil revenues. And the Mexican state had abandoned its attempts to pursue agricultural productivity through land reform after Echeverría.

THREE EPOCHS OF POSTWAR MEXICAN AGRICULTURE

To find the sources of crisis in Mexican agriculture from 1965 to 1980 is to outline the three roles of agricultural growth as well: as engine of growth, as adjunct to industrialization, and as a mechanism for food security.

[10] The estimate comes from John J. Bailey and Donna H. Roberts, "Mexican Agricultural Policy," *Current History* 82:488 (December 1983), 421.

First, in the postwar period, agriculture changed from the engine of growth to the adjunct of industrialization. The specific historical point at which such a transformation took place is impossible to find, however analytically attractive such periodization might be. In any event, a number of indicators suggest the changing role of agriculture in Mexico. First, its contribution to gross domestic product declined after 1950, from a position of importance relative to industry to one of secondary status. By 1979, at the hour of the SAM's birth, agriculture was only an 11 percent contributor to GDP, while industry had grown to over 34 percent.[11] Likewise, in the wake of the oil boom, agriculture had diminished as an important earner of foreign exchange for the Mexican industrialization drive. While such diminution in the importance of export agriculture was never officially recognized—the state maintained an active program of export promotion during the López Portillo years—trade liberalization and the growth of oil revenues made agricultural exports seem critical mainly for their ability to "depetrolize" the oil miracle. In fact, if there existed an inclination in the agricultural bureaucracy, it probably favored increasing domestic market networks for previously exported items, though that programmatic line was never pursued fully. In general, however, the position of agriculture became less crucial as a natural outgrowth of the industrialization drive taking place with such apparent success in the "easy phase" of import substitution industrialization (1940-1958) and the "deepening" integration of industry during the oil boom.[12]

[11] Mexico, NAFINSA, 1981, 23-30.

[12] The term "easy phase" of import substitution industrialization refers to the first wave of consumer goods industrialization typical of Latin American industrialization drives in the 1940s and 1950s. "Deepening" refers to the process of vertical integration in industry, achieved principally by the creation of fully articulated capital goods and intermediate goods sectors. For interesting treatments of these concepts and their relationship to political change, see Albert Hirschman, "The Turn to Authoritarianism in Latin America and the Search for its Economic Determinants," in David Collier, ed., *The New Authoritarianism in Latin America* (Princeton, N.J.: Princeton University

Second, agriculture became an adjunct of industrialization in its role as provider of "cheap food" to the urban population. The combination of urbanization and the increase in wage share of national income (or at least the sectoral shift of wage earners into higher-income categories)[13] meant a lower effective demand for basic foodstuffs and a greater demand for higher-priced food items enhanced (in price, at least) by processing. Because of the high income elasticities of many agricultural products in Mexico, the increasingly urban work force toiling in a regime of wage labor exerted a major influence on rural society by demanding more meat, more oilseeds (especially safflower), more fresh fruits and vegetables, and more agribusiness inputs for processing into canned goods, beverages, and other consumer items of the "modern" table.[14] Such a role for agriculture under the industrialization drive of the postwar era meant three fundamental changes in the impetus for agricultural production: the transformation of the agricultural system from the "independent variable" of the Mexican growth experience to the "dependent variable" of industrialization; the deepening integration of agriculture with agribusiness activities domestically; and the increasing vulnerability of the food system to changes in demand from the urban consumer and the multinational corporation.

We have seen throughout the chapters on agricultural production that the articulation of the countryside with urban markets has been a major tendency of the Mexican agricultural system in the postwar era. The rise in urban demand for animal protein has generated a growing beef herd, a trans-

---

Press, 1979), 61-98; and Guillermo O'Donnell, "Tensions in the Bureaucratic-Authoritarian State and the Question of Democracy," in Collier, 285-318.

[13] See Reynolds for analysis of the sectoral shift of Mexican labor during the industrialization drive of the postwar boom.

[14] For monographic treatments of agribusiness transformation and its impact on specific areas, see Barkin and Suárez, El fin de autosuficiencia alimentaria; Díaz Polanco; and Burbach and Flynn, Chapter 9. For a more general treatment of agribusiness accumulation in Mexico, see U.N. CEPAL, "Las empresas transnacionales en la agroindustria mexicana."

national poultry complex, and a hog industry in transition toward confinement feeding and vertical coordination. In the countryside, that productive response to urban demand has meant shifts in cropping and land use patterns, often with devastating consequences for rural lives and ecologies. In Tabasco, Veracruz, and Chiapas, deforestation for cattle raising and the dispossession of the peasantry progress apace. In the Bajío, the displacement of traditional foodstuffs has coincided with the arrival of the dairy industry (which delivers less than 30 percent of its product to the market as fluid milk) and the rise in hog raising and barley cultivation for the beer industry. In the North, the best rain-fed districts of Tamaulipas are giving way to the production of sorghum for animal feed, and the irrigation districts now yield citrus for the growing urban and export markets. As we have argued in previous chapters, these shifts in cropping have little progressive effect on peasant lives. Most often they result in the industrialization of agriculture at the expense of rural jobs, the concentration of agricultural resources, and the inattention of the food system to the rural crisis in nutrition.

Not only has the food system been transformed into an adjunct of industrialization through the centralization of markets in urban growth areas, but agricultural processes have tended to become industrialized as well, in keeping with the character of Latin American industrialization. In the first blush of import substitution, agribusiness enjoyed effective protection from import competition through the tariff structure, incentives to growth through production incentives and low tax rates, and official state support through programs of export promotion and rural job creation. Under a number of guises—from the beginnings of import substitution to the "rural enterprises" program of Echeverría and the "industrial corridors" proposed by López Portillo—agribusiness has flourished for its putative rural development potential and its attention to the increasingly homogenized and internationalized tastes of the growing urban population.

But the effects of agribusiness growth—however satisfying

they are to the consumers of refined and processed agricultural commodities—have been problematic for the farmer and peasant. Ignoring for the moment the temptation to criticize the nutritive and cultural benefits of much agribusiness processing, two effects are apparent. First, the agribusiness, through its internal necessity to secure adequate and regular supplies of raw materials, tends to try to control the nature of the market or, in more modest terms, to stimulate local producers of inputs through production contracts, financial arrangements, technical assistance, and other interventions in production at the farm level. While this drive to use installed plant capacity at high rates through guaranteeing adequate supplies of raw materials is understandable from the viewpoint of the agribusiness processor, such "rationalization" of agricultural production has also tended to shift the control of food production from farmer and consumer to the intermediary, whether broker or processor.

The growth of agribusiness processing has also meant in many crops the diversion of fresh foodstuffs from the consumer market to industrial processing. The case of pineapple—in which a growing amount of the national product is industrialized in the form of canned slices, chunks, and juice—demonstrates that such agribusiness rationalization also means a rise in the price of fresh foods and an increase in the total price of food products because of the value added in processing. Such price increases translate into the effective proscription of many traditional consumers—rural and poor—from the purchase of the "modern," processed product.[15] Comparable phenomena exist in the use of tomatoes for processing, the elaboration of cheeses and yogurt from milk, the processing of citrus for juice, and the similar transformation of a number of other commodities in the Mexican food system.

[15] For information on the industrialization of Mexican pineapples, see especially the following USDA publications: "Canned Pineapple," "Mexico: Pineapple Report," and "Pineapple Voluntary Report." See also, Mexico, BNCE.

245

More significant, perhaps, is the role of agriculture as an adjunct to industrialization through the rise of the transnational corporation and the state enterprise. As is commonly known (but little analyzed at the level of production), the rise of agribusiness in Latin America has coincided with the appearance of the transnational corporation. From livestock feed to pesticides to jellies and jams, agribusiness activities have borne the brand of Del Monte, Ciba-Geigy, Hoechst, Anderson-Clayton, Ralston-Purina, Bayer, Dekalb, and scores of other international agribusiness luminaries from the moment that import substitution was conceived. As has been argued elsewhere,[16] the import substitution policies of economic nationalism were an open invitation to transnational subsidiaries. As "industries of transformation" and "infant industries" (for all their signs of industrial maturity), transnational agribusinesses found an early home in the rural bulwarks of economic transformation in Mexico. The effects of such transnational influence on agribusiness in Mexico—as we shall see reflected at the political level in recent state agribusiness development policy—have included the international standardization of the character of rural capital accumulation and the creation of an international technological mandate which extends even to the level of the farm itself.

On the first point, the appearance of the transnational agribusiness does not necessarily imply more exploitative relations in the countryside than would exist under domestic agribusinesses, though such greater exploitation may occur in many cases. In fact, the more important dynamic from the viewpoint of the control of agricultural growth relates to the pace transnationals set in agribusiness accumulation. Domestic firms, if they are to compete and create the conditions for their own survival, must adopt many of the labor- and capital-saving devices commonly known to the established agribusi-

[16] See Richard S. Weinert, review of *Global Reach*, in *Yale Review* (Summer 1975), 632, cited in Alfred Stepan, *The State and Society: Peru in Comparative Perspective* (Princeton, N.J.: Princeton University Press, 1978), 252.

nesses of the developed capitalist world. Vertical integration or coordination of primary inputs must replace more ad hoc arrangements with local producers, if domestic agribusinesses are to secure adequate supplies for production. Productivity increases through the application of advanced production techniques (often imported from the advanced capitalist countries) are also necessary. And, as a result, the survival of domestic agribusiness under import substitution protection often means that the firm must replicate at the local level the most advanced, internationally disseminated relations of production and, in effect, become as much like the transnational as possible. In such processes are carried the seeds of agribusiness homogenization; meaningful distinctions between "national" and "transnational" firms evaporate.[17] Such a realization of agribusiness transformation by transnational competition has important implications for state policy and rural development, as we shall see shortly.

The collateral point is that the industrialization of agriculture under a model of import substitution with transnational participation implies a transnational technological mandate as well. That is, in keeping with the influence of transnationals on local relations of production in the agribusiness firm, local producers must also accept to some great degree the techniques of production common to the most advanced agribusiness competitors in the sector. As should be evident from the above discussion, such a transnational technological mandate includes the purchase of modern machinery and production inputs, and the gradual increase in the capital intensity of the firm. It is interesting that—for all the claims that agribusiness is an effective generator of rural employment—the fragmentary data that do exist indicate that the use of labor per unit of capital investment has declined in Mexico.

The real impact of the technological mandate of transnational agribusiness, however, lies in its capacity to gradually

[17] Barkin and Rozo, "L'agriculture et l'internationalization du capital"; Palloix. See also citations from Chapter 1.

transform the nature of agricultural production itself. Because of improved seed, pesticides, fertilizers, farm machinery, and modern processing techniques, the way crops are produced in Mexico has been revolutionized. While there are many salutary aspects of such a revolution—improved yields, better cultivation practices, increased agricultural research with its spin-offs, more agricultural extension and support, higher re-production rates in cattle, shorter maturation times in poul-try—the arrival and proliferation of such modern technologies in agriculture has also meant the industrialization of agriculture at the international level. Wheat yields become a function of transnational seed companies. Entire productive ecologies are threatened by the wanton use of pesticides, often created by transnationals and banned in their "home" countries. Pro-duction contracts depend on the acceptance of specific "tech-nological packages." And the standards for the acceptance of primary goods for agribusiness processing become the stand-ards of the domestic consumer as well. In this technological sense, as well as in the broader shaping force agribusiness represents in the accumulation of capital in the Mexican coun-tryside, Mexican agriculture has become the adjunct of in-dustrialization in two fundamental ways: in the industriali-zation of its processes and in the locus of decision making over the yield of the Mexican *campo* itself. We shall dis-cuss the constraining influence of this transnational model momentarily.

Of course, agriculture has become an adjunct to industrial-ization since World War II in another fundamental way, which has been sensitive to state policies throughout the period. Agriculture is now the producer of wage goods for the in-dustrial labor force and its support structures. That is, under an economic model emphasizing industrialization, agriculture has the primary responsibility of providing the nonfarm work force with food and other agriculture-related consumer items (wearing apparel, leather goods, liquors, fiber products, and the like) at a low price. Since the mid-1950s, the Mexican state has intervened in that process of wage good production by controlling the price of basic commodities through CON-ASUPO and the National Consumer Institute and by subsidizing the costs of production for the same purpose. Such policies have coincided with the emphasis since the 1960s on "export substitution," or the promotion of manufactures for export in order to balance trade and subvert the vulnerability traditionally suffered by economies dependent on the export of primary commodities subject to wild fluctuations in international markets. By attempting to soften the rate of increase in the price of wage goods, the Mexican state also hedges against demands for wage increases commensurate with inflation in consumer prices. Such wage increases are anathema to direct foreign investment and to the competitiveness of Mexican manufactures abroad, particularly in the epoch of booming lower-cost labor markets for light manufactures such as those in Taiwan, South Korea, Hong Kong, and Singapore. Thus, although the point may seem strained in the abstract, the agricultural system of Mexico becomes the adjunct of industrialization through its indirect subvention of the price of labor, which itself responds to the increasing need to demonstrate competitiveness in manufactures internationally.

Whatever advantages might have accrued from harnessing the agricultural miracle of the 1940s to the purposes of industrialization disappeared in the late 1960s and early 1970s, however. The same forces driving the industrialization of Mexico (and the agricultural sector specifically) were also sapping the strength of the rural sector, forcing (or enticing) millions away from the land into the urban slums, changing the structure of rural production and its crops, and, ultimately, aggravating a growing import dependency in basic grains. Such an objectively obnoxious trend came at a particularly sensitive historical moment in public postures toward agricultural modernization and rural development. More importantly, perhaps, the decline of traditional agricultural production in Mexico clashed with the collapse of agrarian populism, the devaluation of the peso, and the first foreign exchange crisis in decades to produce the first tremor of the Mexican food crisis at the national level.

In the transitional decade of the 1970s, the Mexican state's policies toward the agricultural system made another shift in logic. Whereas in the 1940s and 1950s political emphasis had changed from agrarian reform in a sector dubbed the engine of growth to counterreform and subservience to industrialization, now in the 1970s the logic of state intervention shifted to a new concept of agriculture as the motor force of national food self-sufficiency and defender of national food security against the vicissitudes of external markets and the threat of food being brandished as a weapon, perhaps by its always dangerous northern neighbor, the United States.

THE LIMITS OF STATE RESPONSE TO THE FOOD CRISIS

Earlier chapters have described the extent to which the dependence on industrialization and foreign markets affected the ability of the Mexican food system to provide sustenance to all of its population. Equally important to the analysis here, however, is the limited way in which the state maintained control of the agricultural system in the postwar period. In the first place, the state attempted to intervene generally through adjustments to market distortions, that is, through price supports, producer incentives, factor price controls, and similar modest (if expensive) interventions. Second, the state attempted to create markets where none existed, through the expansion of CONASUPO's system of distribution and storage facilities. And third, the state attempted to expand the *frontera agrícola* (agricultural frontier) by bringing new lands into production, expropriating unused and illegally held lands, and maintaining other areas of production in unprofitable crops (e.g., the sugar support program of the 1970s).

The state managed these limited interventions, however, in ways that enhanced agricultural production in most uneven fashion. Public intervention in the private sector seems always to be vulnerable to the fortunes of fiscal policy, and in this respect Mexico was certainly no exception. As we have seen in Chapter 4, the CONASUPO price guarantees were unable to keep up with producer prices, and became less a price floor than a price ceiling. The modest resources (both fiscal and logistical) of CONASUPO prevented the price system from becoming the producer stimulus it might have been. And, of course, part of that equivocal price intervention came from the conflict between the desire to support producer prices as an incentive and the necessity to maintain a cheap food policy in the city. The expense of a dual price support system—high prices to producers and low prices to consumers—fell beyond the reach of a Mexican state with a low tax rate on capital and a rising fiscal deficit.

Other incentives—the crop insurance program, official credit at concessional rates, agricultural extension, water use subsidies, and the like—suffered the same problems of the price mechanism (fiscal and programmatic limits) and the additional distortion which followed from these programs' devotion to the richest agricultural areas, especially the irrigation districts. State intervention in the 1950s and 1960s followed a pattern of agricultural concentration and market exclusion instead of contributing to overcoming those limits to the Mexican food system. The suffering and productive marginalization of the smallholder and *ejidatario* in the rain-fed areas of Mexico actually followed from the elitist politics of market management exercised by the state. The "supply side" of the Mexican food crisis in the peasant zones of Mexican agriculture was a result of not only private sector exclusion but officially sanctioned stratification of the agricultural growth stimuli provided by the public sector.

A more telling limit to state policy in the postwar period involved the state's contradictory desire to maintain its presence in the agricultural sector without asserting a true "steering capacity." In the early agrarian reform, the state had steered the agricultural sector to a much greater extent, though with less public investment and market capabilities. That greater "efficiency" was due to the importance of the reform

251

sector of agriculture—the *ejidatarios* and public constituency (and effective wards) of the credit and usufruct system—compared with the fledgling private sector. As the private forces of agriculture grew with the expansion of the market, the promotion of agricultural exports, the decline of agrarian reform, and the arrival of the great irrigation and infrastructure works, the state increased its public investment exposure in agriculture without gaining power over the output resulting from that investment. Such a result coincided with the desires of many private sector producers that the state play a formative role in agriculture only in those areas not profitable without state presence.

The growing agricultural bourgeoisie over the 1950s and 1960s became increasingly hostile to what it considered improper state meddling in the marketplace, wasted public investment in ejidal credit, "communistic" agrarian reform attacks on private property, and the incitement of the peasantry to exercise its claims under the agrarian reform provisions of the Mexican revolutionary Constitution. In their most reductive statements at the end of the Echeverría experiment, the leading private sector forces in Mexico called for an end to state intervention in civil society.

The possibility that these state-led "perversions" of private sector prerogatives existed more in the minds of defensive agricultural moguls than as actual consequences of state policy is less important than the realization that the state and the private sector operated on an increasingly hostile footing in the post-1965 decline in rural production. That mutual antipathy crystallized under Luis Echeverría's attempt to resuscitate the ghost of *cardenista* agrarian reform and to punish the profligate agriculturalists who were presiding over the decline of Mexico's most precious state treasure: a successful Third World agricultural modernization miracle.

The events and consequences of the Echeverría period (1970-1976) are recounted elsewhere.[18] Suffice it to say for

[18] For some sources in the expanding literature on the Echeverría period,

our purposes that the Echeverría populist remobilization in the countryside had several important results. First, the collapse of *echeverrismo* ended the era of land reform as an agricultural reform tool and a threat to the inefficient use of agricultural resources. Though the new Ley de Fomento Agropecuario (Law of Agricultural and Livestock Promotion) and the Agrarian Reform Law of 1981 provided for the seizure of "idle lands,"[19] the definition of such lands was hazy, and the political coalition which might be invoked to enforce such a provision was nowhere on the horizon of post-Echeverría Mexico. If the likelihood of enforcing the idle lands provisions of the agrarian code was unclear, however, the impossibility of agrarian mobilization was not. López Portillo, in a speech in Bulgaria in 1978, proclaimed the end of the official state-led agrarian reform and called for the "proletarianization of the rural worker at a fair wage,"[20] a quixotic goal for a Mexican president, contradicting the historical experience of the country's rural workers. Likewise, in his Alliance for Production López Portillo promised security in land tenure in return for the repatriation of capital to Mexico after the disastrous exodus of 1976.

In keeping with this post-*agrarista* land policy, reforms imposed on the Agrarian Reform Law by President de la Madrid in late 1983 sought to change the political structure of the *ejido* itself and to devolve more political responsibility to state and local officials, both of which have been traditionally destructive of agrarian reform. In addition, the law now permits

---

see Carlos Arriola, "Los grupos empresariales frente al estado mexicano, 1973-1975," in El Colegio de México, Centro de Estudios Internacionales, *Las fronteras del control del estado mexicano* (Mexico: El Colegio de México, 1976), 33-81; Sanderson, *Agrarian Populism and the Mexican State*; Carlos Tello, *La política económica de México, 1970-1976* (Mexico: Siglo XXI, 1979).

[19] Mexico, "Ley de fomento agropecuario," *Diario oficial*, December 27, 1980, Title V.

[20] "Mexican President Questions Principle of Land Reform," *Latin America Economic Report* 6:23 (June 16, 1978), 180-181.

ejidos to dissolve themselves by popular vote, returning their agrarian rights "freely" to the federal government.[21]

In addition to the political demise of agrarian reform as an agricultural policy tool, however, the Echeverría period also guaranteed that its revolutionary promise of addressing the rural "social question" would require state policy attention in the next sexennium. If the Echeverría agrarian reform fell on hard times under López Portillo, the new administration in 1977 could not ignore the agrarian question altogether, owing at least partly to the bureaucratic necessity of continuing to process petitions and edicts already cemented in the "midnight expropriations" of Echeverría's last days in office.

But, if the agrarian reform was not an alternative to the rural *problemática* in 1977, what would be the new direction for state intervention? Building on past experience and existing state enterprises and bureaucratic agencies, the government turned to the resuscitation of integral agrarian reform. This time, however, the reform had to fulfill several new conditions of the Mexican economy in general and the countryside specifically. The second consequence of the transition from *echeverrismo* to the SAM, then, combined the politically necessary abnegation of land reform responsibilities with the modern realities of oil rich Mexico. In short, that conflation of political retreat and productive stimulus had to involve a solution for the trade and payments impact of the 1976 devaluation on agricultural imports; an alternative to the uncontrolled emigration of rural workers from the countryside to the city; an attempt to resolve the agricultural decline without attacking private property (especially in the important export-oriented irrigation districts); and the ability to conquer recurrent basic food shortfalls in the main market cities of Mexico: Mexico City, Guadalajara, Puebla, Veracruz, and Monterrey. In addition, if the López Portillo food system plan were to be consistent with the industrial promotion plan, it

[21] Reforms to the Ley Federal de Reforma Agraria, published in *Diario oficial*, January 17, 1984.

would require stimulating agricultural inputs to industry, creating rural jobs through agribusiness promotion, and expanding both producer and consumer subsidies as a nonwage benefit of the oil boom.

If one lesson had survived the momentary euphoria of renascent *agrarismo* under Echeverría, however, it was that the agricultural decline was due in part to the failure of the market interventions of the state to regulate precisely those mechanisms required to effect the goals enumerated above. That is, the López Portillo administration was hardly likely to think that the agricultural decline of the 1965-1976 period could be reversed by better managing the commonly accepted agents of that decline: prices, inputs, and markets. In fact, with the arrival of the earliest SAM documents comes the first, full-fledged public attempt to analyze, at the cabinet level, the nature of market insufficiencies in Mexico. But, if the agricultural policy establishment under López Portillo recognized the need for new levels and kinds of policy intervention in agriculture, two major constraints hampered its attempts to intervene effectively: the depth of agricultural internationalization experienced in the postwar period, and the tardiness of the state's attempts to steer an agricultural production system that heretofore had been governed only by the caprice of the market.

In fact, the degree to which the Mexican agricultural system had become internationalized by 1977-1981 affected the ability of the state to control the production of basic foodstuffs for the poor and food security for the nation. The internationalization of Mexican agriculture in the late 1970s involved not only the trade between that country and the United States or other, lesser trade partners. It meant that many goods produced in the Mexican agricultural system went for commodities satisfying the "internationalized" palates of urban consumers, or the input requirements of transnational corporations or their domestic analogs. But, in a deeper sense, the feasibility of steering such an internationalized complex of agricultural relationships had been reduced by a generation of state prostration before the logic of the market, which manifested itself in various ways.

In the 1960s, as the basic grains system became self-sufficient (if we ignore the gross underconsumption by the malnourished), the state turned its grains program to comparative advantage. Under the doctrine of comparative advantage the Mexican agricultural system would, for the next decade, move away from increased grain production in favor of imports from the United States. In return, Mexico would increase its exports of winter vegetables, fruits, live cattle, and other commodities in which it enjoyed advantage. Of course, at the same time, the market-rationalizing mechanisms of vertical coordination and vertical integration dictated that other important lands be given over to agribusiness input crops, oftentimes determined at the international level. In such circumstances, the Mexican state responded in ad hoc fashion to the distorting impact of expanded trade and agribusiness; but it did not exercise its potential to control production.

Aside from the trade imperative of the Mexican agricultural export sector and the impact of agribusiness integration on rural production, the state's agricultural policies were limited by the exchange rate system after the devaluation of 1976. The cheapened Mexican currency initially encouraged more foreign investment in agribusiness and more trade in export commodities, thereby improving gross export volume, but at the cost of aggravating the external dependence of the sector. At the same time, the high cost of imported grains bought with a devalued currency, combined with the necessity to subsidize food prices to consumers in a time of high inflation, meant that the comparative advantage of the 1960s and early 1970s became an intolerable external payments burden at the same time the foreign debt escalated. In response to the first devaluation since 1954, the Mexican system shaped a food self-sufficiency program partly designed to withdraw from the international grain market and to discard the doctrine of comparative advantage in agricultural trade.

256

The Sistema Alimentario Mexicano as a Steering Device for Mexican Agriculture

This is not the place to engage in a full-fledged evaluation of the famous Sistema Alimentario Mexicano. Not only are the data base and documents inadequate to such a purpose, but the future of food self-sufficiency is still unclear. SAM was an amazing phenomenon, having appeared with much fanfare in 1980 and disappeared with a whisper in the change of presidential administrations in 1982. The reappearance of food self-sufficiency (now called "food sovereignty") in the de la Madrid administration suggests that the new PRONAL (Programa Nacional de Alimentación) will attempt to replace the SAM with a more restrictive but intellectually compatible food strategy. In the course of the two years of its life, the SAM promised self-sufficiency in basic grains, improved nutrition for the *campesino*, and the expansion of the agricultural frontier into the many "marginal zones" of the country. The growing literature explaining the origins, purpose, and successes of the SAM[22] will recount its nature more thoroughly than is possible here.

The purpose here is to "explain" SAM tentatively as a national phenomenon: to integrate it into the historical structure of state responses to agricultural modernization problems in the post–World War II epoch. Two concepts can guide such a task: the idea of an expanding public economy, already

[22] In addition to the many SAM documents themselves, see Cassio Luiselli F., "Por qué el SAM?" *Nexos* 3:32 (August 1980), 26-35; Frank Meissner, "The Mexican Food System (SAM)—A Strategy for Sowing Petroleum," and M. R. Redclift, "The Mexican Food System (SAM)—Sowing Subsidies, Reaping Apathy," both in *Food Policy* 6:4 (November 1981), 219-230 and 231-235, respectively; Jack Corbett, "Policy Implementation in a Complex Environment: Production Incentives and the Sistema Alimentario Mexicano," paper delivered at the Western Social Science Association meeting, April 1982; Rose Spalding, "The Mexican Food Crisis: An Analysis of the SAM," Working Paper in U.S.-Mexican Studies, Center for U.S.-Mexican Studies La Jolla, University of California, San Diego, in press; and James W. Wessman, "The Agrarian Question in Mexico," *Latin American Research Review* 19:2 (1984), 243-259.

introduced; and the concept of steering. Specifically, the thesis of such an explanation of the SAM's role in Mexican agricultural history is that the state—faced with the constraints enumerated above and the increasing internationalization of agricultural growth in Mexico—undertook to apprehend agricultural planning through direct producer incentives and risk sharing. The ostensible purpose of such planning was to detach Mexico from volatile international markets as a matter of "food security" and national pride in agricultural patrimony. The poorly hidden "side agenda" involved the necessity of reducing grain imports in such tremendous volumes at a time when critics were pointing out the similarities between Mexico and Venezuela (trading the oil boom for agricultural decline) and when an increasing proportion of foreign exchange generated by the oil boom went for food imports. In this sense, the beneficiaries of SAM policy included not only the nutritionally deprived outlined in the program and the free riders in the private sector, but the urban work force as well. The indirect influences of external disequilibrium would be alleviated by a successful program of national food self-sufficiency.

The SAM was an intensely political program, of course. Not only was it organized under a special team of advisers reporting directly to the president, but it merged the most renowned *campesinistas* in the country with *técnicos* of a less reform-minded persuasion. It never successfully managed to integrate itself into the cabinet, as its functions were hostile to many entrenched bureaucratic interests and its patrons beyond the president unclear. Examples of such difficulties abound. The SAM dictated production goals for the rain-fed districts, for example, but the Secretariat of Agriculture, SARH, was responsible for execution of the programs. The SAM pushed the unification of *ejidal* and smallholder agriculture under the Ley de Fomento Agropecuario of 1981 (a law it had earlier opposed), but the legal entitlement to new *unidades de producción* was left to the legal affairs staff of the SARH. As a result interministerial coordination was poor, execution in the countryside was haphazard, and resentments were many. Where the SAM made recommendations for reform or considered restructuring the agricultural bureaucracy (as in the case of seed manufacture), it lacked the political authority to implement its reforms. But a bureaucratic critique of the SAM is not the central business of this chapter. The first part of analyzing the expanding public phase of Mexican agriculture in the 1980s involves estimating what mechanisms *any* agricultural bureaucracy in a capitalist society might employ for the sake of improving food security and basic grain production.

The first constraint on the bureaucracy—indeed, the political system in general—postulated that the public sector could not challenge the right of unrestricted accumulation in the countryside through an attempt to control or guide economic property. As the leading entrepreneurial groups argued explicitly in the agrarian crisis of 1976, private sector forces would not brook an attempt by a populist regime to expropriate successful properties. The political constraint against meddling in the federal irrigation districts acted as a further qualifier limiting the state's constitutional authority (Article 27) to reform land tenure in a program of food self-sufficiency. From the outset, the political climate of the López Portillo administration stipulated that the irrigated areas dedicated to nonbasic foodstuffs and export crops would not be implicated in the SAM program. In fact, the SAM never argued for including the irrigation districts in a national plan guiding agricultural production under a public system of priorities. The shortcomings of such a perspective have been detailed in Chapters 2 and 4.

Another important determinant of the SAM mandate involved the creation of a "basic foodbasket" (*canasta básica recomendable*) as a standard for SAM incentives and nutritional goals. The SAM was empowered not simply to create better production in the countryside but to improve national nutrition and access to wholesome, cheap foodstuffs. In many instances, that meant including products in the SAM that had little relation to consumer needs in the countryside, and even less to domestic production priorities. The difficulties in fish marketing and consumption in Mexico, for example, were enormous, though the SAM was fond of citing the tremendous untapped resource that fish protein represented. Likewise, the availability and affordability of fresh citrus challenged the SAM's desire to include fresh fruit in every foodbasket. And, to the extent that the two dozen basic commodities reflected an urban bias (an inference easily drawn from the national income and expenditure survey cited earlier), the creation of a broad basic foodbasket diffused support for a rural development program in favor of a "display case" of the basic food groups every consumer should hope to enjoy.

A more important limiting factor in the SAM's mandate involved the mechanisms available to the SAM for steering. If the right of private property were to remain inviolate in the countryside and if agrarian reform were truly "dead" for the term of the López Portillo administration, then the most effective instruments available to the national state for controlling the content and direction of agricultural production would be the same tried and true mechanisms that had led to the agrarian crisis in the first place: price incentives, agricultural crop insurance, concessional credit, and parallel state structures to enhance production, marketing, storage, and distribution. Thus, the main bureaucratic instruments of SAM's field work became the SARH, CONASUPO, and the Ministry of Commerce. As we have already seen to some degree, price incentives and the other mechanisms outlined above have grave limits as well-targeted instruments of public policy toward agriculture.

Before explaining some of the explicit shortcomings of such policy instruments, however, we must finish the litany of constraining influences on the SAM. A critical addition to that list comes in the form of international trade and agribusiness integration—the heart of modern Mexican agricultural growth. In the area of trade, agricultural exports of fresh produce were still among the leading traditional sources of foreign exchange. Coffee, winter vegetables, and strawberries had weathered the storms that had eliminated basic grains from the export bill. In the context of a rapidly growing trade deficit and an overvalued exchange rate, fresh produce trade became more important as a bulwark against the total petrolization of exports. In the increasingly frantic drive to diversify markets and export commodities, the fresh produce traditionally associated with agricultural export enclaves was a natural source for a new wave of export promotion and agribusiness elaboration.

Given such a climate, the SAM was unable to separate its imperative in several crop areas, especially citrus and fresh vegetables, from the more general demands of the national economy in the early 1980s. On the import side, CONASUPO's traditionally heavy involvement in the import of basic grains led to its eventual monopoly over the Mexican grain trade. As a political colleague of the SAM, CONASUPO devised buying policies that took on an explicitly political tone; the agency overbought in 1980 in order to appear to have achieved self-sufficiency in 1981. As CONASUPO also managed coarse grains and their prices, the politics of sorghum purchases and production supports became part of the SAM package, even though they had little to do with the explicit goal structure of the organization.

If CONASUPO purchasing policies were a constraint to the success of the food self-sufficiency system (witness the implicit subsidy to foreign imports offered by CONASUPO in the 1960s and 1970s), a more serious constraint came from agribusiness growth itself. As we have remarked throughout the study, agribusiness growth meant further integration into the international capitalist system, both from the export imperative of "export substitution" plans of the Mexican government itself and from the internationalization of labor processes and technological standards in the agroindustrial complex. Not only were agricultural resources diverted from basic foodstuffs to exports, urban cash crops, and processing inputs, but the entire process of production in the countryside

261

became transformed at the hands of agribusiness processors and intermediaries, whose imperatives included increased profits, greater efficiencies, and rationalized supplies and markets. That meant, in addition to a further displacement of peasants, that the food system of Mexico was driven by the logic of profit and agribusiness expansion, not the values of equitable distribution and improved rural nutrition.

In this context, the agribusiness enterprise—whether agroindustrial processor or commercial agent—ignored the poor markets and inaccessible byways of rural Mexico and concentrated on the key markets of urban Mexico. While the production of Tlaxcala, Oaxaca, Chiapas, and other poor states was integrated into the agribusiness complex, the retail and income possibilities for the consuming poor there were nil. Mexican agribusiness, led by the transnational corporation, never included in its priorities the full extension of the consumer market and the remunerative rural wage labor that that extension would imply.

The final constraint to the SAM became apparent only after June 1981, with the first weaknesses of the international oil market. After that time, the SAM—along with every other Mexican government agency—fought a losing battle against the fundamental arbiter of social policy in Mexico: fiscal austerity. Perhaps it is slightly unfair to assume that the SAM would never have provided the wherewithal for independent rural production by the poor, given its short lifespan and the tremendous fiscal retreat suffered in the last eighteen months of its life. But the political point here is as old as the Cárdenas agrarian reform: as long as the *campesino* relies on the benevolent state apparatus for reform concessions (or food security and redistribution, in the case of the SAM), he will depend on its ability and political will to continue. In the case of the SAM, the fiscal drought of 1982 guaranteed that the programs instituted from the oil patronage dispensed since 1979 could not survive. Ironically, the SAM appeared as a partial response to the fiscal and exchange crisis of 1976 and disappeared as a result of the next crisis of that kind in 1982.

Of course, the fiscal constraint on SAM programs also implies a critique of the SAM's entire approach to the food question itself. The SAM was an essentially liberal redistribution and production program concentrating on the increase of rural production in key areas through the top-down subsidization of crucial inputs and prices. Such a liberal program requires an expanding economy and a national budget sturdy enough to handle the subsidies required. In addition, subsidy programs require effective management and production and price monitoring. As other countries have seen, recession, a change in political administrations, or declining export prices can all affect the ability of such liberal programs to continue with the kind of consistency required for genuine social change. Whether that social change was properly targeted or effectively channeled is another, related dispute.

The Mechanisms of the Sistema Alimentario Mexicano

The SAM began with a set of programs designed to produce more food for Mexico as a hedge against imports, to revive rural production in "marginal zones" defined by the program, and to enhance rural production in general through producer incentives and state intervention. In addition, the SAM hoped originally to improve Mexican nutrition generally, through ambitious designs of public information, attacks on alcoholism, restraints on media advertisements, and the like. Needless to say, in the short life of the SAM these latter goals never amounted to much more than program statements.

On the matter of production, the SAM is not susceptible to straightforward evaluation for several reasons. First, the SAM bureaucracy was only the central focus in a broad set of agencies involved in the food self-sufficiency campaign. SAM involved itself in projects ranging from agroindustrial development under the SARH to portable fruit juicer exhibitions under the CONAFRUT. In between were state purchasing programs in basic grains, improved warehousing of rural production, incentives to small retailers, subsidies to inputs, and a wide range of other programs implemented largely through formally decentralized bureaucratic agencies. Because of the diverse and administratively diffuse programs of the SAM, it is difficult to generalize about the overall state food security strategy at the aggregate level.

Second, it is extremely difficult to isolate SAM interventions in 1981 and 1982 to determine the effects of its crop subsidies and other direct programs on actual production. The harvest year 1981-1982 is generally cited as evidence of the potential successes of the SAM. But that year was blessed by generous and timely rains in addition to SAM programs. The following years' droughts threw the effectiveness of the SAM into question again. In order to evaluate the effectiveness of SAM incentives by themselves, a much broader historical span would be required, a social science luxury not permitted by the current circumstances of the Mexican economy under the de la Madrid administration.

Notwithstanding these formidable difficulties in evaluating the SAM, however, the complex of programs available to the Mexican state as an arbiter of increased production in the countryside was, indeed, limited. The bulk of the SAM's programs came in traditional form: price subsidies to producers, consumer price controls on basic products, expanded crop insurance, a "shared risk" producer incentive program, expanded public credit facilities for poor farmers, and direct management of key inputs from seeds to fertilizer. The political architecture of the SAM never addressed more fundamental questions of agrarian reform or redistribution of the key elements in agricultural production: water, land, access to extension, and so forth.

The form of the SAM programs also disappointed those who argued that the institutional corruption of the Mexican rural system itself provided a major obstacle to improved production and distribution. CONASUPO—for years criticized in its dealings with poor *campesinos*—expanded its influence in rural crop purchases, storage, transport, and distribution under the SAM. PRONASE, the national seed agency so notorious for its improperly treated or inadequately controlled seed, became the vehicle for the SAM's crucial program of improved seed distribution and management. The BANRURAL and FIRA—both well-known leaders in the political management of rural credit—provided the main channels of improved rural credit to the poor. In short, the weakness of the SAM was at least partly an institutional weakness revealed by its exclusive reliance on rural agencies that had, in fact, presided over the disastrous deterioration of rural life in the first place. The SAM's optimistic feeling that such agencies could somehow be transformed from the cooptative mechanisms of social control to the progressive vanguard of rural social change after four decades of evidence to the contrary staggers the imagination and gives credence to a cynical interpretation of the SAM as a sop to elite *campesinistas* and their partisans.

However, even if we accept (or disregard) the matter of intention and organizational potential, the SAM had a more fundamental problem that dogged it throughout its short life. In the style of other top-down blanket authorizations, the SAM had a problem of targeting: how could its programs be designed actually to benefit the intended recipients, and not be diverted in inordinate amounts to "free riders" in the form of rich agriculturalists? On this score, the record of the SAM seems mixed. Clearly, because of the "credit ladder" of the FIRA—by which credit was disbursed at progressively subsidized rates according to the income and capital of the recipient—the SAM was able to enhance the credit opportunities of some small producers, especially in long-term credit traditionally unavailable to them. But it must be remembered also that FIRA is partly a parallel financial agent to draw clients away from the BANRURAL, which is considered by *técnicos* to be the essence of rural corruption. FIRA's explicit bias is toward smallholders and upscale peasants, rather than the poorer clients of the countryside. Likewise, the new crop insurance program that came as a part of the SAM package probably enabled many small farmers to survive, in view of its generous provisions for payment without strict criteria for proof of planting. But its reach and benefit for the poorest of the poor are still open to question.

In other areas, the SAM was likewise unable to target its incentives properly, and mainly provided free riders with a windfall profit in basic goods. Its entire program of price incentives and input subsidies—from seed to fertilizer to pesticides—fell across the board as a boon to any producer who cared to take advantage of them. As a result, undoubtedly many large farmers benefited disproportionately from SAM programs intended to benefit the poor. In the Northwest, high prices for rice and its inclusion in the crop insurance program caused irrigation district farmers to quit vegetables for rice, in contradiction of the government's desire to discourage rice production in Sinaloa in favor of the tropical lowlands of the Gulf of Mexico. Likewise, many irrigation districts increased their corn plantings as a result of government subsidies, further confusing the evidence of SAM successes in marginal zones and raising questions as to the effective use of lands in irrigation districts.

On the consumer side, inadequate targeting was also common. In the price controls exercised over maize, tortillas, and *masa* (tortilla dough), much of the benefit went to chain outlets of tacos and other retailers. The bulk of the beneficiaries also tended to be urban, due partly to the ineffective controls exercised by the National Consumer Institute over prices. And, as always, CONASUPO goods were open to all consumers, regardless of income. Their concentration in wealthy areas and urban zones invariably has an upward class bias, given the Mexican income distribution.

More serious, however, were the deficiencies in the SAM's attempt to build agribusinesses in the countryside. Under the general aegis of the Comisión Nacional de Desarrollo Agroindustrial, the SAM sought to continue the tradition of rural industrialization begun under the import substitution experience and continued under Echeverría's "shared development" plan. The agroindustrial development plan of the SAM dedicated itself to improving the lot of the *campesino* through developing state agroindustries, better commercialization strategies, and alternatives to transnational agroindustrial development. Interestingly, the plan also embraced the goal of rationalizing rural production (also presumably a goal of private sector businesses), and proudly initiated its program with projects including 72 balanced animal feed factories, 155 packing sheds and fruit- and vegetable-processing factories, and 142 of the cryptic but suggestive "agroindustrial units for peasant women."[23] The state, through agroindustrial development, was openly engaged in the rationalized insertion of Mexican agricultural production into an internationalized agroindustrial complex, without any clear indication of understanding the potential consequences for the nature of rural life.

One of the starkest representations of the inadequacy of SAM programs to address the rural crisis as a crisis of agricultural integration into the international capitalist system—a principal point of departure in many SAM documents—came in a model proposed under the Comisión Nacional de Desarrollo Agroindustrial. Under the proposed "collective agroindustrial commercialization contracts" (*contratos de comercialización agroindustrial*) the state attempted to ensure the rationalization of commercial relationships between producers and agroindustries, with the intention of returning more value-added to the producer.[24] In fact, the tripartite structure of such contracts, reminiscent of collective-bargaining organization in Mexican industrial labor, and the specific goals of rationalizing supplies and markets in a program of advanced contracts, suggests a direct imitation of agroindustrial contract production in the private sector. Such agroin-

[23] Mexico, SARH, Comisión Nacional de Desarrollo Agroindustrial, *Plan Nacional de Desarrollo Agroindustrial*, 215-216.

[24] Mexico, SARH, Coordinación General de Desarrollo Agroindustrial, "Documento de enlace para apoyar la implantación del contrato de comercialización agroindustrial," Mexico, April 1981, mimeo.

dustrial contracting, from the viewpoint of this study and the broad base of literature on agroindustrial development in Latin America, has effects obviously contrary to the benefit of populations targeted under the SAM: it leads to the subordination of producers to industry, the disarticulation of production from rural consumption and nutrition, price competition among vulnerable producers, and the like. For the state to embrace such an imaginative program of collective agreements in the countryside, it must have had a rather modest vision of the reform aspects of food self-sufficiency and agroindustrial development, indeed.

THE MINIMUM REQUIREMENTS FOR AN ADEQUATE FOOD SECURITY PROGRAM

Although it is difficult to prove arguments in areas so fresh in history, a critique of the SAM must include some hypotheses offering resolution to its clearer shortcomings. These shortcomings themselves take as their standard the objective goals of greater income and nutrition for the rural poor and a separation from the unqualified integration of agriculture into the international system, goals openly accepted by the SAM. So the critique and proposals offered here do not adopt criteria more exaggerated or ambitious than those implicit in the food security program of the Mexican government itself.

First, this study and the brief life of the SAM suggest that, in order to constitute agriculture as a "public goods" sector for the above goals, the state must satisfy the following requisites.

1. The state must have the political power and will to control key sectors of production and the resources they draw upon. In the Mexican case, the clear implication is that the inadequate control of irrigation districts, water, and agricultural lands, despite the constitutional mandate permitting such control, resulted in the key

sectors of rural life operating under a market mandate inappropriate to food security.

2. The state must "steer" the system early and completely, in order to avoid the erosion of its power over the allocation of rural resources. The implementation of a huge program of rural improvement in the 1940s without any political mission to control the productive apparatus resulting from that program perhaps doomed the SAM thirty years before its birth.

3. State subsidies and programs for food production must be targeted specifically to the benefit of the rural poor in order to avoid the exaggeration of already-great inequalities in the countryside. Such targeting requires refined models of production demands and potential for each economic region, and must be separated from the political criteria of performance at the national level. That is, the revival of the "marginal *campesino*" must not rest with the national performance statistics often based on the concentration of SAM stimuli in the middle peasantry and among the agricultural bourgeoisie.

4. The nutritional and income distribution benefits implied in a food security program must also imply a relatively long-term counterflow of capital away from industry and urban centers to the countryside and small-scale agriculture. If the production of cheap foodstuffs for the urban population had such disastrous effects on the character of rural life throughout industrialization in Mexico, it is hard to see how such imbalances can be redressed without reclaiming the production of agricultural goods as use-values for local consumption and without restructuring the necessary inputs and assistance as a real public good targeted away from free riders among the agricultural bourgeoisie.

The entire issue of reapprehending agricultural production for national purposes and managing the "reform sector" of the agricultural economy as a producer of public goods (i.e.,

269

food and adequate nutrition in a publicly supervised program) leads us back to one of the original premises of this study: that national agricultural development in the broadest sense has been undermined by the internationalization of agriculture in Mexico. While some SAM documents nodded in the direction of international influences on domestic agricultural production, the entire execution of a food security program must base itself on the rejection of unqualified incorporation into the international economic order, dominated by the internationalization of capital itself. In turn, such a realization must be preceded by an understanding of the dynamics of Mexican agriculture, part of which was presented in this study. But, at a more programmatic level, we must understand as well the consequences of the conclusions of this analysis for the traditional course and argument of economic development.

In a more serious way, the shortcomings of the SAM are a product of the structure of Mexican politics itself. In general, comparative political economy has argued that the expansion of the public economy has responded to a progressive "bidding up" of fiscal responsibilities by an electorate mobilized and disposed to turn out state managers who do not attend to their demands.[25] In Mexico, of course, such a model does not apply. In fact, the process of "bidding up" the public agenda is conducted inside the government itself, within a single-party dominant state. In the event that *campesinistas* lose to *técnicos*, or "spending" ministries to "conserving" ministries, the entire political mandate for agricultural production may be lost. In the past two presidential administrations, the *agraristas* lost to the controllers of the budget and the *SAMistas* lost to the fiscal managers of López Portillo. While the discontinuity of Mexican administration allows for a new start and substantial program innovation every six years, such programs generally end up as political grist for the mill in a cabinet system characterized by continuous internal struggles. The

[25] Cameron, 1246.

political base for such programs of redistribution must be broader.

The other influence on the public economy in Mexico is external. Mexico, as a debtor country and as an agricultural system increasingly "open" to the international system, is influenced in its state strategies by external actors and processes. The effects of such externalities are clear. In an expansionary economy, the oil boom and its fiscal windfall allowed the Mexican government to ignore more conventional Keynesian strategies of reducing government expenditures during expansion. Instead, the government expanded social spending and created the SAM in large part as a checkbook political strategy for solving the rural question. There was no painful political process of raising taxes or reallocating scarce resources at the height of the oil boom. The mood was euphoric, and the financial criteria for state programs received less attention. At the same time, the oil boom allowed a redistributive veneer to hide the López Portillo government's reluctance to face the agrarian question squarely.

On the other hand, in times of fiscal austerity—such as pervades the Miguel de la Madrid administration for the foreseeable future—the mandate for such top-down programs evaporates, and little remains at the grassroots level. Popular organizations that might survive under austere budgets do not exist as a result of the SAM. Employment, nutrition, and other social benefits of the SAM have fallen to the red pencil of the IMF and the new president. And, while Mexico has become the first Third World debtor to "obey nurse" in the stabilization of 1983, the rural population has seen the medicine imposed in the form of lower real wages, fewer subsidies for production and consumption, and the general immiserization of low-income families.

In that sense, the oil boom's effect on the rural question did not enhance Mexico's autonomy. Nor did it provide a stable public economy for the provision of basic foodstuffs. The reconstructed state under the terms of fiscal austerity and

271

external stabilization will find the gains of the SAM to be a post-*agrarista* maneuver against the new international division of labor. And the state will have little institutional capability or political power to show for the transformation of Mexican agriculture.

Conclusion

The new administration of Miguel de la Madrid has swept away the euphoric faith in the SAM, if not the conviction that Mexico should attain some sort of meaningful "food security" in the 1980s. To a great extent the SAM was doomed by the international crisis following the fall of oil prices and the disastrous economic policies of the López Portillo administration. In a political system so characterized by bureaucratic positioning and internal power struggles, the SAM, as a little-appreciated newcomer to the administrative hierarchy of the Mexican state, had little chance to survive the greatest fiscal and payments crisis in recent Mexican memory. And, after the drought of 1982, SAM programs were revealed as a mixture of good subsidies and good weather, not as a source of solving the real "agrarian question" of rural Mexico.

So, in market year 1983 (July 1983-June 1984), Mexico imported an estimated 900,000 tons of wheat, 3.5 million tons of maize, and 2.5 million tons of sorghum.[1] The Mexican economy is expected to increase imports and consumption of basic grains throughout the 1980s and to increase consumption of animal protein and feedgrains as well. In each of these categories—basic grains and livestock—Mexico will probably be unable to meet demand with domestic production, with the possible exception of rice.[2]

Likewise, the general crisis of the Mexican economy portends at least a cost-price squeeze in basic commodities. On the one hand, the current administration has abandoned price

[1] USDA, "Grain and Feed Data Update," FAS Report, American Embassy in Mexico, December 1983, mimeo.

[2] Figures are based on unofficial USDA projections.

273

controls: since 1982 the prices of "controlled" items increased faster than free market prices. Practically unqualified price increases in basic foodstuffs have deepened the tremendous suffering occasioned by the economic crisis since 1981. But as stabilization proceeds, the mandate for reinstating real price controls in the current climate of inflation will further discourage the agricultural bourgeoisie of the federal irrigation districts and better rain-fed lands from planting basic crops, instead of the uncontrolled agroindustrial inputs and cattle feed crops that many of them concentrate on now. The logical tendency will be to shift away from price-administered items such as maize, wheat, rice, and other such commodities in favor of livestock, export commodities, and urban foodstuffs that are less price elastic. The impact of such a presumed shift is already being felt in the Mexican countryside. It demands a full-fledged analysis of the impact of economic stabilization strategies on agricultural production, popular nutrition, and state allocation of resources.

But, for all the severity of the current crisis, the focus of this study has not been on the periodic "shaking out" of the Mexican rural economy, in the context of the internationalization of capital, the petrolization of the Mexican "miracle," or the momentary liquidity problems of agroindustrial giants in and outside Mexico. In fact, this study has argued that the agricultural crisis of Mexico—whether considered as an employment, nutritional, distributive, or legitimation crisis—is the product of the everyday mechanisms of international integration, rather than the episodic shudders of world recession or the fluctuations of oil prices. Though the economic disaster that revealed itself in Mexico in late 1981 has, in fact, shaped the current agricultural crisis via the death of the SAM, the withdrawal of agricultural subsidies, and the like, the point of this study has been that *with or without the current economic crisis, there would be a continuing and deepening crisis of agricultural life in Mexico.* That crisis threatens not only the trade balance in agriculture but the very livelihood of the Mexican *campesino.*

Such a conclusion raises serious questions about the credibility of Mexico as an example of nonsocialist agrarian reform and broad-based Green Revolution experience. At a more systemic level, it raises questions about many of the principles of agricultural development and trade theory. In a word, the globalization of the Mexican food system has left the national state without competent mechanisms to govern rural growth and development.

The Gains from Trade

For the past several decades, developmentalists have argued that dynamic comparative advantage offers Third World economies the opportunity to diversify their trade bills, gain foreign exchange, reduce internal prices, and rationally allocate values for development, at least as far as neoclassical notions of "general welfare" allow.[3] While this study does not attempt to question the theoretical bases of comparative advantage per se, in the Mexican case we can see several implicit difficulties that follow from embracing such policies in agriculture. As comparative advantage assumes a bias toward free trade as a positive value, it is particularly apt to consider the merits of trade in the Mexican experience.

First, we have seen in the cases of winter vegetables and live cattle that Mexican producers and the state have chosen to favor exporting commodities in which a number of advantages are obvious. In the case of tomatoes and other winter vegetables, labor is plentiful and cheap, particularly under the

---

[3] The basics of the rich comparative advantage literature may be found in any textbook of international economics. Additional sources that provide interesting insights into Third World problems include Cathy L. Jabara and Robert L. Thompson, "Agricultural Comparative Advantage under International Price Uncertainty: The Case of Senegal," *American Journal of Agricultural Economics* 62:2 (May 1980); Timothy Josling, "World Trade in Basic Foodstuffs," *International Journal* 34:4 (Winter 1978-1979), 39-52; F. Mansour, "World Trade or Stable Agriculture?" *Ecologist Quarterly* 1:3 (August 1978), 187-203; Myint; and Aníbal Pinto, "The Opening up of Latin America to the Exterior," *CEPAL Review* 11 (August 1980), 31-56.

current regime of migratory wage labor. Technological benefits are readily assimilated in a market of free exchange among competitors from the United States. Water, fertilizer, agricultural extension, and pesticides have all been subsidized through various mechanisms, making Mexican export producers more competitive with their competitors in the United States. And, of course, regional comparative advantage must not be forgotten, as the winter vegetable industry sits in a favorable climate on a 2,000-mile border with the United States, near a burgeoning produce market.

In the case of live cattle, it is not the productivity of labor or its low cost that encourages the production of feeders for export to the United States. In addition to the regional advantage spun off from the change in cattle feeding in the United States, the separation of the northern Mexican cattlemen from the domestic market, their technological link with transnational corporations and southwestern U.S. feedlots, and the relative availability of low-cost land for cattle raising all have contributed to the rise of the frontier beef cattle complex. In other commodities—from garbanzo to table grapes— the viability of exports has been determined by the attractiveness of the U.S. market, a relationship due to the unique geographic attachment of two countries of such disparate wealth and power.

But, if we examine comparative advantage in the Mexican case from the perspective of domestic welfare in a broader sense, major questions arise as to the gains from trade. We can concede that foreign exchange is important to Third World economies. And, despite the deterioration of agriculture as a generator of foreign exchange, it still maintains great importance in an economy such as Mexico's. But, looking at the sector as a whole, we can see that the export promotion of agriculture has also played an important part in the concentration of agricultural resources in Mexico, the diversion of labor away from basic commodities, and the internationalization of much of the sector through trade. Thus, trade has also generated a dynamic by which Mexico is increasingly import dependent, as well as export dependent in agriculture. Gone are the days of relative food self-sufficiency in Mexico, and they are gone not only because of the diversion of resources to trade but because of the related inattention of the agricultural system to the productive and nutritive needs of the rural population being displaced by agricultural modernization.

The gains from trade can be faulted on another score as well. Insofar as cheap food policies contribute to a "stable" wage (i.e., low and slowly rising), agriculture shores up the export competitiveness of manufactures, in which Latin America—led by Brazil, Colombia, and Mexico—is seen to be a growing competitor in the 1980s and 1990s. To a certain extent, the export growth of Mexican manufactures will be carried on the back of Mexican agriculture and cheap food policies. In a more serious way, as we shall discuss shortly, exports in manufactures depend for inputs on agricultural commodities. Those inputs further deepen the insertion of domestic agriculture into the new international division of labor.

Thus, the gains from trade are problematic. They include foreign exchange, but with a new import dependence in agriculture as well. Trade generates employment, but at extremely low wages on a migratory labor circuit. Trade increases import capacity, but imports are insufficiently targeted to those displaced by the export-led aspect of Mexican agriculture. And, of course, a guiding principle of comparative advantage or free trade or export promotion ultimately has had to confront the prospect of not being able to import sufficient quantities of basic grains, now disarticulated from those who produce exportable agricultural commodities.

The Rise of Agribusiness

If trade has been an important traditional impulse to agricultural modernization in Mexico, agribusiness shares the credit. As we have seen throughout this study, one of the values of agricultural modernization has been to incorporate more of the Mexican agricultural system into a market nexus, guided and dominated by capitalist forces and relations of production. In commercial relations, brokers now rationalize production for the marketplace, whether for retail sale or processing. Agroindustries contract for production in many sectors of activity from tobacco to cattle feed. Agribusiness interests in general offer credit, technology, pesticides, and entire "packages" to farmers who have been described as contract laborers for the processing mill.

In this process of agribusiness growth, value is added to primary commodities, and production is undoubtedly made more efficient. Exports of manufactures—led by the food and beverage industries—are likewise enhanced by agribusiness growth. And off-farm jobs, the critical bellwether of industrial development strategy in Mexico's labor-abundant society, undoubtedly increase as a result of agroindustrial expansion. But the value that is added in agroindustrial processing or commercial sales rarely accrues to the farmer, as has been noted repeatedly in the United States and other agricultural systems. Industrial exports and manufactures for the domestic market have little to do with the nutritive needs or consumer possibilities of the rural population that creates the primary good in the first place. Contract markets improve price stability but also trap producers in a deeper web of commitment than auction prices without production contracting. And the generation of off-farm jobs in agroindustry has been all too modest for the capital invested in the sector. Of course, in Latin American policy circles, it goes without saying that the prominent role of transnational corporations in agribusiness is open to serious criticism.

In fact, the agricultural sector has been undone by industrialization and agribusiness development policies from the first. Import substitution gave tremendous subsidies to agribusiness "infant industries" that have rationalized agricultural production from avocados to *zempoaxochitl*. Transnational corporations participated and flourished in that environment, linking their growth to the transformation of the Mexican countryside and its integration into global strategies of accumulation. Simultaneously, Mexico, like other underdeveloped countries, reveled in the growing availability of "modern" consumer goods, such as wheat bread, canned vegetables and fruits, and fine industrial fibers that wove the production of cotton into synthetic blends impelling the stagnation of cotton as a leading Third World commodity. Through the transnational and national corporations in agribusiness processing and marketing, Mexicans and international consumers alike benefited from the growing farm sector, and fresh commodities found their ways to canneries and factories more often than to produce markets. The stagnation of the Mexican agricultural economy so often cited in traditional arguments about the food crisis did not come in those goods critical to agribusiness. Citrus for oil and frozen orange juice concentrate, pineapples for canned chunks and slices, strawberries for freezing and preserving—all these commodities grew rapidly, while the basic foodstuffs sector barely grew at all. And, of course, such agribusiness-processed commodities are rarely consumed in the countryside, and even more rarely contribute to a well-balanced and financially reasonable diet for the *campesino*.

The Character of State Intervention in Agriculture

Mexico is also a great example of state intervention in the agricultural sector. Not unlike other societies that come to industrialization late, Mexico has found a serious role for state financing, infrastructure, and industrial control since the 1930s. In agriculture, that control began with the creation of the federal irrigation districts and rural banking system in the 1920s, but only "took off" to assume its present form beginning in the presidency of Miguel Alemán (1946-1952). Similarly, the Mexican state has had a unique mandate over rural property since the inauguration of the revolutionary Constitution of 1917. These two forms of state intervention—

through the control of inputs and substantial public investment in the sector and through the constitutional capacity to
reform the control of economic property in the countryside—
have resulted in a high profile for the Mexican state, with
problematic effects.

Though such arguments are speculative, one of the con-
cluding hypotheses of this study is that the state was forced
to separate the productive transformation of agriculture
through economic subsidies and infrastructure from the political mandate to reform rural life. Such a forced separation
came from the very logic of capital accumulation in the private
sector, which demanded absolute security in private property
and the right to accumulate capital as prerequisites for investment. The corollary to this proposition is that, once the
state abandoned the connection between productive modernization and economic reform, it lost its fundamental steering
capacity to the private sector, which was simultaneously becoming more international by virtue of the very exigencies of
capital accumulation in Mexican agriculture.

The second hypothesis regarding state control is that the
high visibility of the state in agriculture makes it vulnerable
to a true legitimation crisis connected with the food crisis.
This is true, not only because of the long and deeply felt
agrarian reform tradition in Mexico, but because a state-in-
tervened agricultural sector implies that economic crisis be
laid at the feet of the state presiding over agricultural growth,
export promotion, and the allocation of public resources to
the sector.

The combination of this hypothesis with the first allows us
to view the fundamental difficulty of the Mexican state in
regard to the future of its agricultural sector: the economic
growth and productive success of agriculture is the burden of
the state, precisely at a time when its capacity to influence
such outcomes is undermined by the internationalization of
the economy and by its own restricted mandate to steer the
sector through controls over property. In fact, the separation
of production increases from agrarian reform leads to a highly

undesirable effect: the state's modes of intervention in the agricultural economy—price subsidies, purchasing programs, agroindustrial development—have been shown to *enhance* the internationalization of the Mexican agricultural system, not to challenge it.

The state, as we saw in several chapters, acts less as the spokesman for food security than as the intermediary for rationalizing production inputs to agroindustry, extending market networks into the countryside, standardizing technologies along international lines, and—to paraphrase former president López Portillo—"proletarianizing the *campesino* at a fair wage." Needless to say, oftentimes the lack of steering capacity, along with the exigencies of export competition, do not permit the state to monitor the fair wage as closely as necessary.

But if the state is left as the part-time manager—but not the owner—of the powerful Mexican agricultural complex, such an incomplete position must also reveal certain political directions for the 1980s. If the agricultural leadership of the Mexican state is to manage a real food security program— and its will to do so is open to question—it must challenge those leading elements of agricultural internationalization which have led to its weakening position and the dependence of Mexico's peasantry on a propitious future niche in agricultural capitalism. First, the "commanding heights" of the agricultural economy cannot continue to be the exclusive domain of the agribusiness giants of Mexico, whether we are speaking of Impulsora Agrícola or the *tomateros* of Sinaloa. Currently, the state maintains two standards in the irrigation districts, both flawed. On one hand, peasant credit, water, and other inputs are available only for crops deemed useful to the agencies of the state. Often this has meant that *campesinos* have gone without credit for beans, or contracts with CONASUPO for their purchases, or improved seed. On the other hand, the substantial national patrimony available for distribution in the federal irrigation districts—land, labor, credit, and water—has not been controlled in the case of the agribusiness enterprise. Private entrepreneurs escape government control largely through their financial independence and political power at the local level; and the agencies of the state rarely monitor or withhold key inputs with the same vigor applied to peasant farmers.

In fact, the model for allocation of Mexican agricultural resources in the countryside describes a market relationship, in which those entrants into the market with economic power do well, and those without do poorly. As of mid-1984, the allocation of agricultural resources under strong state supervision in Mexico has, in fact, never departed from a market model of distribution. If the market is supervised by the political authority of the SARH and its sibling agencies, the protection and nurture of economic power in the countryside has never been challenged by a full-fledged redistribution of resources, or a new model of distribution of future increments of growth. The determination of the Mexican state to deal with agriculture as a public good under the SAM was fatally flawed by the "impurity" of the good—i.e., its appropriability and divisibility according to market logic—and the incapacity of the state to steer the sector properly toward its professed political goals. This critique does not even challenge the more fundamental problem of whether the state's various agencies actually ever prosecuted the SAM honestly at all.

What such a challenge to market prerogatives and internationalizing agents might mean in Mexico is problematic. Clearly, few familiar with the Mexican agricultural landscape would advocate more centralized control over decision making among state agencies. Nor would a haphazard plan of irrigation district nationalization necessarily contribute to a solution to the current food crisis. In fact, to some degree, suggesting solutions to such a complex and historically well-formed crisis borders on arrogance. Two more parsimonious suggestions are apparent, however.

First, in order to move in the direction of food security, Mexico must husband its resources more carefully, which implies clearly less waste of water, land, and labor in exploitative and unremunerative—in the broad sense—activities such as the export of white asparagus and other luxury comestibles. A number of relatively modest political vehicles already tested in Mexico, from water rights management to crop insurance programs, might be used to effect such disincentives to the export of food security resources.

Second, in pursuing a "public goods" approach to agricultural resource allocation, the Mexican state must target recipients more acutely, withhold favor from rich free riders, and cement a progressive relationship in the countryside through the free formation of *campesino* political organizations. As has been noted by Mexican *campesinistas*, the SAM without peasant organization is ultimately useless to the rural dweller, as are other programs permanently dependent on the benevolence of the state.

Naturally, this discussion has assumed the formation of a much different political coalition at the national level than apparently guides Mexican agricultural policy today. The emergence of such a reform coalition presumes the national activity of the *campesino*, the aggravation of the rural crisis, and the inadequacy of the Mexican food system to sustain itself in the next two decades—all assumptions well within the potential political horizon of Mexico under the current presidential administration. The consequences of such a shift in the national political coalition to such a reform position would undoubtedly challenge some of the most basic assumptions of power since the failure of *echeverrismo*. But those are the topics of future study.

For now, the danger signals to Mexican rural life are clear. The "streamlined" PRONAL food program is led by *técnicos* in the Finance and Planning ministries, not by *campesinistas* or ministries with a traditional agrarian constituency. The Agriculture Ministry has been eclipsed by the president's multiagency *gabinete económico* in the indicative planning process; Agrarian Reform is a vestigial organ of traditional agrarian populism. And the rationalization of food security and rural development in such a political context has removed political power from the rural dweller, targeted wealthier peasants and agricultural capitalists as the proper clientele of the public rural credit system, and signaled an end to the expansion of the agricultural frontier. In the language of economic stabilization and "fiscal responsibility," the agricultural policy elite of the new administration has set the rural poor adrift and relegated the agrarian question to a back burner, where it will surely simmer.

Bibliography

PRIMARY SOURCES

Affidavit of the West Mexico Vegetable Distributors Association (WMVDA) to the U.S. Department of Commerce. May 29, 1979.

Banco Nacional de México (BANAMEX). *Examen de la situación económica de México.* Various issues.

Bergland, Robert. *A Time to Choose: Issues in the Structure of U.S. Agriculture.* Washington, D.C.: U.S. Department of Agriculture (USDA), 1981.

Brief of Respondents Union Nacional de Productores de Hortalizas and West Mexico Vegetable Distributors Association. Submitted to U.S. Department of Commerce, 1979.

"Consignment Sales Irk Bergland." *The Packer* 87:17 (April 26, 1980), 1.

Emerson, L. P. Bill, Jr. "Preview of Mexico's Vegetable Production for Export." USDA Foreign Agricultural Service Report, 1980.

Food Marketing Institute Brief to the U.S. Department of Commerce. February 29, 1980.

Hawkins, Wayne. "A Statement of the Florida Tomato Industry to the House Agricultural Committee Concerning the General Agricultural Situation in the United States as It Applies to Florida Tomatoes." February 9, 1978. Manuscript.

————. "Statement on the Views of the Florida Tomato Industry to the Subcommittee on Foreign Agricultural Policy of the Senate Committee on Agriculture, Nutrition and Forestry Concerning Imports of Tomatoes." March 22, 1978. Manuscript.

————. "Statement on the Views of the Florida Tomato Industry to the Subcommittee on Trade of the House Committee on Ways and Means Concerning Relief from Unfair Trade Practices." April 12, 1978. Manuscript.

Inter-American Development Bank (IDB). *Economic and Social Progress in Latin America.* Washington, D.C.: IDB, 1981.

BIBLIOGRAPHY

Inter-American Development Bank (IDB). *Economic and Social Progress in Latin America: The External Sector.* Washington, D.C.: IDB, 1982.

————. *Nutrition and Economic Development in Latin America.* Washington, D.C.: IDB, 1978.

Kredietbank. "The New International Division of Labor." Kredietbank *Weekly Bulletin* 33:37 (October 6, 1978).

McDonald, Alonzo. "U.S. Agriculture's Stake in the MTN." *U.S. Department of State Bulletin* 79 (August 1979).

Mexico. "Decreto por el que se reforma, adiciona y deroga diversas disposiciones de la Ley Federal de Reforma Agraria." *Diario oficial,* January 17, 1984.

————. "Ley de fomento agropecuario." *Diario oficial,* December 29, 1980.

————. "Ley federal de reforma agraria de 22 de marzo de 1971." *Diario oficial,* May 1, 1971.

————. "Reglamento de inafectabilidad agrícola y ganadera del 23 de septiembre de 1948." *Diario oficial,* October 9, 1948.

————. Banco de México, S.A. *La distribución del ingreso en México.* Mexico: Fondo de Cultura Económica, 1974.

————. *Informe anual.* Various years.

————. Banco Nacional de Comercio Exterior (BNCE). "Piña enlatada." *Comercio exterior,* April 1980, 403-411.

————. Cámara Nacional de Industrias de Transformación (CANACINTRA). Sección de Fabricantes de Alimentos para Animales. *La industria alimenticia animal en México (en cifras).* Mexico: CANACINTRA, 1978.

————. CONASUPO. *CONASUPO en cifras.* Mexico: CONASUPO, 1982, 1983.

————. Coordinación General del Plan Nacional de Zonas Deprimidas y Grupos Marginados (COPLAMAR). *Mínimos de bienestar.* Six volumes. Mexico: Secretaría de la Presidencia, 1979.

————. Instituto Mexicano de Comercio Exterior (IMCE). *El comercio exterior y los comités para la promoción de las exportaciones.* Mexico: IMCE, September 1980.

————. Nacional Financiera, S.A. (NAFINSA). *La economía mexicana en cifras.* Mexico: NAFINSA, 1978, 1981, 1982.

————. Oficina de Asesores del C. Presidente. Sistema Nacional de Evaluación, Sistema Alimentario Mexicano (SINE-SAM). "La exportación de becerros y sus alternativas de engorda." Two volumes. November 1980. Mimeo.

————. *El Sistema Alimentario Mexicano: primer plantamiento de metas de consumo y estrategía de producción de alimentos básicos para 1980-1982*. Mexico: SINE-SAM, March 1, 1980.

————. "Sistema global de alimentos para ganado." Mexico, September 1981. Discussion document.

————. "Sistema integral de carne de ganado bovino." Five volumes. Mexico, May 1981. Discussion document.

————. Presidencia de la República. "Decreto por el que se reforman y adicionan varios artículos de la ley federal de reforma agraria." *Diario oficial*, December 11, 1980.

————. Secretaría de Agricultura y Ganadería (SAG). *El extensionismo pecuario en la situación actual de la ganadería nacional y en su proyección para 1983*. Mexico: SAG, 1976.

————. *Plan nacional ganadero, 1975-1980. Bovinos productores de carne*. Mexico: SAG, 1975.

————. *Síntesis de la problemática de la ganadería bovina productora de carne en México*. Mexico: SAG, 1976.

————. Secretaría de Agricultura y Recursos Hidráulicos (SARH). *Anuario estadístico: Año agrícola 1977-1978*. Mexico: SARH, 1979.

————. *Anuario estadístico de la población pecuaria de los Estados Unidos Mexicanos*. Mexico: SARH, 1977.

————. *Anuario estadístico de la producción agrícola de los Estados Unidos Mexicanos, 1977*. Mexico: SARH, 1979.

————. *Determinación de los precios de garantía para los productos del campo*. Mexico: SARH, 1978.

————. "Documento de enlace para apoyar la implantación del contrato de comercialización agroindustrial." Mexico: Coordinación General de Desarrollo Agroindustrial, April 1981. Mimeo.

————. *Econotecnia agrícola: consumos aparentes de productos agrícolas para los años de 1925-1978*. Mexico: SARH, 1979.

————. *Econotecnia agrícola: panorama sobre el comportamiento del sector agropecuario nacional, 1977-1979 y algunas consideraciones sobre el mercado internacional*. Mexico: SARH, 1980.

————. *Estadística agrícola en los distritos y unidades de riego*. Mexico: Dirección General de Distritos y Unidades de Riego, various years.

————. *Estadística pecuaria en las unidades de riego. Ciclo agrícola 1977-1978*. Mexico: SARH, 1980.

Mexico. *Estudio de mercado de la uva.* Mexico: SARH, 1974.

——. *Informes de labores de la Secretaría de Agricultura y Ganadería.* Mexico: SARH, 1979.

——. *Ley de fomento agropecuario.* Mexico: SARH, 1981.

——. *Ley federal de aguas.* Publicación legal #13. Mexico: SARH, 1972.

——. *Plan nacional de desarrollo agroindustrial.* Mexico: Comisión Nacional de Desarrollo Agroindustrial, 1980.

——. *Programa siembra-exportación de tomate, temporada 1978-1979.* Mexico: SARH, 1979.

——. "Valorización de la producción agrícola, año agrícola 1980: datos estimativos." Mexico, 1981. Mimeo.

——. *Valorización de producción de cultivos.* Mexico: SARH, 1979.

——. Secretaría de Industria y Comercio (SIC). *V censo agrícola, ganadero, y ejidal, 1970.* Mexico: Dirección General de Estadística, 1972.

——. *IX censo general de población, 1970.* Mexico: Dirección General de Estadística, 1972.

——. Secretaría de la Presidencia. *Cuarto informe de gobierno del C. José López Portillo. Anexo III.* Mexico: Secretaría de la Presidencia, 1980.

——. *Quinto informe de gobierno del C. José López Portillo. Anexo III.* Mexico: Secretaría de la Presidencia, 1980.

——. Secretaría de Programación y Presupuesto (SPP). *Agenda estadística.* Mexico: SPP, 1977.

——. *Manual de estadísticas básicas: sector agropecuario y forestal.* Mexico: SPP, 1979.

——. *Manual de estadísticas básicas de la economía mexicana.* Volume II. *Sector industrial.* Mexico: SPP, 1981.

——. *México: estadística económica y social por entidad federativa.* Mexico: SPP, 1981.

——. *La población de México, su ocupación, y sus niveles de bienestar.* Mexico: SPP, 1979.

——. *El sector alimentario en México.* Mexico: SPP, 1981.

——. SPP and Banco de México, S.A. *Sistema de cuentas nacionales de México.* Volume I. *Resumen general.* Mexico: SPP, 1981.

——. Secretaría de Recursos Hidráulicos (SRH). *Estudio de mercado de la piña.* Mexico: SRH, 1974.

————. Unión Nacional de Empacadoras, T.I.F. (UNE). *Industria-lización del ganado en México*. Mexico: UNE, 1970.

New York Herald. October 8, 1847.

United Nations. Centre on Transnational Corporations. *Transna-tional Corporations in Food and Beverage Processing*. New York: U.N., 1981.

————. Comisión Económica para América Latina (CEPAL). "Las empresas transnacionales en la agroindustria mexicana." Mexico, May 1981. Mimeo.

————. *La industria de la carne de ganado bovino en México*. Mexico: Fondo de Cultura Económica, 1975.

United States. Agricultural and Food Act of 1981 (95 Stat. 1213).

————. Federal Meat Inspection Act (52 Stat. 1235). 1964.

————. The Wholesome Meat Act (81 Stat. 584). 1964.

————. Congress. Senate Committee on Agriculture and Forestry. Hearings. *Policies and Operations of PL 480*. 84th Cong., 1st sess., 1957.

————. Department of Agriculture (USDA). *Agricultural Situation: Western Hemisphere. Review of 1980 and Outlook for 1981*. Washington, D.C.: Economic Research Service, 1981.

————. "Brazil: Agricultural Situation, 1981." Foreign Agricultural Service Report. American Embassy, Brasilia, March 5, 1982. Mimeo.

————. "Canned Pineapple." Foreign Agricultural Service Report #MX-0020. American Embassy in Mexico, 1980. Mimeo.

————. *Cattle on Feed*. Washington, D.C.: Statistical Reporting Service, January 18, 1982.

————. *Citrus in Mexico*. Foreign Agricultural Service Report. May 1981.

————. *Country Market Profile: Mexico*. Washington, D.C.: Economic Research Service, 1982.

————. "FAS Official Sees Bright Oilseed Export Outlook." *Foreign Agriculture* 16:8 (September 1978), 2-3.

————. "Feeding Trials Boost Mexican Use of U.S. Soybean Meal." *Foreign Agriculture* 16:8 (August 1978), 8-9.

————. "Grain and Feed Data Update." Foreign Agricultural Service Report. American Embassy in Mexico, December 1983. Mimeo.

————. *Livestock and Meat Situation*. Various years.

————. "Meat Boom Sparking Latin American Demand for U.S. Soy Products." *Foreign Agriculture* 16:7 (July 1978), 2-5.

BIBLIOGRAPHY

United States. "The Mexican Beef Cattle Industry." *Foreign Agriculture* 8:11 (November 1944), 244-265.

———. "Mexican Government Concerned over Lag in Meat Production." *Foreign Agriculture* 18:4 (April 1980), 10-11.

———. *Mexico: Agricultural and Trade Policies.* Foreign Agricultural Service Report #306. October 1981.

———. "Mexico: Annual Feed and Grain Report." Foreign Agricultural Service Report #MX-1028. American Embassy in Mexico, June 9, 1981. Mimeo.

———. "Mexico: Pineapple Report." Foreign Agricultural Service Report #MX-1015. American Embassy in Mexico, April 2, 1981. Mimeo.

———. *Mexico's Livestock and Meat Industry.* Foreign Agricultural Service Report #M-27. November 1957.

———. "Mexico's Transportation System Strains to Meet Demands of Booming Economy, Rising Trade." *Foreign Agriculture* 18:10 (October 1980), 10-11.

———. "Pineapple Voluntary Report." Foreign Agricultural Service Report #MX-1037. American Embassy in Mexico, 1981. Mimeo.

———. Untitled memorandum. July 17, 1979.

———. Untitled memorandum from Under Secretary for International Affairs and Commodity Programs to Deputy Secretary of Agriculture. May 30, 1979.

———. *U.S. Fed Beef Production Costs, 1976-77, and Industry Structure.* Agricultural Economic Report #424. Washington, D.C.: Economics, Statistics and Cooperatives Service (ESCS), June 1979.

———. "U.S., Mexico Sign First Trade Agreement in 35 Years." *Foreign Agriculture* 16:3 (March 1978), 7-9.

———. Department of Commerce. International Trade Commission (ITC). *Conditions of Competition in U.S. Markets between Domestic and Foreign Live Cattle and Cattle Meat for Human Consumption.* Washington, D.C.: U.S. Government Printing Office, 1977.

———. *U.S. Imports for Consumption and General Imports.* Washington, D.C.: Bureau of the Census, various years.

Zepp, G. A. and Simmons, R. L. *Producing Fresh Tomatoes in California and Baja California: Costs and Competition.* USDA Economics, Statistics, and Cooperatives Service (ESCS) Report. February 1980.

————. *Producing Fresh Winter Vegetables in Florida and Mexico: Costs and Competition*. USDA ESCS Report. November 1979.

SECONDARY SOURCES

Agribusiness Associates, Inc. *The Poultry Breeding Industry and Mexican Development*. Wellesley Hills, Mass.: Agribusiness Associates, 1981.

Aguilar Camín, Héctor. *La frontera nómada: Sonora y la revolución mexicana*. Mexico: Siglo XXI, 1977.

Alt, James E. and Chrystal, K. Alec. *Political Economics*. Berkeley and Los Angeles: University of California Press, 1983.

Anderson, Alexander D. *Mexico from the Material Standpoint*. N.p., 1884. Pamphlet.

Andrews, Bruce. "The Political Economy of World Capitalism: Theory and Practice." *International Organization* 36:1 (Winter 1982), 135-163.

Applebaum, Harvey, and Victor, A. Paul, editors. *Basics of Antidumping and Other Import Relief Laws: Multilateral Trade Negotiations Update*. New York: Practicing Law Institute, 1979.

Arnould, Richard J. "Changing Patterns of Concentration in American Meatpacking, 1880-1963." *Business History Review* 45 (Spring 1971), 18-34.

Arriola, Carlos. "Los grupos empresariales frente al estado mexicano, 1973-1975." In El Colegio de México, Centro de Estudios Internacionales, *Las fronteras del control del estado mexicano*, 33-81.

"Asparagus Acreage Drop Associated with Imports." *Western Grower and Shipper* 52:2 (February 1981), 14-15.

Assael, Hector. "The Internationalization of the Latin American Economies: Some Reservations." CEPAL *Review* 7 (April 1979), 41-55.

Austin, James E. *Agribusiness in Latin America*. New York: Praeger, 1974.

Aziz, Sartaj, editor. *Hunger, Politics and Markets: The Real Issues in the Food Crisis*. New York: New York University Press, 1975.

Bailey, John J. "Agrarian Reform in Mexico: The Quest for Self-

Sufficiency." *Current History* 80:469 (November 1981), 357-360ff.

———, and Roberts, Donna H. "Mexican Agricultural Policy." *Current History* 82:488 (December 1983), 420-424ff.

Bancroft, Hubert Howe. *History of Arizona and New Mexico, 1530-1888.* Albuquerque: Horn and Wallace, 1962. Reprint of 1889 edition.

Barchfield, John W. *Land Tenure and Social Productivity in Mexico.* University of Wisconsin Land Tenure Center Paper #121. Madison, 1979.

Barkin, David. *Desarrollo regional y reorganización campesina: La Chontalpa como reflejo del problema agropecuario mexicano.* Mexico: Editorial Nueva Imagen, 1978.

———. "Mexico's Albatross: The U.S. Economy." *Latin American Perspectives* 2:2 (Summer 1975), 64-80.

Barkin, David, and Esteva, Gustavo. "El papel del sector público en la comercialización y la fijación de precios de los productos agrícolas básicos en México." Mexico: U.N. CEPAL, 1981. Mimeo.

Barkin, David, and King, Timothy. *Regional Economic Development: The River Basin Approach in Mexico.* Cambridge: Cambridge University Press, 1970.

Barkin, David, and Rozo, Carlos. "L'agriculture et l'internationalization du capital." *Revue tiers-monde* 88 (October-December 1981), 723-745.

———. "La producción de alimentos y la internacionalización del capital." *Trimestre económico* 50:3 (1983), 1603-1626.

Barkin, David, and Suárez, Blanca. *El complejo de granos en México.* Mexico: Centro de Ecodesarrollo, 1979.

———. *El fin de autosuficiencia alimentaria.* Mexico: Editorial Nueva Imagen, 1982.

Bee, Edward. "Prospects for Basin Fresh Vegetable Exports." Federal Reserve Bank of Atlanta *Caribbean Basin Economic Survey* 4:4 (July-August 1978), 12-15.

"Beef Extra: The Changing Face of Cattle Feeding." *Farm Journal* 106:1 (January 1982), 1-4ff.

Benassini, Oscar. "Estudio general de gran visión del aprovechamiento de los recursos hidráulicos del Noroeste." *Ingeniería hidráulica en México* 8:4 (1954), 18-31.

Berlan, Jean Pierre, Bertrand, Jean Pierre, and Lebas, Laurence. "The

Growth of the American 'Soybean Complex.' " *European Review of Agricultural Economics* 4:4 (1977), 395-416.

Bhagwati, Jagdish N., editor. *The New International Economic Order: The North-South Debate*. Cambridge, Mass.: MIT Press, 1977.

Billington, Ray A. *Westward Expansion: A History of the American Frontier*. Fourth Edition. New York: MacMillan, 1974.

Bluestone, Barry, and Harrison, Bennet. *The Deindustrialization of America*. New York: Basic Books, 1982.

Bowles, Samuel, Gordon, David M., and Weiskopf, Thomas E. *Beyond the Wasteland: A Democratic Alternative to Economic Decline*. New York: Doubleday, Anchor, 1983.

Brack, Gene M. *Mexico Views Manifest Destiny, 1821-1846: An Essay on the Origins of the Mexican War*. Albuquerque: University of New Mexico Press, 1975.

Brand, Donald D. "The Early History of the Range Cattle Industry in Northern Mexico." *Agricultural History* 35:3 (July 1961), 132-139.

"Broiler Boom in Mexico." *Poultry International* (May 1980).

Burbach, Roger, and Flynn, Patricia. *Agribusiness in the Americas*. New York: Monthly Review Press, 1980.

Business International. *Trading in Latin America: The Impact of Changing Policies*. New York: Business International Corporation, 1981.

Cameron, David. "The Expansion of the Public Economy: A Comparative Analysis." *American Political Science Review* 72:4 (December 1978), 1243-1261.

Caporaso, James A., editor. "Dependence, Dependency and Power in the Global System: A Structural and Behavioral Analysis." Special issue of *International Organization* 32:1 (Winter 1978), 13-44.

———. "Industrialization in the Periphery: The Evolving Global Division of Labor." *International Studies Quarterly* 25:3 (September 1981), 347-384.

Cardoso, Fernando Henrique, and Faletto, Enzo. *Dependency and Development in Latin America*. Berkeley and Los Angeles: University of California Press, 1979.

Cauley, T. J. "Early Business Methods in the Texas Cattle Industry." *Journal of Economic and Business History* 4 (November 1931-August 1932), 461-486.

Ceceña C., José Luis, et al. *Sinaloa: crecimiento y desperdicio.* Mexico: UNAM, Instituto de Investigaciones Económicas, 1973.

Centro de Investigaciones Agrarias (CDIA). *Estructura agraria y desarrollo agrícola en México.* Mexico: Fondo de Cultura Económica, 1974.

Chávez, Adolfo. "Nutrición: problemas y alternativas." In Pablo González Casanova and Enrique Florescano, editors, *México, hoy.* Mexico: Siglo XXI, 1979.

Chayanov, Alexander. *The Theory of Peasant Economy.* Daniel Thorner et al., editors. Homewood, Ill.: Richard D. Irwin, 1966.

Chevalier, François. *Land and Society in Colonial Mexico: The Great Hacienda.* Translated by Alvin Eustis. Edited by Lesley B. Simpson. Berkeley and Los Angeles: University of California Press, 1963.

Chilcote, Ronald H., and Edelstein, Joel C., editors. *Latin America: The Struggle with Dependency and Beyond.* Cambridge, Mass.: Shenkman, 1974.

Choi, Wonyoung. "The Cattle Cycle." *European Review of Agricultural Economics* 4:2 (1977), 119-136.

Cline, Howard. "The 'Aurora Yucateca' and the Spirit of Enterprise in Yucatan, 1821-1847." *Hispanic American Historical Review* 27:1 (February 1947), 30-60.

Coatsworth, John. "Railroads, Landholding, and Agrarian Protest in the Early Porfiriato." *Hispanic American Historical Review* 54:1 (February 1974), 48-71.

Collier, David, editor. *The New Authoritarianism in Latin America.* Princeton, N.J.: Princeton University Press, 1979.

Conner, J. Richard, and Rogers, Robert W. "Ground Beef: Implications for the Southeastern U.S. Beef Industry." *Southern Journal of Agricultural Economics* 11:2 (December 1979), 21-26.

Connor, Seymour V., and Faulk, Odie. *North America Divided: The Mexican War, 1846-1848.* New York: Oxford University Press, 1971.

Cooper, Richard N. *The Economics of Interdependence.* New York: Columbia University Press, 1980.

Corbett, Jack. "Policy Implementation in a Complex Environment: Production Incentives and the Sistema Alimentario Mexicano." Paper delivered at the Western Social Science Association Meeting, April 1982.

Córdova, Arnaldo. *La política de masas del cardenismo*. Mexico: Ediciones ERA, 1974.

Cosío Villegas, Daniel, editor. *Historia moderna de México*. Mexico: Editorial Hermes, various years.

Cossío Silva, Luis. "La agricultura." In Daniel Cosío Villegas, editor, *Historia moderna de México*, Volume VIII, Tome I, second edition. *El porfiriato: la vida económica*. Mexico: Editorial Hermes, 1974.

Dabdoub, Claudio. *Historia del valle del Yaqui*. Mexico: Editorial Porrúa, 1964.

Dahlberg, Kenneth. *Beyond the Green Revolution: The Ecology and Politics of Global Agricultural Development*. New York and London: Plenum Press, 1979.

Dale, Edward Everett. *Cow Country*. Norman: University of Oklahoma Press, 1943.

———. *The Range Cattle Industry*. Norman: University of Oklahoma Press, 1930.

de Janvry, Alain. *The Agrarian Question and Reformism in Latin America*. Baltimore: The Johns Hopkins University Press, 1981.

———. "Agriculture in Crisis." *Society* 17:6 (September-October 1980).

de la Peña, Sergio. *La formación del capitalismo en México*. Second edition. Mexico: Siglo XXI, 1976.

Destler, I. M. "United States Food Policy, 1972-1976: Reconciling Domestic and International Objectives." In Raymond F. Hopkins and Donald J. Puchala, editors, *The Global Political Economy of Food*, 41–77.

Díaz Polanco, Héctor. "Estructura de clases y comercialización: un caso mexicano." In Ursula Oswald, editor, *Mercado y dependencia*, 125-164.

———. *Teoría marxista de la economía campesina*. Mexico: Editorial Juan Pablos, 1977.

Dietrich, R. A., Martin, J. R., and Ljungdahl, P. W. *The Capital Structure and Financial Management Practices of the Texas Cattle Feeding Industry*. College Station: Texas Agricultural Experiment Station, December 1972.

Dobie, J. Frank. *The Longhorns*. Austin: University of Texas Press, 1980. Reprint.

Dorronsoro, José María. "La mecanización de la agricultura en los distritos de riego en México." *Ingeniería hidráulica en México* 18:1-2 (January-June 1964), 102-111.

Dougherty, James E., and Pfaltzgraff, Robert L., Jr. *Contemporary Theories of International Relations*. Second edition. Philadelphia: Lippincott, 1980.

Downs, Robert B. "Afterword" to Upton Sinclair, *The Jungle*. New York: Signet, 1960.

Dyer, I. A., and O'Mary, C. C., editors. *The Feedlot*. Philadelphia: Lea and Febiger, 1977.

Ebeling, Walter. *The Fruited Plain: The Story of American Agriculture*. Berkeley and Los Angeles: University of California Press, 1980.

Eckstein, Salomón. *El ejido colectivo en México*. Mexico: Fondo de Cultura Económica, 1966.

El Colegio de México. *Estadísticas económicas del porfiriato*. Volume I. *El comercio exterior de México, 1877-1911*. Mexico: El Colegio de México, 1960.

——. *Estadísticas económicas del porfiriato*. Volume II. *Fuerza de trabajo y actividad económica por sectores*. Mexico: El Colegio de México, 1963.

——. *Estadísticas sociales del porfiriato*. Mexico: El Colegio de México, 1966.

——. Centro de Estudios Internacionales. *Las fronteras del control del estado mexicano*. Mexico: El Colegio de México, 1976.

Emerson, L. P. Bill, Jr. "Grape Output in Mexico Rising Rapidly." *Foreign Agriculture* 18:9 (September 1979).

——. "Mexican Strawberry Industry Strong Despite Problems." *Foreign Agriculture* 16:7 (July 31, 1978), 2-4.

Esteva, Gustavo. "La experiencia de la intervención estatal reguladora en la comercialización agropecuaria de 1970 a 1976." In Ursula Oswald, editor, *Mercado y dependencia*, 207-246.

——. *The Struggle for Rural Mexico*. Mexico: V World Congress of Rural Sociology, 1980.

Evans, Peter. *Dependent Development: The Alliance of Multinational, State, and Local Capital in Brazil*. Princeton, N.J.: Princeton University Press, 1979.

Fagen, Richard R. "Mexico and the United States: The Inescapable Relationship." *Wilson Quarterly* 3:3 (July 1979).

——, editor. *Capitalism and the State in U.S.-Latin American Relations*. Stanford: Stanford University Press, 1979.

Falcón, Romana. *El agrarismo en Veracruz: la etapa radical, 1928-1935.* Mexico: El Colegio de México, 1977.

Feder, Ernest. *El imperialismo fresa.* Mexico: Editorial Campesina, 1977.

———. *Lean Cows, Fat Ranchers: The International Ramifications of Mexico's Beef Cattle Industry.* Berlin: Research Institute of the Berghof Stiftung for Conflict Research, 1978.

Feinberg, Richard. *The Intemperate Zone: The Third World Challenge to U.S. Foreign Policy.* New York: Norton, 1983.

Fernández Ortiz, Luis Má., and Tarrio G. de Fernández, María. "Cattle Raising, Farmers, and Basic Grain Products: A Study in Chiapas." Mexico, 1980. Manuscript.

———. "Ganadería y estructura agraria en Chiapas." Mexico, 1979. Manuscript.

Ferns, H. S. *Britain and Argentina in the Nineteenth Century.* London: Cambridge University Press, 1960.

Fitzgerald, E.V.K. "Oil and Mexico's Industrial Development Plan." *Texas Business Review* (May-June 1980).

Fogarty, John. "Staple Theory and the Development Experiences of Argentina, Australia and Canada." Paper delivered at the International Congress of Americanists, Manchester, England, September 1982.

Ford, A. G. "British Investment and Argentine Economic Development, 1880-1914." In David Rock, editor, *Argentina in the Twentieth Century*, 12-40.

Fornari, Harry D. "The Big Change: From Cotton to Soybeans." *Agricultural History* 53:1 (January 1979).

Foweraker, Joe. *The Struggle for Land: A Political Economy of the Pioneer Frontier in Brazil from 1930 to the Present Day.* Cambridge: Cambridge University Press, 1981.

Frank, André Gunder. *The Development of Underdevelopment.* New York: Monthly Review, 1966.

Fuller, John D. P. *The Movement for the Acquisition of All Mexico, 1846-1848.* Baltimore: The Johns Hopkins University Press, 1936.

Furtado, Celso. *Economic Development of Latin America.* Second edition. Cambridge: Cambridge University Press, 1976.

Galtung, Johan. "A Structural Theory of Imperialism." *Journal of Peace Research* 2 (1971), 81-118.

Girvan, Norman. *Corporate Imperialism: Conflict and Expropriation.* White Plains, N.Y.: M. E. Sharpe, 1976.

Goldberg, Ray. *Agribusiness Management for Developing Countries—Latin America.* Cambridge, Mass.: Ballinger, 1974.

Gomes, Gerson, and Pérez, Antonio. "The Process of Modernization in Latin American Agriculture." CEPAL *Review* 8 (August 1979), 55-74.

González Navarro, Moisés. *La Confederación Nacional Campesina: un grupo de presión en la reforma agraria mexicana.* Mexico: Costa-Amic, 1968.

Goodman, Louis W., and Domike, Arthur. *The Improved Seed Industry: Issues and Options for Mexico.* A Document of the Joint Program of SINE-American University, Center for International Technical Cooperation. Washington, D.C.: The American University, 1982.

Goodman, Louis W., Sanderson, Steven E., and Shwedd, Kenneth. *Agricultural Policy Making in Mexico.* Monograph prepared as a part of a Joint Agreement between the Economic Research Service, USDA, and the Latin American Program of the Woodrow Wilson International Center for Scholars, Washington, D.C., 1985.

Gregg, Josiah. *Commerce of the Prairies.* Dallas: Southwest Press, 1933. Reprint of 1844 edition.

Griffin, Keith. *The Political Economy of Agrarian Change: An Essay on the Green Revolution.* Cambridge, Mass.: Harvard University Press, 1974.

Grindle, Merilee Serrill. *Bureaucrats, Politicians and Peasants in Mexico: A Case Study in Public Policy.* Berkeley and Los Angeles: University of California Press, 1977.

"Hands Off the IMF." *The Economist* 284:7253 (September 4, 1982), 15-16.

Heimpel, Gretchen. "Mexico: Agricultural and Trade Policies." USDA Foreign Agricultural Service Report, 1981.

Helleiner, G. K. "Transnational Enterprises and the New Political Economy of U.S. Trade Policy." *Oxford Economic Papers* 29:1 (March 1977).

Herz, John H. "Political Realism Revisited." Symposium in Honor of Hans J. Morgenthau. *International Studies Quarterly* 25:2 (June 1981), 182-197.

Hewitt de Alcántara, Cynthia. *Modernizing Mexican Agriculture:*

Socioeconomic Implications of Technological Change, 1940-1970. Geneva: United Nations Research Institute for Social Development, 1976.

Hirschman, Albert O. "The Turn to Authoritarianism in Latin America and the Search for its Economic Determinants." In David Collier, editor, *The New Authoritarianism in Latin America*, 61-98.

Hopkins, Raymond F., and Puchala, Donald J. *Global Food Interdependence: Challenge to American Foreign Policy.* New York: Columbia University Press, 1980.

————, editors. *The Global Political Economy of Food.* Madison: University of Wisconsin Press, 1978.

Hymer, Stephen. "The Internationalization of Capital." *Journal of Economic Issues* 6:1 (March 1972), 91-111.

"Increased World Livestock Needs Will Strengthen U.S. Grain Trade, Study Says." *Feedstuffs* 53:14 (April 6, 1981), 9.

Jabara, Cathy L., and Thompson, Robert L. "Agricultural Comparative Advantage under International Price Uncertainty: The Case of Senegal." *American Journal of Agricultural Economics* 62:2 (May 1980).

Jackson, Hillard, and Malphrus, Lewis D. *The South's Hog-Pork Industry and Vertical Coordination.* Southern Cooperative Series Bulletin #179 (September 1973), 20-22.

Jardines Moreno, José Luis. "Los distritos de riego por bombeo del centro y norte de Sonora." *Recursos hidráulicos* 5:1 (1976), 8-25.

Jauregui, Jesus, et al. *TABAMEX: un caso de integración vertical de la agricultura.* Mexico: Nueva Imagen, 1980.

Jiménez Villalobos, Ángel, "Condiciones de las aguas subterráneas en el Distrito de Riego #51, Costa de Hermosillo, Sonora." *Ingeniería hidráulica en México* 19:3 (1965), 65-80.

Johnson, Robert. "The Florida Tomato War." *Florida Trend* (June 1979).

Josling, Timothy. "World Trade in Basic Foodstuffs." *International Journal* 34:4 (Winter 1978-1979), 39-52.

Katzenstein, Peter J. "International Interdependence: Some Longterm and Recent Changes." *International Organization* 29:4 (Autumn 1975), 1021-1034.

Keohane, Robert, and Nye, Joseph. *Power and Interdependence: World Politics in Transition.* Boston: Little, Brown, 1977.

Krasner, Stephen D., editor. "International Regimes." Special issue of *International Organization* 36:2 (Spring 1982).

Kujovich, Mary Yeager. "The Refrigerator Car and the Growth of the American Dressed Beef Industry." *Business History Review* 44 (Winter 1970).

Lappé, Frances Moore, and Collins, Joseph. *Food First: Beyond the Myth of Scarcity.* Boston: Houghton Mifflin, 1977.

Lawrence, Paul R., and Dyer, Davis. *Renewing American Industry.* New York: Free Press, 1982.

Link, John. "Mexican Oil and U.S. Agricultural Trade." *USDA Agricultural Outlook* (January-February 1979).

"Look for More Forage Fed Cattle." *The Farmer's Digest* 41:9 (March 1978), 81-84.

Louis, Arthur M. "Squeezing Gold out of Oranges." *Fortune* 103:2 (January 26, 1981), 78-82.

Luiselli, Cassio F. "Agricultura y alimentación: premisas para una nueva estrategia." In Nora Lustig, *Panorama y perspectivas de la economía mexicana*, 83-111.

―――. "¿Por que el SAM?" *Nexos* 3:32 (August 1980), 26-35.

Lustig, Nora, editor. *Panorama y perspectivas de la economía mexicana.* Mexico: El Colegio de México, 1980.

Machado, Manuel A., Jr. *An Industry in Crisis: Mexican-United States Cooperation in the Control of Foot-and-mouth Disease.* University of California Publications in History, Volume 80. Berkeley and Los Angeles, 1968.

―――. *The North Mexican Cattle Industry, 1910-1975: Ideology, Conflict, and Change.* College Station: Texas A & M Press, 1980.

Magee, Stephen P. "Information and Multinational Corporation: An Appropriability Theory of Direct Foreign Investment." In Jagdish N. Bhagwati, editor, *The New International Economic Order*, 317-340.

Mansour, F. "World Trade or Stable Agriculture?" *Ecologist Quarterly* 1:3 (August 1978), 187-203.

Mares, David. "The Evolution of U.S.-Mexican Agricultural Relations: The Changing Roles of the Mexican State and Mexican Agricultural Producers." Working Papers in U.S.-Mexican Studies, #16. La Jolla: University of California, San Diego, 1981.

Martín del Campo, Antonio. "Transformación agraria y nuevas opciones para el desarrollo." In Nora Lustig, *Panorama y perspectivas de la economía mexicana*, 48-79.

Martinez, Orlando. *The Great Landgrab: The Mexican-American War, 1846-1848*. London: Quartet Books, 1975.

McBride, George McCutchen. *The Land Systems of Mexico*. New York: Condé Nast Press, 1923.

McCoy, J. *Livestock and Meat Marketing*. Westport, Conn.: AVI Publishers, 1979.

McDonald, Alonzo. "U.S. Agriculture's Stake in the MTN." *U.S. Department of State Bulletin* #79 (August 1979), 41-43.

McGhee, Allan W. "A Comeback in Cornbelt Cattle Feeding?" *Farmer's Digest* 44:4 (October 1980), 60-61.

Meissner, Frank. "The Mexican Food System (SAM)—A Strategy for Sowing Petroleum." *Food Policy* 6:4 (November 1981), 219-230.

"Mexican President Questions Principle of Agrarian Reform." *Latin America Economic Report* 6:23 (June 16, 1978), 180-181.

Mighell, Ronald, and Jones, Lawrence. *Vertical Coordination in Agriculture*. USDA report, 1963.

Montañez, Carlos, and Aburto, Horacio. *Maíz: política institucional y crisis agrícola*. Mexico: Nueva Imagen, 1979.

Moran, Theodore H. "Foreign Expansion as an 'Institutional Necessity' for U.S. Corporate Capitalism." *World Politics* 25:3 (April 1973), 369-386.

Morgan, Dan. *Merchants of Grain*. New York: Viking, 1979.

Morrissy, J. David. *Agricultural Modernization through Production Contracting: The Role of the Fruit and Vegetable Processor in Mexico and Central America*. New York: Praeger, 1974.

Mosk, Sanford A. *Industrial Revolution in Mexico*. Berkeley and Los Angeles: University of California Press, 1950.

Muñoz, Heraldo, editor. *From Dependency to Development: Strategies to Overcome Underdevelopment and Inequality*. Boulder, Colo.: Westview Press, 1981.

Myint, H. "The Gains from International Trade and the Backward Countries." *The Review of Economic Studies* 22:2 (1954-1955), 129-142.

O'Donnell, Guillermo. "Tensions in the Bureaucratic-Authoritarian State and the Question of Democracy." In David Collier, editor, *The New Authoritarianism in Latin America*, 285-318.

BIBLIOGRAPHY

O'Donnell, Guillermo, and Linck, Delfina. *Dependencia y autonomía*. Buenos Aires: Editorial Amorrortú, 1973.

Olson, Mancur. "Introduction." In Todd Sandler, editor, *The Theory and Structures of International Political Economy*, 3-16.

Orive Alba, Adolfo. "Programa de irrigación del C. Presidente Miguel Alemán: posibilidades de un financiamiento parcial." *Ingeniería hidráulica en México* 1:1 (January-March 1947), 17-32.

Oswald, Ursula, editor. *Mercado y dependencia*. Mexico: Nueva Imagen, 1979.

Paarlberg, Robert L. "Food, Oil, and Coercive Resource Power." *International Security* 3:2 (Fall 1978), 3-19.

Palloix, Christian. *Las firmas multinacionales y el proceso de internacionalización*. Mexico: Siglo XXI, 1977.

Paré, Luisa. *El proletariado agrícola en México: ¿campesinos sin tierra o proletarios agrícolas?* Mexico: Siglo XXI, 1977.

Parker, Joel R. "Basin Exporters Move to Stabilize Coffee Prices." *Caribbean Basin Economic Survey* 6:2 (May-June 1980), 7-10.

Parks, Richard W. "The Role of Agriculture in Mexican Economic Development." *Inter-American Economic Affairs* 18:1 (Summer 1964), 3-27.

Pinto, Aníbal. "The Opening up of Latin America to the Exterior." CEPAL *Review* 11 (August 1980), 31-56.

————. "The Periphery and the Internationalization of the World Economy." CEPAL *Review* 9 (December 1979), 45-67.

"Plan Would Bring Mexican Cattle to U.S." *Feedstuffs* 53:14 (April 6, 1981).

Pletcher, David M. *Rails, Mines and Progress: Seven American Promoters in Mexico, 1867-1911*. Ithaca, N.Y.: Cornell University Press, 1958.

Powell, Fred W. *The Railroads of Mexico*. Boston: The Stratford Company, 1921.

Raine, William MacLeod, and Barnes, Will C. *Cattle*. Garden City, N.Y.: Doubleday, 1930.

Rama, Ruth, and Rello, Fernando. "El estado y la estrategia del agronegocio transnacional: el sistema soya en México." Mexico, n.d. Manuscript.

Rama, Ruth, and Vigorito, Raúl. *El complejo de frutas y legumbres en México*. Mexico: Nueva Imagen, 1979.

Redclift, M. R. "The Mexican Food System (SAM)—Sowing Subsidies, Reaping Apathy." *Food Policy* 6:4 (November 1981), 231-235.

Regier, Donald W. "Feed Demand in the World GOL Model." *Agricultural Economics Research* 30:2 (April 1978), 16-24.

Reich, Robert. *The Next American Frontier.* New York: New York Times Books, 1982.

Restrepo, Iván, and Eckstein, Salomón. *La agricultura colectiva en México: la experiencia de la Laguna.* Mexico: Siglo XXI, 1975.

Revelt, Mary. "Developing the Caribbean: Its Implications for U.S. Agriculture." *Foreign Agriculture* 20:6 (June 1982), 4-7.

Reynolds, Clark W. *The Mexican Economy: Twentieth Century Structure and Growth.* New Haven: Yale University Press, 1970.

Rippy, J. Fred. *The United States and Mexico.* New York: Alfred A. Knopf, 1926.

Rock, David, editor. *Argentina in the Twentieth Century.* Pittsburgh: University of Pittsburgh Press, 1975.

Rojko, Anthony S., and Schwartz, Martin W. "Modeling the World Grain-Oilseeds-Livestock Economy to Assess World Food Prospects." *Agricultural Economics Research* 28:3 (July 1976), 89-98.

Rosecrance, Richard, et al. "Whither Interdependence?" *International Organization* 31:1 (Winter 1977), 83-105.

Rosenzweig, Fernando. "El comercio exterior." In Daniel Cosío Villegas, editor, *Historia moderna de México*, Volume VII, Tome I, *El porfiriato: la vida económica.*

Ross, Eric B. *Beyond the Myths of Culture: Essays in Cultural Materialism.* New York: Academic Press, 1980.

Rothstein, Robert L. *Global Bargaining: UNCTAD and the Quest for a New International Economic Order.* Princeton, N.J.: Princeton University Press, 1979.

———. *The Weak in the World of the Strong.* New York: Columbia University Press, 1977.

Rubio Valdez, Humberto. "Perspectivas de producción y exportación de tomate a los Estados Unidos y Canadá para la temporada 1978-1979." *Comercio y desarrollo* 8 (November-December 1978).

Sánchez Burgos, Guadalupe. *La región fundamental de economía campesina en México.* Mexico: Editorial Nueva Imagen, 1980.

Sanderson, Steven E. *Agrarian Populism and the Mexican State: The*

303

Struggle for Land in Sonora. Berkeley and Los Angeles: University of California Press, 1981.

———. "The Complex No-Policy Option: U.S. Agricultural Relations with Mexico." Working Papers of the Latin American Program, Woodrow Wilson International Center for Scholars, Washington, D.C., 1983.

———. "The Emergence of the 'World Steer': Internationalization and Foreign Domination in the Latin American Cattle Industry." Paper presented at the 44th International Congress of Americanists, University of Manchester, England, September 1982.

———. "Florida Tomatoes, U.S.-Mexican Relations and the International Division of Labor." *Inter-American Economic Affairs* 35:3 (Winter 1981), 23-52.

———. *Trade Aspects of the Internationalization of Mexican Agriculture: Consequences for Mexico's Food Crisis.* Center for U.S.-Mexican Studies, Monograph #10. La Jolla: University of California, San Diego, 1983.

———, editor. *The Americas in the New International Division of Labor.* New York: Holmes and Meier, 1985.

Sandler, Todd, editor. *The Theory and Structures of International Political Economy.* Boulder, Colo.: Westview, 1981.

Schejtman, Alejandro. "Economía campesina y agricultura empresarial: tipología de productores del agro mexicano." Mexico: U.N. CEPAL, 1981. Limited circulation manuscript.

Schmitz, Andrew; Firch, Robert S.; and Hillman, Jimmye S. "Agricultural Export Dumping: The Case of Mexican Winter Vegetables in the U.S. Market." *American Journal of Agricultural Economics* 63:4 (November 1981), 645-654.

Schoonover, Thomas. *Dollars over Dominion: The Triumph of Liberalism in U.S.-Mexican Relations, 1861-1867.* Baton Rouge: Louisiana State University Press, 1978.

Schwanz, Lee. "Your Customers Demand the Hamburger Steer." *The Farmer's Digest* 41:10 (April 1978).

Scobie, James R. *Revolution on the Pampas: A Social History of Argentine Wheat, 1860-1910.* Institute for Latin American Studies, Latin American Monographs, No. 1. Austin: University of Texas Press, 1964.

Shwedel, Kenneth. "Los precios agrícolas: una perspectiva histórica." Mexico, 1982. Manuscript.

———. "El sector agropecuario mexicano versus el resto de la

economía: un análisis de transferencias." Mexico, 1982. Manuscript.

Simmons, Richard L. "An Updated Comparison of U.S. and Canadian Prices of Mexican Winter Vegetables." Washington, D.C., February 1980. Mimeo.

Simpson, Eyler. *The Ejido: Mexico's Way Out.* Chapel Hill: University of North Carolina Press, 1937.

Simpson, James R. "An Assessment of the United States' Meat Import Act of 1979." University of Florida, 1979. Manuscript.

———. "The Cattle Cycle: A Guide for Cattlemen." Food and Resource Economics Staff Paper, Institute for Food and Agricultural Sciences (IFAS), University of Florida, 1978.

———. "World Cattle Cycles and the Latin American Beef Industry." Food and Resource Economics Department Staff Paper, IFAS, 1979.

Smith, Peter H. *Politics and Beef in Argentina: Patterns of Conflict and Change.* New York: Columbia University Press, 1969.

Solís, Leopoldo. "Hacia un análisis general a largo plazo del desarrollo económico de México." *Demografía y Economía* 1:1 (1967).

Sonnichsen, C. L. *Colonel Greene and the Copper Skyrocket.* Tucson: University of Arizona Press, 1974.

Spalding, Rose. "The Mexican Food Crisis: An Analysis of the SAM." Working Paper in U.S.-Mexican Studies, Center for U.S.-Mexican Studies. La Jolla: University of California, San Diego, in press.

Spero, Joan Edelman. *The Politics of International Economic Relations.* Second edition. New York: St. Martin's, 1981.

Spicer, Edward H. *Cycles of Conquest: The Impact of Spain, Mexico and the United States on the Indians of the Southwest.* Tucson: University of Arizona Press, 1962.

Stepan, Alfred. *The State and Society: Peru in Comparative Perspective.* Princeton, N.J.: Princeton University Press, 1978.

Story, Dale. "Trade Politics in the Third World: A Case Study of the Mexican GATT Decision." *International Organization* 36:4 (Autumn 1982), 767-794.

"Strano Farms." A Case Study prepared for the Harvard Business School, July 1980. Mimeo.

Sunkel, Osvaldo. "Capitalismo transnacional y desintegración nacional en América Latina." *Estudios internacionales* 4:16 (January-March 1971), 3-61. In English, "Transnational Capitalism and National Disintegration in Latin America." *Social and Economic Studies* 22:1 (1973), 132-176.

Tello, Carlos. *La política económica de México, 1970-1976.* Mexico: Siglo XXI, 1979.

Texas Agriculture in the 1980s: The Crucial Decade. College Station: The Texas Agricultural Experiment Station, 1980.

Torres Gaytán, Ricardo. "Sector agropecuario y desarrollo económico y social de México." *Comercio exterior* 31:6 (June 1981), 619-626.

Tucker, Robert W. *The Inequality of Nations.* New York: Basic Books, 1977.

Uceda, Gustavo. "Prospects for Expanding Beef Production in the Basin." Federal Reserve Bank of Atlanta *Caribbean Basin Economic Survey* 5:4 (September-October 1979), 10-16.

Venezian, Eduardo L., and Gamble, William K. *The Agricultural Development of Mexico: Its Structure and Growth since 1950.* New York: Praeger, 1969.

Vernon, Raymond. "International Investment and International Trade in the Product Cycle." *The Quarterly Journal of Economics* 80:2 (May 1966), 190-207.

Wallerstein, Immanuel. *The Modern World-System: Capitalist Agriculture and the Origins of the European World-Economy in the Sixteenth Century.* New York: Academic Press, 1974.

Wares, William A. *The Theory of Dumping and American Commercial Policy.* Lexington, Mass.: D. C. Heath, 1977.

Watkins, Melville H. "A Staple Theory of Economic Growth." *The Canadian Journal of Economics and Political Science* 29:2 (May 1963), 150-158.

Webb, Walter Prescott. *The Great Plains.* Boston: Ginn and Co., 1931.

Weber, William T. "The Complexities of Agripower: A Review Essay." *Agricultural History* 52:4 (October 1978), 526-537.

Weinert, Richard S. Review of *Global Reach* in *Yale Review* (Summer 1975).

Wessman, James W. "The Agrarian Question in Mexico." *Latin American Research Review* 19:2 (1984), 243-259.

"Western Producers Visit Mexico, Report 'Good' Market for U.S. Sheep." *Feedstuffs* 53:47 (November 16, 1981).

Whetten, Nathan. *Rural Mexico*. Chicago: University of Chicago Press, 1948.

Winrock International. *Technical Report: The World Livestock Product, Feedstuff, and Food Grain System*. Morrilton, Ark.: Winrock International, 1981.

Wionczek, Miguel. "La aportación de la política hidráulica entre 1925 y 1970 a la actual crisis agrícola mexicana." *Comercio exterior* 37:4 (April 1982), 394-409.

Wolf, Eric. *Europe and the People without History*. Berkeley and Los Angeles: University of California Press, 1982.

Wood, Charles. "The Political Economy of Infant Mortality in São Paulo, Brazil." *International Journal of Health Services* 12:2 (1982).

Wortman, Sterling, and Cummings, Ralph W., Jr. *To Feed This World: The Challenge and the Strategy*. Baltimore: The Johns Hopkins University Press, 1978.

Yates, Paul Lamartine. *El campo mexicano*. Two Volumes. Mexico: Ediciones El Caballito, 1978. In English. *Mexico's Agricultural Dilemma*. Tucson: University of Arizona Press, 1981.

"You're a Winner—If You Can Raise Lean Beef." *Progressive Farmer* 96:9 (September 1981), 18-20.

Index

313

LIBRARY OF CONGRESS CATALOGING IN PUBLICATION DATA

Sanderson, Steven E.
  The transformation of Mexican agriculture.

  Bibliography: p.
  Includes index.
    1. Agriculture and state—Mexico. 2. Agriculture—
Economic aspects—Mexico. 3. Food supply—Mexico.
4. International division of labor. I. Title.
HD1793.S26 1985   338.1'0972   85-42701
ISBN 0-691-07693-6 (alk. paper)
ISBN 0-691-02239-9 (pbk.)